TOO LITTLE TOO LATE

THE CAMPAIGN IN WEST AND SOUTH GERMANY, JUNE-JULY 1866

Michael Embree

Hardback edition produced in a strictly limited printing of 1,000 individually numbered and signed copies.

This is copy number 797 of 1,000

M G Embree

Too Little Too Late

The Campaign in West and South Germany, June-July 1866

Michael Embree

Helion & Company

Helion & Company Limited
26 Willow Road
Solihull
West Midlands
B91 1UE
England
Tel. 0121 705 3393
Fax 0121 711 4075
Email: info@helion.co.uk
Website: www.helion.co.uk
Twitter: @helionbooks
Visit our blog http://blog.helion.co.uk/

Published by Helion & Company 2015
Designed and typeset by Bookcraft Ltd, Stroud, Gloucestershire
Cover designed by Paul Hewitt, Battlefield Design (www.battlefield-design.co.uk)
Printed by Gutenberg Press Limited, Tarxien, Malta

Text and maps © Michael Embree 2015.
The publishers and author express their thanks to Bruce Weigle for the maps.
Images © as individually credited.

Front cover: The death of Major Rohdewald, commander of the Lippe Detmold
Füsilier Battalion, at Kissingen, July 10 1866, by Ludwig Burger (*Erinnerungs-
Blätter aus dem Feldzüge der Main-Armee 1866*); Rear cover: The Oldenburg Brigade
at the crossing of the Tauber near Hochhausen engage Baden troops, July 24 1866
by Ludwig Burger (*Erinnerungs-Blätter aus dem Feldzüge der Main-Armee 1866*).

ISBN 978-1-909384-50-7

British Library Cataloguing-in-Publication Data.
A catalogue record for this book is available from the British Library.

For details of other military history titles published by Helion & Company Limited
contact the above address, or visit our website: http://www.helion.co.uk.

We always welcome receiving book proposals from prospective authors.

Despite Tapas!

Contents

List of Illustrations

Images in colour section

Key to image credits:

Cohn: Cohn, Martin & Mels, August, *Von der Elbe bis zur Tauber. Der Feldzug der Preußischen
Main-Armee im Sommer 1866,* (Velhagen & Klasing, Bielefeld & Leipzig 1867)
Deutsche Uniformen: Knötel, Herbert & Lezius, Martin, *Deutsche Uniformen. Album 3:
Das Zeitalter der Deutschen Einigung 1864-1914. Band 1: Die Kriege von 1864 und 1866*
(Sturm Zigaretten, Dresden, 1933)
Erinnerungs-Blätter aus dem Feldzüge der Main-Armee 1866: Burger, Ludwig, *Erinnerungs-
Blätter aus dem Feldzüge der Main-Armee 1866* (Korn, Berlin, 1870)
Fontane: Fontane, Theodor, Der *Deutsche Krieg von 1866* (Volume II), *Der Feldzug in West
und Mitteldeutschland,* (Royal Press, Berlin 1871)
Illustrirte Kriegs-Chronik: *Illustrirte Kriegs-Chronik. Gedenkbuch an den Feldzug von 1866 in
Deutschland und Italien* (J.J. Weber, Leipzig 1867)
Regensberg/*Mainfeldzug*: Regensberg, Friedrich, *Der Mainfeldzug,* (Frankh, Stuttgart 1908)
Uniformenkunde: Knötel, Richard, *Uniformenkunde: lose Blätter zur Geschichte der
Entwicklung der militärischen Tracht in Deutschland* (Babenzien, Rathenow, 1890-19??)

List of Maps

In colour section.

Glossary of Terms

Military units are commonly represented by numbers and/or words placed either side of an oblique stroke. A Roman numeral preceding the oblique would indicate an infantry battalion, whereas an Arabic numeral would indicate a company or squadron. For example, the symbol I/II Hanoverian Regiment would represent the First Battalion of the Second Hanoverian Infantry Regiment. Conversely, Prussian 1/IR15 represents the First Company of the Prussian 15th Infantry Regiment.

Bad	Literally 'Bath'; used as a prefix, and indicating a Spa town, as in Bad Kissingen.
Cuirassiers	Heavy Cavalry, generally wearing a metal breast (and in some cases back) plate. Prussian cuirassiers were no longer so equipped.
Diet	Governing body of the German Confederation. Used interchangeably with Parliament.
Dragoons	'Heavy' Cavalry
Ersatz	Replacement (as in military unit
FML	Lieutenant-General (Austrian)
Foot (distance)	A contemporary unit of measurement, varying in length, according to local jurisdiction; generally near 300 millimetres. A Prussian foot was 313 millimetres, and a Bavarian, 292, although local exceptions also existed.
Gefreiter	Lance-Corporal, PFC
General of Cavalry	Lieutenant-General
General of Infantry	Lieutenant-General
German Confederation	Loose organisation of German states from 1815-1866, with its capital in Frankfurt on Main
Hussars	Light Cavalry
I, II after a surname/last name	I indicates oldest son, II, next oldest etc.
Jäger	Light Infantry
Landwehr	Militia
Leib (Regiment)	Life Guards (Can apply to Infantry or Cavalry)
Main (River)	The Main (pronounced 'Mine'), is a German river which flows from Kulmbach, in Franconia, westward, to the Rhine. Some 570 kilometres long, it is the principal tributary of the latter.
Mile (unit of distance)	A German unit of measurement varying in length, according to local jurisdiction; generally close to 7,500 metres. A contemporary Prussian mile measured 7,532 metres, and a Bavarian, 7,415 metres.

Needle-Gun	Prussian breech-loading rifle/carbine. This was the standard Prussian personal weapon for NCO's and men. A number of different models existed.
'Ober'	In rank, 'senior'.
Oberlieutenant	Lieutenant/1st Lieutenant
Odenwald, The	An area of low mountains located east of the Rhine, and south of the River Main and the Spessart.
Parliament	Governing body of the German Confederation. Used interchangeably with Diet.
Premier Lieutenant/ Premierlieutenant	Lieutenant/1st Lieutenant
Ritter	Knight
Schützen	Light Infantry
Rhön, The	A formation of low mountains, partly formed by volcanic activity, the Rhön lies at the south-east end of the Hessian Highlands, separated from the Vogelsberg by the River Fulda.
Saale (River)	There are two German rivers bearing the name 'Saale'. The Saale discussed in this study is the Franconian Saale. The other river, the Saxon Saale, lies further to the east, and has no bearing on this study. (See Map 1)
Spessart, The	The Spessart is a low mountain range in north-western Bavaria and southern Hesse, bordered on three sides by the River Main. The two most important towns located at the edge of the Spessart are Aschaffenburg and Würzburg.. It forms a roughly circular mountain range, its most prominent ridge lying from the southwest to the northeast. To its south-west is the Odenwald, and to the north and east, the Rhön.
Unterlieutenant	Second-Lieutenant

Acknowledgements

Stephen Allen, Jean-Claude Brunner, Bruce Bassett-Powell, Michael Gandt, Oliver Heyn, Tom Hill, Glenn Jewison, Martijn Nicasie, Daniel Speir, Tim O'Brien, Shane Pinkston, Duncan Rogers, Bruce Weigle, and, as ever, Sally and Kathryn.

Introduction

The War of 1866 was a defining moment in European history, and, given that it occurred in the middle of the 19th Century, it was also, for a short time, of worldwide importance. As a direct result, the modern nation of Germany rapidly came into being, itself to be a world power for almost 80 years. Although this war was primarily between the Kingdom of Prussia and the Austrian Empire for effective control of 'Germany', there were, of course, deep concerns within all of the political entities involved as to what form any possible unified 'Germany' might take. What, then, of the conflict which took place in the summer of that year, actually inside the German Confederation itself? The answer to this question went back just over 50 years, to the time of the French Emperor, Napoleon.[1]

---

1   Many would refer to the Emperor as Napoleon I. The author considers him the Emperor Napoleon.

1

'Germany' after 1815

After the Treaty of Vienna, in 1815, the various independent states which together were termed to be a part of 'Germany' had been included within the loosely defined German Confederation. This organisation, and its new Parliament, were both based in the city of Frankfurt on the (River) Main, in western 'Germany'. The Confederation, the existence of which was first agreed under the Treaty of Paris in 1815, formally came into existence in November 1816. It then comprised 39 separate states, including four 'Free' cities, the latter of which had originally been granted charters by Holy Roman Emperors. These four, were themselves the historical 'survivors' of 51 previously existing such entities. Though united in language, the various states of the German Confederation presented a most diverse body of political, religious, and economic views. The one over-riding factor which had provided general agreement at that time was a fear of France, and after more than 20 years of almost continuous warfare against or on behalf of that country, this was, understandably, both the initial cement and the prime function for the Confederation's existence.

The Confederation's Presidency constitutionally fell to Austria, then generally still considered to be the overseeing power, as successor to the Holy Roman Empire. For important or urgent issues, a plenary session would be held, in which member states were accorded a set number of votes, also formally allocated in the organisation's constitution. These were initially as follows:

Austria, Prussia, Saxony, Bavaria, Hanover, and Württemberg—four votes each

Baden, Electoral Hesse, Grand Duchy of Hesse, Holstein, and Luxembourg—three votes each

Brunswick, Mecklenburg-Schwerin, and Nassau—two votes each

Saxe-Weimar, Saxe-Gotha, Saxe-Coburg, Saxe-Meiningen, Saxe-Hildburghausen, Mecklenburg-Strelitz, Holstein-Oldenburg, Anhalt-Dessau, Anhalt-Bernburg, Anhalt-Cothen, Schwarzburg-Sondershausen, Schwarzburg-Rudolstadt, Hohenzollern-Hechingen, Saxe-Gotha, Liechtenstein, Saxe-Coburg, Hohenzollern-Sigmaringen, Waldeck, Reuss, Elder Branch, Reuss, Younger Branch, Schaumberg-Lippe, Lippe, and the Free Cities of Lübeck, Frankfurt-on-the Main, Bremen, and Hamburg—one vote each

Total votes—69[1]

---

1   It should also be noted that there were also several anomalies. Until 1837, the British Monarch was also King of Hanover. In addition, until 1864, The King of Denmark sat as the Duke of

17

For a measure to be passed, generally, a two-thirds majority was required.

Membership of the Confederation, however, remained fluid throughout its existence, with the status of various, usually smaller states, altering as they expanded, split, or were absorbed. For example, the Duchy of Anhalt-Köthen was inherited by the Duke of Anhalt-Dessau in 1847, and simply ceased to exist as a separate entity.

An additional responsibility of the Confederation was the maintenance and garrisoning of the so-called Federal Fortresses, which had also been designated in the Treaty of Paris. The cost of these was also, then, paid for by France. The cities of Mainz, Luxembourg, and Landau were originally so appointed, with Rastatt and Ulm being added in the early 1840s. Mainz, due to its strategic position on the River Rhine, southwest of the Federal, capital Frankfurt on the Main, was popularly known as 'Germany's Bulwark'. These 'German' fortresses were, of course, in addition to those which were the sole and specific possession and responsibility of various individual members of the Confederation.[2]

Holstein, and the King of the Netherlands for the Duchy of Luxembourg. Also, large areas of both the Austrian Empire and the Kingdom of Prussia were actually outside the Confederation, especially of the former.

2   Very late in the life of the Confederation, it was proposed that the fortress of Rendsburg, in Holstein, should also be designated at as Federal Fortress. The Schleswig-Holstein War of 1864 precluded any further discussion on the matter.

2

Metternich to Bismarck – 1848: The Year of Revolution

For over 25 years, the Parliament in Frankfurt was largely a talking shop, and the whole organisation was actually completely dominated by the Austrian Chancellor, Prince Metternich. Appointed Chancellor in 1821, he remained in control until the 'Year of Revolution' 1848.

Many factors came to the fore during the major disturbances of that year in much of Europe, a dangerous synthesis of nationalism, constitutional unrest, and economic depression. For the most part, the peasantry was uninvolved, and though some political concessions were instituted in a number of states, these were primarily window-dressing. Crucially, the majority of the military forces had remained loyal. However, Metternich and his personal grip on Europe had finally gone, leaving something of a vacuum. This vacuum would later be filled by an aristocratic Prussian lawyer-diplomat turned politician, ironically himself born in 1815.

Hesse-Cassel Crisis of 1850

Without the guiding hand of Metternich, inevitably, the competing interests of Prussia and Austria, especially, could not fail to clash. Prussia's developing aspirant leadership of a fully federal German State was the complete opposite to Austria's ideal of a loose confederation, as originally promulgated, over 30 years earlier. The initial clash between the two came to a head, not over Denmark, as expected by many, but actually over the affairs of The Electorate of Hesse-Cassel.

The situation in the Electorate, in the Spring of 1848, was one of serious general public discontent, as elsewhere. Friedrich Wilhelm had succeeded upon his father's death, on November 20 1847. He found himself forced to dispense with his entire conservative ministry, headed by Hans Hassenpflug, and to agree to implement a comprehensive programme of democratic reform. This policy, however, was but short lived. After the breakdown of the Frankfurt Parliament, the Elector considered which path to follow. In May 1849, he sent envoys to a short-lived Erfurt Parliament.[1] As the Habsburg Empire regained its strength, though, he reconsidered his position.

On February 23 1850, Hassenpflug was again placed at the head of the Electorate's affairs, and threw himself with renewed zeal into the struggle against the constitution and into opposition to Prussia. On September 2 the Diet was dissolved, and martial law

---

1   The Erfurt Parliament was a short-lived attempt to establish an alternative German Parliament, sponsored by Prussia, in March and April 1850.

declared. Taxes continued to be paid, and calm prevailed. Neither the Elector nor his Minister, however, could depend upon the army to enforce it. The two men left Cassel on October 15, and appealed for help from the reconstituted Federal Parliament, which willingly passed a decree of "intervention". On November 1 an Austrian and Bavarian force marched into the Electorate.

This was a direct challenge to Prussia, which under conventions with the Elector had the right to the use of the military roads which ran through the Electorate. These roads were Prussia's only route to her Rhineland Provinces. War seemed imminent, and both sides began to mobilise. Prussian troops entered the country, and shots were actually exchanged between some outposts. Austria, however, under the strong leadership of Prince Felix Schwarzenberg, as Minister-President, was in the ascendant. Prussia was in no condition to take up the sword. After a minor skirmish between Austro-Bavarian and Prussian troops over access to a road, and with Saxony also leaning towards the Habsburgs, Baron Manteuffel realised that, with Prussian mobilisation in a complete mess, force would not succeed.[2]

The diplomacy that followed was deeply humiliating for Prussia. Her Foreign Minister, Josef von Radowitz stated that, "Prussia abandons the German cause in return for concessions by Austria which impose no obligations upon her." Both sides were to demobilise, but Prussia's was to take place first, and was to be complete. This was humiliation indeed! The agreement, the "Punctation of Olmütz", was signed on November 29 1850. Hesse-Cassel, itself was surrendered to the Federal authorities.

In April 1852, the Frankfurt Parlament issued a new provisional constitution for the Electorate. The subsequent Electoral Diet had, under this document, very narrow powers; and the Elector was free to carry out his policy of amassing money, while halting the construction of railways and factories, and imposing a strict orthodoxy on churches and schools. The Minister responsible for these problems was none other than Hassenpflug, who had been reinstated by the Elector. In 1855, however, he was, for the second time, dismissed

After a further period of seemingly endless agitation, on May 14 1862, permission was granted by the consent of the Federal Parliament to restore the constitution of 1831. This decision had been due to a threat of Prussian occupation. Indeed, so obdurate was he, that it needed another such threat to persuade the Elector to reassemble the Chamber, which he had dismissed at the first sign of opposition. Affairs in Hesse-Cassel remained unsettled.[3]

The Rise of Prince Otto Bismarck

The man who would eventually challenge the Habsburgs would prove to be Prince Otto Eduard Leopold, Prince of Bismarck, Duke of Lauenburg. This son of an East Prussian Junker was born in the fateful year of 1815, in the month of the escape of Napoleon from Elba. Politically conservative, and very ambitious, he naturally gravitated towards politics. In 1851, luck and influence landed him the Prussian seat in the Federal Parliament

---

2   The only fatality was a Prussian trumpeter's horse, since known as "The White Horse of Bronzell".
3   Ward, Vol. I, p. 531.

in Frankfurt. He found an organisation loosely dominated by the Austrian Empire, largely to the satisfaction of the smaller states.

Subsequently, Bismarck joined the diplomatic service, being posted first in St. Petersburg, and then Paris. He proved to be a diplomat of some skill. While in Russia, he developed the strong view that good relations with that Empire were of great importance to Prussia, a view that never left him.

As ambassador to Paris, he remained a staunch supporter of the King, with Wilhelm replying with genuine affection. The King also had something else in mind. On September 18 1862, Bismarck was summoned to Berlin by the War Minister, Count Roon. Four days later he attended Babelsberg Palace, the Royal Summer Residence at Potsdam. He left as Chancellor of Prussia.[4] From this point, not only the King would pursue aggressive policies aimed at furthering Prussian interests – so would the King's Chief Minister.

Schleswig-Holstein

Only the new Chancellor of Prussia had a crystal clear view of the model 'Germany' which he wished to create; a united one dominated by Prussia, effectively meaning himself. To achieve this, the future 'Iron Chancellor' now sought to remove Danish influence from the northern Duchies of Schleswig and Holstein.

One of the by-products of the revolutions of 1848 had been a conflict between Denmark and the German Confederation over the Duchies. Both were members of the Confederation, and equally, both under the Danish Crown. An on-off military campaign lasted until 1850, ultimately achieving nothing. The crisis waned, although no solution had surfaced.

The issue resurfaced in late 1863, with the death of the Danish King, Frederick VII. Since constitutional matters concerning the two Duchies had never actually been resolved, and had now reappeared, Bismarck would now achieve a solution by military force, with the help of Austria, cloaked by some dubious dealings in Frankfurt, and aided by Danish obstinacy. On February 1 1864 an Austrian/Prussian army of some 39,000 men crossed the River Eider, opening hostilities. The military campaign lasted until July, the Danes being defeated, and losing both Schleswig and Holstein.

Now, Bismarck sought to exclude Austria itself from German affairs. Initially, after the conflict with Denmark, Austrian troops occupied Holstein, and Prussian, Schleswig. For the Habsburgs, though, neither Schleswig nor Holstein held any interest as possessions. Although willing, in principle, to consider a financial settlement with Prussia on the matter, Vienna was far more inclined in obtaining territory elsewhere in exchange for her new interests north of the River Eider.[5]

As so often, the Prussian Chancellor's supposed negotiations were illusory. Certainly, he was sure of the conflict with Austria to come, as he was of the necessity of the dissolution of the German Confederation. War was again on the horizon.

---

4   Ibid., Vol. II, p. 81.
5   Jaehns, Vol. II, p. 375 & Carr, pp. 135-136.

3

Prelude to War in Germany – Prussia or Austria?

On April 8 a new twist in the situation was announced. Italy had earlier made overtures to Vienna for the transfer of Venetia to the Italian Kingdom. These had been rebuffed. Consequently, on this date, Prussia signed an offensive/defensive treaty with Italy. Although not entirely binding on Prussia, it virtually ensured that Austria would bee engaged on two fronts.[1]

Mobilisation Begins

Prussia announced a partial call-up on May 3, followed by a series of further decrees until, by the 12th, a full-scale mobilisation was in force.[2]

Part of the mobilisation, of course, necessitated the movement of Prussian troops and materiel eastward, from the Rhine Provinces. At the height of these movements, between May 27 to June 5, 12 troop trains per day from Cologne and Coblenz rolled through Hanover, on their way to Halle, carrying Eberhard Herwarth von Bittenfeld's VIII Corps, towards the Austrian frontier. At the same time, another eight daily trains transported the Prussian VIII Corps (minus the 13th Division) through Cassel, also to the east. Neither movement elicited any obvious concern in Hanover or Hesse-Cassel, though the starkly obvious implications cannot have gone unnoticed in either capital, or indeed, anywhere else.[3]

The question now facing the various German states was simple; either support Prussia, or fight her. Neutrality, as would be seen, was not an option, although some still naively believed it to be possible. Indeed, matters would now proceed with considerable speed.

Attempted Assassination of Prince Bismarck

Amidst the frenetic activity of mobilisation, on the afternoon of May 7 an attempt was made on Chancellor Bismarck's life, in Berlin. A radical former student from Baden, who had graduated from Hohenheim Agricultural Academy only weeks before, Ferdinand Cohen-Blind, like many, was greatly worried by the possibility of war within the German Confederation. For this, the 22 year old squarely blamed the Prussian Chancellor. After graduating, he had gone on a walking holiday in the countryside of

---

1 Malet, pp. 154-155.
2 GGS, pp. 16-18.
3 Ibid., pp. 29-34, & Ward & Wilkinson, p. 247.

Bavaria and Bohemia. During this trip, he resolved to kill Bismarck, believing, perhaps rightly, that only this extreme step would prevent such a conflict.

He arrived in Berlin on May 5, there checking into the Hotel Royal 'Unter den Linden'. Two days later, armed with a revolver, he waited in this famous street, near the Royal Palace. At about 17:00, as the Chancellor, who was walking home, passed the Russian Embassy, Cohen-Blind fired two shots at him, from behind. A struggle between the two men ensued, in which the assailant fired a further three rounds, before being apprehended by soldiers on Guard at the palace, and handed over to the police. That night, Cohen-Blind cut his own throat in his cell at the city Central Police Station.

Bismarck was later examined by the Royal Physician, Doctor von Lauer. Remarkably, three of the bullets merely only caused grazes, and the other two, it was said, were deflected by the Chancellor's ribs!![4]

Prussian Occupation of Holstein

The immediate spark that lit the fuse to hostilities occurred in the former Danish Duchy of Holstein. The second war over the Duchies of Schleswig and Holstein, two years earlier, had resulted in the Treaty of Gastein, whereby Schleswig was to be administered by Prussia, and Holstein, by Austria. Fortunately, the two commanders involved both behaved in a sensible manner.

The Prussian force, some 12,000 strong, was commanded by Major-General von Manteuffel. His Austrian counterpart, FML Gablenz, had a force of some 4,800. Gablenz fell back before the slow Prussian advance, Manteuffel ensuring that the Habsburg troops had sufficient time to embark on trains, and leave.[5]

Crisis at Frankfurt

The Federal Diet met in 'extraordinary' Session on the 11th. The Habsburg delegate, Baron von Kübeck, stated that the Prussian action in Holstein was in breach of previous agreements, and that it was now a matter for the Parliament. The Baron now proposed the immediate mobilisation of all 'Federal' military contingents, apart from that of Prussia. He further insisted that this operation be completed, with all forces being on a war-footing in 14 days! Prussia, unsurprisingly, contested these proposals. Indeed, her delegate further moved that Austria itself now be excluded from the 'Bund'.

After three days of debate, proposal, and counter-proposal, a vote was taken on the original Habsburg measure. This was duly passed by a vote of nine votes to six. Thereupon, the Prussian minister, Karl Friedrich von Savigny, simply declared that he

---

4   Schoeps, Julius H., *Bismarck und sein Attentäter. Der Revolveranschlag Unter den Linden am 7. Mai 1866*. Some sources relate that Bismarck was wearing some form of body armour. An altogether more 'rip-roaring' version can be found in, *Bismarck: His authentic biography*, New York 1877, pp.389-393. Fantasy apart, the reader is invited to consider the reality of the situation, had the Chancellor been killed in this attempt.

5   GGS, pp. 24-25 & Malet, pp. 182-184.

had no more business in Frankfurt, and departed from the city.[6] For the anti-Prussian forces, matters were less clear-cut.

Any possible lingering doubts about a conflict were swiftly clarified. On June 12 the Diet voted that the Confederation's Army be mobilised, apart from the Prussian contingent. For Prussia, and her allies, however, the vote was a spur to even more frenetic action.

Possibly, many of the states, especially the smaller ones, had hoped that the vote would actually intimidate Prussia. If so, Bismarck's determination soon disabused them of this notion, and, in any case, the wheels of mobilisation, as seen, were already turning. Force, not votes, would now decide the fate of Germany.

While the major campaigns would be fought between the primary forces of Austria, Prussia, and Italy, outside the territory of the Confederation, not insignificant armies would also clash in Germany itself. Every member of the Confederation would, in some way, be involved, there being no place to hide. What then, of the forces which were about to contest the German Question on its home soil?

The 'Army' of the German Confederation

The Federal Constitution of 1815 had specified that a Confederation army be formed with ten Army Corps, all to be furnished by member states. Austria was to supply I, II, and III Corps, Prussia IV, V, and VI, while Bavaria provided VII Corps. VIII Corps was mainly composed of troops from Württemberg, Baden, and the Grand Duchy of Hesse, and IX Corps, by the Electorate of Hesse, Lemberg, Luxembourg, and Nassau. Finally, X Corps was to be constituted with men from Bremen, Brunswick, Hamburg, Hanover, Holstein, Lauenburg, Lübeck, Mecklenburg, and Oldenburg. All of this, of course, was predicated upon an outside external threat.

The military forces of the Confederation were, of course, intended to overawe, or if necessary, fight, any outside enemy. In practice, in 1815, this meant, as seen, France. It had not, of course, occurred to anyone at that time that any threat to peace could possibly come from within the organisation itself. Inevitably, therefore, there were no contingency plans for such an unthinkable eventuality. Equally, Prince Bismarck would, as he had with the two former Danish Duchies less than two years before, turn this unprecedented situation to Prussia's, and thus his own, advantage. In the event of some form of a 'civil war', what forces, then, would be potentially available to 'each' side?

---

6   Malet, pp. 188-192.

4

Opposing Forces[1]

KINGDOM OF PRUSSIA

A Note on the Prussian forces engaged in South and West 'Germany'

Of the huge might of the Prussian Army, only a small proportion was engaged in Western and Southern Germany in the summer of 1866. What would initially become the rather grandly named Army of the West, commanded by Lieutenant-General Vogel von Falckenstein, comprised three infantry divisions, the already existing 13th Division, and the other two, rapidly formed 'combined' divisions, these formations at first commanded respectively by Lieutenant-General Goeben, Major-General von Manteuffel, and Major-General Beyer.[2] Prior to the outbreak of hostilities, Manteuffel's troops had been stationed largely in Holstein, whereas many of Beyer's troops had been in various garrisons, including the fortresses of Mainz, Rastatt, Luxembourg, and some also in the Federal Capital, Frankfurt-on-Main. In contrast to the primary theatre, this hastily assembled force had no separate artillery reserve. These formations initially totalled some 48,000 men, altogether, including 36 battalions of infantry.[3] Later in the campaign, the contingents from the north German Hanseatic towns, Oldenburg, and some newly-raised Landwehr infantry and cavalry would also join these forces.

Falckenstein's initial task was two-fold. First, he was tasked to occupy Hanover and Hesse-Cassel, and then also to prevent the Hanoverian Army from linking up with the Bavarian and other Federal German forces to the south. This latter task was considered of prime importance by both Prince Bismarck, and the Prussian Chief of Staff, Count Moltke. Indeed, four years earlier, Moltke, musing on a future conflict, had written:

> Hanover can expect no immediate support from the other contingents of the 10th Federal Corps, or from Southern Germany. Her position must be immediately divined, or the Hanoverian Contingent must be attacked and disarmed. For this, II Corps and possibly one division of the Guard should suffice.[4]

---

1   It will be noted that the Army of the Kingdom of Saxony is not discussed in this volume. This is because, upon the outbreak of hostilities, the Saxon forces withdrew into Bohemia and Moravia, and fought exclusively there, together with the great majority of the Austrian Imperial forces. For details of specialist troop terminology, see Glossary.

2   From July 1 renamed as the 'Army of the Main', after the river of that name. Manteuffel's command had initially been referred to as a 'corps'. Note that a number of very minor states' forces have not been separately described.

3   See Appendix I.

4   Moltke, *Moltkes Militärische Korrespondenz, Aus dem Dienstschriften des Krieges 1866*, p.19. In the same letter, though, Moltke also considers that Bavarian intervention would be unlikely, unless

Vogel von Falckenstein. (Cohn)

The 69 year old von Falckenstein, a veteran of the 1813-14 campaigns against Napoleon, had last seen active service two years earlier, in the Second Schleswig War against Denmark, initially as the chief of staff of the Prussian forces there, and later, as Governor of Jutland. Upon the advent of the growing crisis in early 1866, he was transferred from command of the 7th Corps, and appointed to that of the Prussian forces in Western Germany, as discussed. Unfortunately, Falckenstein, who held large estates in Silesia, considered Moltke to be his social inferior, and was inclined to take his lead from Bismarck, rather than the Chief of Staff. The irascible old General's own immediate subordinates presented sharp contrasts.

The senior of the three, 49 year old Lieutenant-General August von Goeben, finding garrison life tedious, had resigned his commission and fought in the Carlist Wars in Spain, later writing a book on the subject. Re-joining the Prussian service in 1842, Goeben rapidly gained prominence for his intellectual consideration of military affairs, and headed a military mission to Morocco in 1860, observing the Spanish colonial campaign there. In 1864, he commanded a brigade in the Danish Campaign. He had been promoted to lieutenant-general in 1865.

Next in seniority, Major-General Baron Edwin von Manteuffel had entered the army in 1826, and only reached the rank of captain in 1843. Chance placed him at the King's side in the revolutionary year of 1848, and his loyalty at that time was subsequently repaid. In 1857, Manteuffel was appointed to head the Military Cabinet, the committee

---

France comes to her support!!!

which decided, among other matters, officers' promotions, dismissals, and retirements. Widely considered utterly ruthless, he was most unpopular in many quarters. Though also a favourite of the present King, Manteuffel was on less than good terms with von Falckenstein.[5]

Vogel von Falckenstein's third divisional commander was 54 year old Major-General Gustav Friedrich Beyer, a Berliner. Beyer had entered the army 1835, and saw active service as a brigade adjutant during the revolutionary disturbances in the Duchy of Baden in 1849. He had been promoted to the rank of major-general in 1861.

Later in the campaign, as mentioned, an additional 'Prussian' force was briefly introduced into the German campaign. This would be the newly organised II Reserve Corps, commanded by the staunch Prussian ally, the 43 year old Grand Duke Friedrich Franz, of Mecklenburg-Schwerin.[6] The Grand Duke's corps would see brief and limited, though important, action in north-eastern Bavaria during the latter part of operations there.

Arms & Services in the German Theatre

Infantry

The Infantry arm of the Army of the Kingdom of Prussia, in 1866, was composed of 81 three-battalion regiments, nine of which were Guards, and ten independent Jäger battalions. Only one of the latter served in the German Theatre. This newly-raised unit, the 9th Battalion, joined The Army of the Main late in the campaign, on July 22. Battalion organisation was as for the rest of the infantry.

The Prussian infantry, other than the Landwehr, was, during the conflict, armed exclusively with models of the famous Zündnadelgewehr, or 'needle-gun', a single shot breech-loading rifle, invented by Johann Nicolaus Dreyse. Dreyse's weapon used a long needle to pierce, and ignite the cartridge. As early as 1827, Dreyse had offered a prototype model to the Prussian War Ministry, but no interest was shown in the weapon. He, however, was persistent to the point well beyond annoyance, and by the mid 1830's, the weapon was finally being tested by the Prussian Army. After a number of trials, a modified weapon was officially adopted at the end of 1840, and, until 1855, all weapons were manufactured at Dreyse's own factory at Sommerda, north of Erfurt. Beginning in that year, production also commenced at the Royal Arsenal at Spandau. The weapon was faster to load than any muzzle-loader, and could be loaded in the prone position, although its range was actually somewhat less than that of many Minié-type rifled muskets.

The first troops slated to receive the new weapons were the Guards Infantry and the Fusilier Battalions of the II, III, and IV Army Corps. By 1852, 14 Guard and 32 Line battalions were so equipped. Production of these weapons continued until 1865, when a new model, the M. 1862, an improved version with higher production values, was adopted. All infantry regiments engaged in the war of 1866 carried the original versions

---

5   Blankenburg, p.446.
6   See Appendix VI.

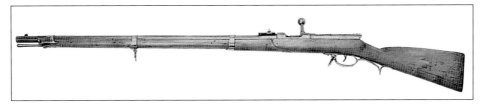

A Model 1841 Prussian Dreyse 'Needle Gun' infantry rifle, 15.4mm.
(Author's collection)

of the M.1841, although some units uncommitted to the conflict had actually been re-equipped with the M. 1862.[7]

The Landwehr infantry formations were armed with older Minié-type muzzle loading weapons. This caused some difficulties, quite apart from the obvious possible logistical ones. At the action of Langensalza, the Landwehr troops, who had been trained to use Dreyse weapons during their own military service, actually found themselves in action using unfamiliar muzzle-loaders.

The first two of the three battalions of a Prussian line infantry regiment were designated musketeer battalions, while the third was the fusilier battalion. In the case of a Fusilier Regiment, however, the battalions were numbered simply I, II, & III. These traditional terms belied the actual identical training and employment of all of the units, as did the titles of Grenadier and Guards regiments.

A battalion comprised four companies, each company having one captain (company commander), one premier-lieutenant, the three second-lieutenants (one acting as battalion adjutant), one cadet, one feldwebel, four sergeants, 19 obergefreiter, 10 gefreiter, four musicians, one orderly, and 204 men. The battalion staff was composed of the commanding officer, normally a major, a battalion surgeon, an assistant surgeon, a paymaster, quartermaster, a feldwebel or vice-feldwebel, a drum major, and two orderlies. The regimental staff included the commanding officer (Colonel or Lieutenant-Colonel, the adjutant (a lieutenant), and the regimental surgeon. Attached were a Senior Warrant Officer/Regimental Sergeant Major, a drum major, and the Quartermaster (an official, not a commissioned officer),

Cavalry

Of the mounted arm of King Wilhelm's army, once again, only a comparatively small percentage would see service in the 'German' campaign.

Artillery

Once again, only a very small portion of the army's artillery arm served in the campaign in Germany. Significantly, there was no siege train attached. The field artillery organisation

---

7   Von Menges, p.74, and also quoted in Walter, p.34. Several other models of the needle-gun existed, including models for Jäger and cavalry troops.

called for one Guard and eight Line Regiments. Each regiment was composed of three foot and one horse 'battalions', the regiment possessing 96 guns in all. Any discussion of higher organisation or employment of artillery is largely irrelevant to the campaign studied here, as no use of guns 'en masse' took place. The 1866 conflict caught the Prussian artillery in transition between rifled and smoothbore weapons. By then, 54 out of an initial total of 144 batteries had been so re-equipped.

Four types of field battery comprised the Army of the Main's artillery arm. These were:

Six pounder breech-loader battery: equipped with six of these Krupp-designed and manufactured weapons. Personnel numbered one captain, one premier-lieutenant, two second-lieutenants, four sergeants, four unteroffizier, eight obergefreiter, eight gefreiter, and 114 gunners.

Four pounder rifled muzzle-loader battery: Another Krupp designed weapon, the four pounder battery comprised six of these weapons. Commanded by a captain, the battery also had a premier-lieutenant, a second-lieutenant, and a Portepee-fähnrich. Non-commissioned ranks were four sergeants, four unteroffizier, eight obergefreiter, eight gefreiter, and 108 gunners.

Twelve pounder smoothbore horse artillery battery: One captain, three subaltern officers, one assistant medical officer, one Portepee fähnrich, one feldwebel/wachtmeister, three sergeants, eight unteroffizier, six obergefreiter, 12 gefreiter, and 124 gunners.

Twelve pounder smoothbore foot battery: One captain, one premier-lieutenant, two second-lieutenants, two sergeants, eight unteroffizier, 12 bombardiere, corporals, two trumpeter,eight obergefreiter, nine gefreiter, and 114 gunners.

It may be noted that half of the batteries in the Army of the Main were equipped with the older twelve pounders. Also, as with many regulations, establishments allowed numerical flkexibility.

KINGDOM OF BAVARIA

In the southern German Kingdom of Bavaria, the revolution of 1848 had been relatively peaceful. King Ludwig I, unwilling to bow to change, had abdicated in favour of his son, Maximilian I. The latter managed to weather the potential political storm reasonably well, although in the following year, more serious unrest in the Palatinate, a Bavarian province on the west bank of the Rhine, did emerge, and the King therefore requested (and received) Prussian troops to quell it.

Equally fortunately for Bavaria, she was not directly involved in the Schleswig-Holstein crisis and war of 1863-64. However, after a short illness, King Maximilian himself died on March 10 1864, his 18 year old son, Ludwig II, succeeding him. In the spring of 1866, the young King would not have the luxury of neutrality with the coming storm between Austria and Prussia. Inaction being impossible, Bavaria chose Austria's side in the conflict. Her mobilisation, however, proved to be both cumbersome and slow, an unfortunate precursor to the army's field performance in the campaign to come

Organisation of the Army

The sizeable, though neglected, military forces of 20 year old King Ludwig II lay in the hands of 70 year old Prince Karl Theodor. The Prince had last seen active service

Prince Karl of Bavaria. (*Illustrirte Kriegs-Chronik*)

at the end 0f the Napoleonic Wars, over 50 years before, and, inevitably, therefore, had no experience of high command. The Bavarian Army itself, as discussed, provided one complete corps of the Federal Army, although a full mobilisation could theoretically have increased this number considerably. As it was, the mobilisation actually undertaken was effected slowly enough.

The Bavarian Army constitutionally provided all of the troops for VII Corps of the Army of the German Confederation, although the Kingdom was also supposedly capable of assembling another similar sized force. VII Corps itself was eventually composed of four infantry divisions, one reserve infantry brigade, a cavalry reserve, and an artillery reserve.[8]

Infantry

The infantry arm consisted of 16 infantry regiments. Each of these comprised three battalions, with every battalion composed of four fusilier and two schützen companies. The fusilier companies were numbered sequentially through the regiment from 1 to 12, and the schützen, from 1 to 6. The unnumbered Leib Regiment held guard status, with the other regiments being numbered from 1-15. The Jäger battalions contained four companies apiece.

---

8   See Appendix III.

The infantry battalions were each allocated to one of nine brigades, eight of which formed the core of the four Bavarian divisions. The remaining brigade, organised subsequently, was classified as the Reserve Infantry Brigade.

A fusilier company, at mobilised combatant strength, consisted of three officers, these being one captain, one oberlieutenant, and one unterlieutenant. NCOs and men numbered one feldwebel, three sergeants, one writer, six corporals, two vice-corporals, three musicians, two pioneers, eight gefreiters, and 112 men, a total of 144 officers and men. There were also three unarmed stretcher bearers. A schützen company had the same complement, with the addition of an additional unterlieutenant. These strengths, however, varied greatly in reality.

The Bavarian army first adopted cap lock weapons in 1839, after long and comprehensive research, with the first arms being produced at the Royal Arsenal at Amberg, three years later. Many of the early weapons were conversions of already existing arms. At this stage, no serious thought was given to the adoption of rifled weapons.

In 1853, though, a new Director of the Arsenal was appointed, 44 year old Captain Baron Philipp von Podewils. An innovator, the Baron introduced, in 1858, a rifled muzzle-loading musket for the infantry, which was to bear his name. The Podewils was produced in three models, all in a calibre of 13.9mm. These were a 'standard ' Model 1 for the infantry, a shorter Model 2 for Jäger and schützen troops, and a carbine Model 3 for specialist marksmen. By 1862, the infantry had been completely equipped with the various appropriate versions of the Podewils.

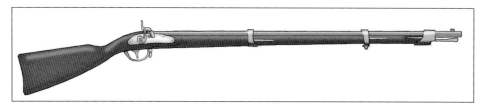

A Model 1858 Bavarian 'Podewils' rifled musket, 13.9mm. (Author's collection)

Jäger

Eight Jäger battalions composed this arm, numbered from one to eight. A Jäger company had a mobilised strength of five officers and 162 NCOs and men. In practice, though, the number of men varied, even though the army's mobilisation was rather slow. Like the schützen, most of the Jäger were armed with the Model 2 Podewils rifled musket, a shorter model than that of the line infantry.

Cavalry

The Kingdom's cavalry force was composed of 12 regiments. Three of these were cuirassier regiments, numbered one to three. Most numerous were the six chevauleger regiments, also consecutively numbered, as also were the three uhlan regiments. On mobilization, four and a half chevauleger regiments were allocated to divisional/brigade duties, leaving the remainder to form the 'Reserve Cavalry', organized in three brigades.[9]

Immediately before mobilization, in mid-June, the internal organisation of the mounted regiments was changed. The regiment continued to be formed with four squadrons, but the size of these squadrons was reduced. At the same time, regiments were also charged with raising two additional second echelon squadrons! With regiments supposedly numbering 415 combatant officers and men, the reality was a wide variation.

Artillery

The field artillery of the Kingdom comprised four regiments, the 1st, 2nd, and 4th designated as foot artillery, and the 3rd, horse. The first two regiments were each composed of two batteries of rifled breech-loading six pounder cannon, and three batteries of twelve pounder muzzle-loading smoothbores. In addition, both regiments, for administrative reasons, contained a further seven batteries, designated as 'Foot Batteries', which, in fact, were actually assigned either to the Artillery Park, or duty in fortresses. The 4th Regiment also contained of two batteries of rifled breech-loading six pounders, but had only two batteries of muzzle-loading twelve pounders, in addition to eight 'foot batteries'. For operational purposes, the foot artillery regiments operated in 'divisions', arbitrarily formed of two, three, or four batteries each. Field foot batteries were large, each having eight guns, divided into two sections.

The 3rd Artillery Regiment was, as noted, deemed to be horse artillery. It contained, unlike the other regiments, four batteries of muzzle-loading twelve pounders. Each of these batteries fielded six cannon.

In terms of personnel, until shortly before the conflict, the mobile batteries all had a wartime complement of 200, other than the six pounder batteries, which had 203. Unfortunately, immediately prior to hostilities, the numbers in six pounder and twelve pounder batteries fell dramatically to 145 combatants and 61 non-combatants, and 144 and 62 respectively. The confusion may be imagined. Most batteries initially hovered around the 130 combatants mark, with four-five of these being officers, the commanding officer being a captain.

Engineers

The Engineer Corps comprised a staff and an engineer regiment. The latter was composed of eight companies, numbered 1 to 8. The first four were designated for field service, and the latter four as fortress companies. In the field, a company, commanded by a captain, comprised five officers, a sergeant-major, two sergeants, one lance-sergeant, three trumpeters, 24 lance-corporals, and 176 men.

---

9   See Appendix IV.

KINGDOM OF HANOVER[10]

The Army of the blind King George V, along with the troops of the Duchy of Brunswick, constituted the 1st Division of the German Confederation's X Corps. The King's army had last seen active service against Denmark in the First Schleswig-Holstein War, which ended in 1850. In December 1863, six battalions, six squadrons, and three artillery batteries were mobilised for possible action, once again against Denmark, but in the event, although war did subsequently break out, the Hanoverian force was fortunate enough not to see any action in it.

The invasion of Hanover itself, in June 1866, came so rapidly that the theoretical organisation of the army had to be immediately and completely improvised, much of it actually on the march. This, in itself, was a salutary and remarkable achievement. The actual plan for mobilisation called for the existence of two infantry divisions, and one of cavalry.[11]

König von Hannover.

King George V of Hanover.
(Author's collection)

Line Infantry

The Royal Hanoverian Army's infantry arm was composed of eight regiments, each having two battalions. These regiments were grouped into four brigades, with these latter forming two divisions of two brigades each. Due to the rapid occurrence of events in the spring and early summer of 1866, this theoretical organisation did not actually come into being, as noted. Instead, an ad hoc order of battle was adopted, based upon four mixed brigades

The core elements of each of these brigades were the two infantry regiments, each having two battalions. The regiments themselves were numbered 1 to 8. A battalion was composed of four companies, with each one having a theoretical four officers, six NCOs, seven corporals, three musicians, and 198 men. With the battalion staff, this totalled 880 officers and men. The chaotic nature of the mobilisation inevitably caused extreme difficulties, and regimental strength varied considerably, no unit coming close to its establishment.

---

10 See Appendix II.

11 Though, no doubt, a great deal of luck was involved in this feat, the sheer determination and devotion to duty of all concerned must be recognised.

Jäger

The four Jäger battalions, one being Guard, and the other three line units, had the same company organisation as the line infantry units. With the battalion staff, this theoretically totalled 893 officers and men. The 3rd Battalion somehow initially actually exceeded its establishment, unlike the other units.

The line infantry were armed with two Minié-type rifled muskets. Unfortunately, these were in two different calibres, the M. 1842 being 16.5mm, and the M. 1855, in 16.1mm. The Jäger troops carried the M. 1858 rifle, this in yet another calibre, 15.7mm. Even without the enforced hurried withdrawal from the city of Hanover to the south, this situation would have been difficult. With the army literally carrying all of the ammunition which it possessed, it was critical.

Cavalry

General Ahrentsschildt's mounted arm consisted of six regiments, two of which were combined with an artillery battery to form a cavalry brigade. The other four regiments were each assigned to the individual self-standing mixed brigades, which composed the majority of the rest of the army.

Cavalry regiments were composed of a staff, and four squadrons. As with the rest of the army, many niceties went out the window, due to the immediacy of the emergency. The authorised establishment of 499 combatants was simply unachievable, a total of under 400 being the highest, and there was a continuous ebb and flow during the brief campaign.

Artillery

As with the rest of the army, the frantic pace of mobilisation precluded attention to many details which would have been necessary for more extended operations. As it was, frenetic activity on the part of two officers, Colonel Stolzenberg and Major Hartmann, produced eight field batteries which were at least capable of taking the field, along with a munitions column. Three of the army's brigades was assigned a battery each, and the 4th Brigade, two. The remaining three batteries formed the Artillery Reserve. As with the cavalry, a chronic shortage of horses added to all the other difficulties. Remarkably, even a small, but serviceable artillery park was brought into being, at least for the short-term!

Engineers

The two pioneer companies of the army, one pioneer and the other pontonnier, were, upon the commencement of hostilities, both attached to the 4th Brigade. The latter was equipped with a Birago-type pontoon train. Together, they nominally comprised 13 officers, 25 NCOs, four musicians, and 192 men.

KINGDOM OF WÜRTTEMBERG

This well-to-do Kingdom, which as such pre-dated the Confederation itself by only 10 years, lay in the extreme south of Germany, between Baden, to the west, and Bavaria, to the east. Formerly a Duchy, it was raised to the status of Kingdom by the great Napoleon, himself. Upon the formation of the Confederation, in 1815, Württemberg became, and remained, a constant thorn in the side of Prussia. The population, in 1864, was just over 1.7 million.

The military forces of King Karl I provided the 1st Division of the Federal VIII Army Corps, and was commanded by Lieutenant-General von Hardegg. It was formed by three infantry brigades, one cavalry brigade, and supporting artillery, with ancillary arms. The troops were recruited by conscription, although the use of substitutes was permissible. A conscript, although theoretically liable for six years' service in the line, followed by six in the Landwehr, could actually expect to serve some 18 months. Like much of VIII Corps, the division was top-heavy with inexperienced senior officers. The mobilisation itself was a messy affair, with alterations being made to the tables of organisation whilst it was actually under way.

Infantry

The infantry arm, as mobilised in 1866, consisted of three brigades, each formed with two regiments, also themselves of two battalions apiece. Attached to each brigade was one of the three existing Jäger battalions. Two of infantry regiments, the 4th, and the 6th, were not included in VIII Corps. The 4th Regiment was not committed to the field until despatched to join the garrison of the Federal Fortress of Mainz, in early July, where it remained until the end of the campaign. The 6th Regiment was sent to occupy the small Prussian principality of Hohezollern-Hechingen, one of the roots of the House of Hohenzollern, much to the annoyance of the Prussians.

Before 1866, a battalion was composed of four companies. The confusion of the mobilisation before the campaign then was finally resolved into a five-company battalion establishment, with a company itself comprising three officers/aspirants, four NCOs, eight corporals, four gefreiters, four musicians, two pioneers, and 136 men. Without the regimental staff, a regiment numbered 1,700 officers and men, but field strength was considerably lower.

Jäger

By 1866, three battalions of Jäger troops existed in the Kingdom's army, the third having been raised only the previous year. A battalion was composed of four companies, a company being formed along the same lines of the infantry.

The Württemberg infantry and Jäger were both armed with the Model 1857 'Vereinsgewehr', originally developed in cooperation with Hesse-Darmstadt and Baden. Designed and manufactured at the Royal Armoury, in Oberndorf, this was a normal Minié-type rifled musket, manufactured in 13.9mm calibre.

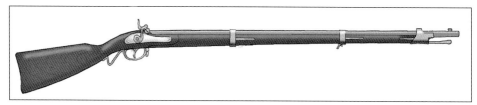

A Model 1857 Vereinsgewehr rifled musket, used by several German states, 13.9mm.
(Author's collection)

Cavalry

The cavalry force comprised a division of four mounted (Reiter) regiments, numbered 1 to 4. Each regiment was composed of five squadrons, one of which was the depot. Theoretical wartime strength was 715 officers and men, with 647 horses. The mobilisation, however, was slow, and ill-organised. The 1st and 4th regiments fielded four squadrons each, and the 3rd, five. The 2nd Regiment was only able to field two. On June 18, the 4th Mounted Regiment comprised 17 officers and 583 men.[12]

Artillery

From 1855, the artillery was officially designated a brigade, with one branch acting as the technical centre for a number of functions. The other branch was the army artillery itself. This latter consisted of four battalions, three of these being field artillery, and the fourth as the fortress artillery.

Upon mobilisation in 1866, six batteries were put in the field, with VIII Corps. Three of these were allocated to the 1st (Württemberg) Division of the corps, two with the Corps Artillery Reserve, and the other one to the Corps Cavalry Reserve. These batteries were all unusually large.

The two batteries of the horse artillery (First Battalion) were equipped with eight guns each, the 1st battery having Krupp rifled six pounders, and the 2nd Battery, six Austrian muzzle-loading rifled four pounders. The 6th and 7th Foot Batteries (Second Battalion) were each armed with eight Krupp rifled six pounders. Finally, the 1st and 4th Foot Batteries (Third Battalion) fielded eight smoothbore twelve pounders apiece.

The Fortress Battalion, composed of three companies, providing two for Federal fortresses, and one for field use.

GRAND DUCHY OF BADEN

The south-west German state of the Grand Duchy of Baden, ruled by Grand Duke Friedrich, possessed an army, which provided the 2nd Division of the Federal VIII Corps. It was composed of 10 battalions, 11 squadrons, five batteries, and ancillary troops. In the field, this force would be commanded by Lieutenant-General Prince Wilhelm of

---

12 Starklof, p.256.

Baden.[13] The Prince's command was trained and equipped after the Prussian model, and, indeed there were some sympathies within Baden for the Prussian cause. Service was theoretically universal, with some exceptions, but substitution was freely allowed.

Infantry

The infantry arm of the Field Division consisted of two brigades, each composed of two regiments, also of two battalions each. In addition, both brigades possessed an additional battalion. In the case of the 1st Brigade, this was the Jäger Battalion, and in the 2nd Brigade, it was the 2nd Fusilier Battalion, giving the force a total of 10 infantry battalions. Unique among the Federal forces, the Baden troops were armed with the Prussian needle-gun, having previously carried the Minié-type Model 1857 'Vereinsgewehr'.

In addition to the troops of the Field Division, there was a replacement contingent, composed of the 1st Fusilier Battalion, and three replacement battalions. Finally, the two battalions of the 4th Infantry Regiment were a part of the garrison of the Federal fortress of Rastatt.

An infantry company, on a war footing, was composed of five officers, 19 NCOs, four musicians, and 210 men, a total of 238 combatants. A battalion comprised 22 officers, 78 NCOs, 17 musicians, and 840 men, a total of 957 combatants. The two battalion regiment, at full strength should number 47 officers, 157 NCOs, 45 musicians, and 1,680 men, a theoretical total of 1,929. Most, if not all units, however, were understrength.

Cavalry

The Baden cavalry comprised three dragoon regiments. Each of the regiments consisted of four squadrons. All three units were part of the Field Division, apart from one squadron assigned to Rastatt. There were also two replacement squadrons. From 1854, a squadron was composed of five officers, five NCOs, six corporals, 12 carabiniers, and 75 'riders'. The regiment had a full strength of 487, all ranks, but this was not achieved in the campaign.

Artillery

The Field Division had five artillery batteries assigned to it. One battery was designated as horse artillery, and was armed with six smoothbore six pounders. The remaining four foot batteries were equipped with six rifled six pounders each. Attached was also a munitions column. One six pounder foot battery, armed with six pounder smoothbores, was also assigned to the replacement contingent. A foot battery had four officers, one official, 145 NCOs and men, and nine non-combatants, a total of 159 personnel.

Other Troops

Attached to the Field Division were a Pioneer detachment, a bridging train, and a medical unit.

---

13   See Appendix V.

ELECTORATE OF HESSE

The western German state of Electoral Hesse, or Hesse-Cassel, with a population of some three-quarters of a million, had an army which, in a normal situation, would have formed a part of the Federal IX Corps. In 1866, however, the situation forced the Elector and his government to choose, like everyone else, between Prussia and Austria. Unlike most of the other states, however, the Electorate was stranded, even more than Hanover to south, between Prussian dominated areas. The state's military establishment consisted of one infantry division, a cavalry brigade, and an artillery brigade, all organised along Prussian lines.

In the event, of the whole force, only two squadrons of hussars actually saw field service in the Main Campaign. The rest of the contingent, being judged as unfit for field operations by the commander of VIII Corps, was posted to the Federal fortress of Mainz, where some minor sporadic action took place.

Infantry

The infantry division comprised four infantry regiments, each of two battalions. The senior regiment was entitled The Life Guards, and the other three line regiments were numbered 1 to 3. There were also two light infantry battalions, these being the Schützen Battalion, and the Jäger Battalion. Each regiment, on a war footing, was to have numbered 1,600 officers and men, but the entire electorate was overrun so quickly by the invading Prussians, that mobilisation proved to be impossible. The quick action of the army commander, General Loßberg, did allow a significant portion of the force to escape Prussian captivity.

Cavalry

The Elector's cavalry brigade was composed of three regiments, these being the Gardes du Corps (cuirassiers), and two hussar regiments. In the event, only two squadrons of this force would actually participate in field operations.

Artillery

Hesse-Cassell's artillery contingent consisted of one 'brigade', composed of three foot artillery batteries and one horse battery. The foot batteries were equipped with twelve pounder smoothbore muzzle-loaders, rifled breech-loading six pounders, or six pounder smoothbore muzzle-loaders. The horse artillery battery possessed smoothbore muzzle-loaders. All four batteries had six cannon each. None of the individual formations actually had even 100 total personnel.

GRAND DUCHY OF HESSE AND BY RHINE

Also colloquially known as Hesse-Darmstadt, the Grand Duchy was composed of three provinces in southern Germany, to the north of the Duchy of Baden. The Grand Duke, Ludwig III, possessed an army which furnished the entire 3rd Division of the Federal

VIII Corps, with additional elements at corps level. This division consisted of two infantry brigades, one independent battalion, a cavalry brigade of two regiments, and four artillery batteries.

Infantry

The Grand Duchy's infantry arm consisted of two infantry brigades, each of two regiments and one Jäger company. The regiments were numbered 1 to 4, the 1st Regiment having Guard status as the 'Leib' Regiment. In addition, there existed the battalion-sized Schützen, or 'Sharpshooter Corps'.

The wartime complement of an infantry regiment was 1,666, including 38 officers. A battalion, commanded by a major (himself, attended by a soldier of the military train), comprised a staff of an adjutant (a lieutenant), one junior adjutant, two other lieutenants, one colour-bearer, one battalion drummer, one senior doctor, with assistant medical officer, and three officer attendant soldiers of the military train. Three other men of the military train were also attached to battalion headquarters. Each battalion was composed of four companies. Unfortunately, during the mobilisation, three different organisations were promulgated, and a fifth company added, theoretically for open order fighting.

A company was composed of a captain, an oberlieutenant, one lieutenant (two in a schützen company), an oberfeldwebel, four feldwebels, eight corporals, one trumpeter, three drummers (only four trumpeters in a schützen company), four gefreiters, one pioneer, 10 sharpshooters, and 130 men.

The troops were armed with the Minié-type M. 1857 'Vereinsgewehr', in a calibre of 13.9mm.

Scharfschützen-Corps

A specialist light infantry formation, the Scharfschützen-Corps (Sharpshooter Corps) was established in the summer of 1861, but little was done, as so often, until the possibility of conflict actually threatened. A battalion-sized unit, this was apart from the line formations, though it happily poached as many men as it could from them.

The corps had four companies, each to be composed of one captain, one oberlieutenant, two lieutenants, one oberfeldwebel, four feldwebels, eight corporals, four trumpeters, four gefreiters, two pioneers, 120 men, and four men of the military train. A theoretical strength of 880 was never approached, and an initial total of under 600 is likely.

Cavalry

The Hessian cavalry comprised only two regiments, the 1st and 2nd Mounted Regiments. The 1st Regiment was a part of the Hessian Division, while the 2nd was an VIII Corps asset, being assigned to the Reserve Cavalry. Both mobilised regiments theoretically included one colonel, one other field officer (lieutenant-colonel or major), four captains, five premier-lieutenants, eight second-lieutenants, a doctor, a junior doctor, a veterinarian, a trumpet-major, a quartermaster, 56 other NCOs, 16 musicians, 16 lance-corporals, and 452 men.

Artillery

Hesse-Darmstadt's artillery consisted of three foot artillery batteries, one horse battery, and a fortress battery. The three foot batteries were each equipped with six Krupp six pounder breech-loaders, while the horse battery was a hybrid, with two of the Krupp breech-loader, and four twelve pounder muzzle-loaders. Complement was theoretically 238 all ranks. A small depot battery was also formed.

A pioneer company of three officers, 12 NCOs, and 127 men, with bridging equipment also took the field.

GRAND DUCHY OF MECKLENBURG-SCHWERIN

A close ally of Prussia, the Grand Duchy effectively furnished a reinforced brigade of some 5,500 men to the Prussian cause, around which the II Reserve Corps was then formed. Commanded by Grand Duke Friedrich Franz II, this force took to the field in eastern Bavaria in late July.

Infantry

The Grand Duke's infantry consisted primarily of two regiments, each one composed of two battalions, with all battalions numbered sequentially from one to four. The 1st Battalion held Guard status, and had a 36-man band attached. Wartime battalion complement was 18 officers, 65 NCOs, and 798 men. Attached were one doctor, with four medical orderlies, one train NCO, and 20 train soldiers.

In addition to the above, a two-company Jäger 'battalion' existed. Each company had a theoretical mobilised combatant strength of four officers, an officer aspirant, four NCOs, six corporals, three musicians, and 144 men.

Cavalry

The Grand Duke's cavalry consisted of one dragoon regiment, composed of four field and one depot squadrons. The four squadron regiment took the field with combatants numbering two majors, four captains, 15 lieutenants, two officer-aspirants, 50 NCOs, 15 musicians, and 508 men.

Artillery

Two field batteries comprised the Grand-Ducal artillery, the 1st Battery being armed with smoothbore muzzle-loading twelve pounders, and the 2nd, with Krupp breech-loaders, each battery having six guns. Each unit was commanded by a captain, and had a premier-lieutenant, two second-lieutenants, an officer-aspirant, two sergeants, four corporals (three), three musicians. 15 lance corporals (12), 56 mounted gunners (42), 42 drivers (36), of whom 12 were senior gunners, 27 (21) reserve gunners, four (three), and one doctor (assistant). There was also a small munitions column, and a pioneer detachment.

DUCHY OF NASSAU

Duke Adolph's modest military forces, during the 1866 campaign, consisted of an infantry brigade and two artillery batteries. The infantry brigade consisted of two regiments, each composed of two battalions, and also a single Jäger battalion. All five infantry arm battalions had five companies apiece. An infantry company comprised four officers, 15 NCOs, 12 gefreiters, four pioneers, four musicians, and 164 men. A full strength regiment numbered 2,066 combatants. The single Jäger Battalion numbered 808 combatants. The troops were armed with variants of the Bavarian Podewils rifled musket, known in its Nassau incarnation as the M. 1861.

The Duke's artillery, as prescribed in May 1866, consisted of two batteries, each of eight guns. The batteries were, themselves, operationally subdivided into half batteries. One battery was equipped with eight smoothbore muzzle-loaders, and the other with eight rifled Krupp breech-loaders. These were serviced by two small munitions columns. There was also a pioneer company, consisting of a premier-lieutenant, three NCOs, and 81 men

AUSTRIAN EMPIRE

As was the case with Prussia, but even more so, the overwhelming majority of the Empire's military forces were in other theatres, in this case, Bohemia/Moravia and northern Italy. Indeed, the Imperial forces in the Theatre, hastily assembled from depots and various Federal fortresses, were comparatively completely insignificant. These seven battalions, and two artillery batteries, were formed into an ad-hoc brigade, under the command of Major-General Hahn. Brigaded with the Nassau Brigade, this force constituted the 4th Division of the Federal VIII Corps.

Infantry

Austrian infantry involved in the German campaign consisted of only one complete three battalion infantry regiment, individual battalions of three others, and one Feld-Jäger Battalion, the 35th. An infantry battalion was composed of six companies, each company comprising one captain, one oberlieutenant, two lieutenants, 14 NCOs, 16 senior privates, 130 privates, one trumpeter, and two pioneers. The Jäger battalion had a combatant strength of 963.

Artillery

Two Imperial-Royal artillery batteries were present during the Main Campaign, one four pounder foot battery, and the other, a twelve pounder battery. Each battery was equipped with eight rifled muzzle-loading cannon.

MINOR STATES

A number of very minor states which half-heartedly favoured Prussia in the conflict managed to prevaricate their way through it. Some were actually able to avoid committing troops until hostilities had actually ended. The participation or otherwise of these entities was, of course, made no material difference at all to the outcome of the conflict, but showed perhaps, that in the mid 19th Century, irrelevance still helped!

Anhalt

The pro-Prussian Duchy of Anhalt, though having a population of almost 200,000, only possessed a military establishment of two infantry battalions, each of four companies, and two sharpshooter companies. The two battalions together mustered a little over 1,900 officers and men including some men transferred from the sharpshooters. The contingent later joined the II Reserve Corps in Eastern Bavaria.

Duchy of Brunswick

The staunchly pro-Prussian northern Duchy of Brunswick proved particularly reticent when called upon to assist its mentor. Only on July 21, after considerable pressure from Berlin, did the Duke reluctantly mobilise his forces. The Ducal forces comprised an infantry regiment of two battalions, each battalion having four companies, a four-company 'Leib' Battalion, a six-company Landwehr Battalion, a hussar regiment, and an artillery battery.

Oldenburg-Hanseatic Brigade

Brigaded together in the coming conflict were the armed forces a number of Prussian allied north German states. These comprised the military forces of Bremen, the Grand Duchy of Oldenburg, Hamburg, and Lübeck. The units of the brigade took the field late in the campaign, but significantly, as part of the Army of the Main, rather than the II Reserve Corps.

Free City of Frankfurt (on the Main)

The Free City of Frankfurt, which also housed the Federal German Parliament, possessed a modest military establishment of one single infantry battalion. This force, divided into six companies, occupied a barracks in the centre of the city. The strength of the unit was under 750 officers and men, when the Prussian marched into the city, and no opposition was offered. The battalion was swiftly disbanded, and, later, the city itself annexed by Prussia.

Lippe-Detmold

This close ally of Prussia consisted of a number of separated landholdings, having a population of some 100,000. Its military force consisted of one ('fusilier') battalion, trained and organised along Prussian lines. This unit joined the Prussian Army of the Main in early July.

The Mecklenburg Grand Duchies

Despite its imposing title, the Grand Duchy of Mecklenburg-Schwerin was a poverty-stricken entity, comprised of two separate entities, in north Germany, separated by its sister Duchy, Mecklenburg-Schwerin, with which it co-operated in military matters.

The Grand Duchy's army comprised two infantry regiments, each of two battalions, a two-company Jäger battalion, a four squadron dragoon regiment, two artillery batteries, and a pioneer detachment. A band was attached to the 1st (Guard Grenadier) Regiment.

The theoretical strength of a four-company infantry battalion was 18 officers, 65 NCOs, 17 musicians, and 798 men. Medical and ancillary personnel added another 27 men. The Jäger battalion took the field with 11 officers, one official, two doctors, 25 NCOs, 11 buglers, 273 men, and 17 other personnel.

The Dragoon Regiment, commanded by a major, had a staff of two officers, one doctor, one junior doctor, a trumpet-major, two officials, and 10 men. The main body of the regiment comprised two captains, two oberlieutenants, 13 second-lieutenants, two aspirants, 50 NCOs, 15 trumpeters, one doctor, two assistant doctors, 508 men, and 41 other personnel.

The Grand-Ducal artillery consisted of two six-gun batteries, the 1st equipped with smoothbore twelve pounder cannon, and the 2nd with Krupp rifled six pounders. The former, commanded by a captain, comprised an oberlieutenant, two second lieutenants, a sergeant-major, an officer aspirant, two sergeants, four corporals, three trumpeters, 15 lance corporals, 56 unmounted gunners, 42 drivers, 27 reserve gunners, four transport men, and a smith.

The Krupp battery had a slightly smaller complement, having one fewer corporal, three lance corporals, 14 dismounted gunners, six drivers, and six reserve gunners.

Leaning, as did it sister Duchy, toward Prussia, Mecklenburg-Strelitz's very modest military forces amounted to one four-company infantry battalion, and a six-gun battery of Krupp six pounder breech-loaders. Pressure was applied by Berlin to involve the Duchy in the conflict, and thus, the Grand Ducal troops found themselves on occupation duty in Saxony.

Schaumburg-Lippe

Another very minor state, in north-western Germany, this member of the Bund adopted, possibly in error, an anti-Prussian stance. This move resulted in its rapid occupation by Prussian troops. The principality's two infantry companies were subsequently added to the Confederation garrison of Mainz.

The Schwarzburg Principalities

Both of the small Schwarzburg states were pro-Prussian, and, upon the outbreak of hostilities declared support for that Kingdom. Both contingents saw limited employment in the operations in Germany.

The Schwarzburg-Rudolstadt contingent, a four-company fusilier battalion, after a period of administrative confusion, attained a strength of some 700, all ranks. After a short time at the fortress of Erfurt, the battalion joined the force blockading the Federal fortress of Mainz.

Its sister principality, Schwarzburg-Sonderhausen, likewise contributed a four-company fusilier battalion to the Prussian cause. It, too, was committed to the blockade of Mainz.

The Thuringian Duchies

The four Duchies of Saxe-Altenburg, Saxe-Coburg-Gotha, Saxe-Meiningen, and Saxe-Weimar-Eisenach all lay in the region of north Germany known as Thuringia. All had their origins in the Duchy of Thuringia, which ceased to exist in 1440. In 1866, three states declared for Prussia, while the fourth found itself opposing her.

The Saxe-Altenburg Fusilier Regiment was composed of two four-company battalions. The contingent, 30 officers and 1,233 NCOs and men, spent most of the campaign in the garrison of the Prussian fortress at Erfurt.

The Saxe-Coburg-Gotha troops would see arduous service on Prussia's behalf. The Duchy's two-battalion infantry regiment saw initial service in the campaign against Hanover, and then in the subsequent Main Campaign. For the latter, the mobilised strength was 29 officers, one officer aspirant, nine senior NCOs, and just under 1,500 other ranks. There was also a band.

Opposing Prussia, the small armed force of Saxe-Meiningen, a two-battalion infantry regiment, was marched, in mid-June, to the Federal fortress of Mainz, where it remained as part of the garrison, throughout the campaign. Its strength, at this time, was about 900 officers and men.[14]

The Duchy of Saxe-Weimar-Eisenach was one of the winners of the 1815 Congress of Vienna, gaining land, and beoming a Grand Duchy. In 1866, though having close ties with Prussia, Karl Alexander attempted to remain neutral. This resulted in a declaration for Prussia, while the contingent of troops were sent to join the garrison of the anti-Prussian garrison of Mainz. This force comprised three weak battalions totalling under a thousand, all ranks.

Reuss-Greiz & Reuss-Schleiz

Upon the crisis, these small states split over the issue, with Reuss-Greiz voting against Prussia. Each provided a battalion to the opposing sides. In true comic opera fashion, both battalions subsequently came to form the garrison of Rastatt, without any hostilities taking place.

Waldeck & Pyrmont

A small pro-Prussian Principality, north of Electoral Hesse, Waldeck possessed, in 1866, a military force of one four-company infantry battalion, some 750 strong, all ranks. This unit was mobilised, and served in a garrison/occupation capacity.

---

14   See Appendix XI.

THE FEDERAL VIII CORPS – The 'Bundes-Armee'

Prince Alexander of Hesse.
(*Illustrirte Kriegs-Chronik*)

Command of the Federal VIII Corps was given to 42 year old Prince Alexander of Hesse, the third son of Grand Duke Ludwig II. The Prince was commissioned as a second-lieutenant in his father's army at the age of 10, before entering the Russian Imperial Guard in 1840. He subsequently saw service in the campaign in the Caucasus in 1845, gaining him promotion and also the Knight's Cross of the Order of Saint George. Later, in the Austrian service, Alexander again saw action, in Italy, at the battles of Montebello and Solferino in 1859, winning the Knight's Cross of the Order of Maria Theresa for his conduct at the latter. By the Spring of 1866 Alexander commanded the Austrian VII Corps, in northern Italy. Upon the outbreak of hostilities, he resigned his Imperial commission, and accepted the command of the Federal VIII Corps.[15]

The corps was, of course, a microcosm of much of the Confederation itself. It was plagued by rivalries, petty jealousies, and differing interests. There were also considerable differences in weapons and equipment, levels of command, training, and doctrine. It would have been a difficult command for anyone to fully control, but it was to prove to be almost beyond the Prince, who, nevertheless, acted throughout with great dignity. Like its Bavarian counterpart, the corps was top heavy, having too many senior officers, including no less than eight lieutenant-generals. It is also most significant to note that VIII Corps had never actually been mobilised, thus rendering the difficulties of command and control even more difficult!

THE TOPOGRAPHY OF THE SEAT OF WAR

The area within which the campaign in Germany would take place encompassed a varied landscape from the open heath in the north of Hanover to mountains and thick forests further south. The first-hand account of an acute observer of these events, a British officer of the Royal Engineers, the then Captain Charles Cornwallis Chesney, gives a good description of the differing terrain as it then was:

15 Had he not done so, the Prince would, presumably, have retained his command, and fought against the Royal Italian Army.

The theatre of the events we propose to trace lies mainly in the district which separates the rich and varied Westphalian possessions of Prussia from the tamer provinces of Brandenburg and Saxony. Starting from the north, we glance from the Elbe (River) across a flat and sandy country, with a few ranges of hills about the (River) Weser, forming the chief part of the Kingdom of Hanover. To the south-west this plain may be followed out to Frankfurt through the Electorate of Hesse-Cassel, becoming more hilly as the Rhine is neared; but to the south-east it is distinctly shut off from Saxony by an irregular mass of broken country rising to mountainous elevations, traversed by few roads, and known as the Hartz (Harz Mountains).

A line drawn due north and south through the capital of Hanover would divide its whole territory into nearly equal parts, pass clear of the Hartz through the eastern portion of Hesse-Cassell, and strike, twenty miles west of Eisenach, on the apex of the mountainous triangle known as the Thuringian Forest, which fills the space north of the (River) Main from Bamberg to Aschaffenburg, being about 70 miles deep (around 112 kilometres), and 90 (some 145 kilometres) wide from east to west at its base. The eastern side of this triangle is connected by minor ranges of hills with the great Bohemian mountains; the western overlooks the Hessian Plain, and throws its last branch nearly out to Frankfurt.

The great railroad from that city into Saxony turns the forest by running north-east to Cassell, and then south-east to Eisenach, where an opening of a few miles wide is left by nature between the Hartz and the Thuringian (mountain) chains. Another line is conducted along the south of the latter from Frankfurt to Bamberg, up the Main, being first carried over the hills to Aschaffenburg to escape one deep bend in the river, and cutting off another by crossing a fine plain between the stream and the mountains beyond the city of Wurtzburg (Würzburg).

Rugged as are the Hartz and Thuringian districts by nature are, German industry has crossed their hills and valleys with numberless fine carriage-roads, and rendered the movement of troops of all arms practicable in any given direction by a division of the columns rather greater than that practised in an easier country.[16]

---

16   Chesney, C. C., 'The Campaign in Western Germany', *Blackwood's Edinburgh Magazine*, January 1867, pp.68-69.

5

Hostilities begin – The Campaign of Hanover and Electoral Hesse

The Prussian Occupation of Electoral Hesse

The Electorate of Hesse was first state to be forcibly occupied by Prussia in 1866. Presented with the crisis at hand, the myopic parliamentarians of the Electorate had insisted upon a neutral stance in the matter, absorbed as they were with internal matters. The unreality of their position quickly became evident.

The Prussian division of Major-General Beyer, then concentrated around Wetzlar, to the west of the Electorate, assembled near Giessen, on the night of June 15.[1] At 02:00 the following morning, Beyer crossed the border into Hesse-Cassel, heading directly for the capital, Cassel. On his orders, on the morning of the 16th, a detachment of 80 men of FR39 in wagons, and a troop of hussars, was pushed forward to the town of Marburg, where the force surprised and captured three officers and 60 men of the Kur-Hessian 2nd Infantry Regiment.[2]

The Glümer Brigade entered Cassel, the Electorate'scapital, on the 19th, and the rest of the division, on the following day, after a hard march of some 110 kilometres from Wetzlar. The Elector, Friedrich-Wilhelm I, fully understanding the overall situation, had already ordered his troops to muster and march south towards Bad Hersfeld, with a view to linking up with the other elements of Federal VIII Corps assembling around Frankfurt and Mainz, the latter of which already had some Hessian troops as part of its fortress garrison.

Major-General von Loßberg, commander of the Elector's army, swiftly took control of the very rapidly assembling Kur-Hessian troops, and by further prompt action was able to transport over 4,000 men, nearly 1,000 horses, and 16 guns, by rail as far as Hünfeld. From there, von Loßberg then moved in the direction of Hanau via Fulda, adding the garrisons of these two towns to his command. Subsequently, he marched towards Frankfurt to link with the Federal forces assembling in that area. On June 23, the force was placed at the orders of Prince Alexander of Hesse. General Loßberg had served his sovereign well, though the latter was unable to benefit from it.

On the 29th, the Prince himself was able to carefully inspect General von Loßberg's troops, later confiding his disappointment to his campaign diary:

---

1   Hiltl, p.37.
2   Rintelen, *Geschichte des Niederrheinischen Füsilier-Regiments Nr.39*, p.178.

Inspection of the Electoral Hessian division, 4,600 strong, under General von Loßberg, at Hanau. My former intention to allow the Electoral Hessians to join VIII Corps, had to be given up, because these troops require a longer period to become combat ready. I will now move them to reinforce the garrison of Mainz, where they will be set on a war footing, provided that the partial occupation of the Electorate by the enemy allows for it.[3]

Only two squadrons of hussars were considered fit to join Alexander's field force. These troops were duly posted as the divisional cavalry of the 4th Division of VIII Corps. General Loßberg, most especially after his admirable exertions in assembling and leading his men to join the main force, must also have felt completely humiliated by this slight. The great bulk of the Elector's force subsequently assembled in the fortress of Mainz, as ordered, remaining there throughout the campaign.

Curiously, the Elector himself had courageously remained in Cassel, defiant of the invaders. Regardless of the purpose of his stand, he was quickly arrested by the Prussian authorities, and taken to the fortress of Stettin, far to the east, in Pomerania, where he remained as a prisoner for the duration of hostilities. The Electorate was itself quickly abolished, becoming a part of Prussia. Two Prussian battalions, I/IR 30 and II/IR 70, were then retained on occupation duty in Cassel for just over a month.[4]

Prussian Troops enter the Kingdom

On the morning of June 15, the Prussian Minister to Hanover, Prince Ysenburg, presented an ultimatum to King George, at the same time as similar notes were presented to the Kingdom of Saxony and the Electorate of Hesse. As unsatisfactory replies were received (ie capitulation), Prussia declared war on all three the same day. On the 16th, Prussian forces then invaded all three states. The capital of Electoral Hesse, Cassel, was quickly occupied, as discussed, as was Dresden, the Saxon capital. It was an absolute imperative for the Prussians that both Hanover and Electoral Hesse be rapidly overrun, since they lay directly between the western and eastern provinces of Prussia itself.[5]

At the point when hostilities commenced, the Prussian forces in Western Germany comprised three widely separated components. The 13th Division of Lieutenant-General von Goeben was near the town of Minden, some 55 kilometres west of the Kingdom's capital, the city of Hanover. As noted, the Combined Division of Major-General Baron Manteuffel was to the north, in Holstein. Another Combined Division, that of Major-General von Beyer, was, as also noted, in the Prussian enclave of Wetzlar, sandwiched between Hesse-Darmstadt and Nassau. These formations, the Western Army, under the command of General of Infantry Vogel von Falckenstein, then moved as described above, as well as against Hesse-Darmstadt.

---

3   Prince Alexander, *Feldzugs-Journal des Oberbefehlshabers des 8ten deutschen Bundes-Armee-Corps im Feldzug des Jahres 1866 in Westdeutschland*, pp.4-5. Significantly, Colonel Booms considered that, as a whole, VIII Corps, "...was unfit as an instrument of war.", Booms, p.5.

4   Both units rejoined General Beyer's division on July 21.

5   It is interesting to note that Prussia declared war on these three states amost a week before she did so to Austria!

Hanoverian Mobilisation and Initial Moves

Upon receipt of the first Prussian note, an immediate concentration of the Hanoverian Army, which fortunately was already partially mobilised for summer manoeuvres, was ordered. All available infantry and artillery were hurriedly moved from the capital by train to the city of Göttingen, almost 100 kilometres to the south, with formations elsewhere instructed to follow on as best they could. The cavalry was also directed there, but travelled by road. Once the troops had left Hanover, every effort was made to send as large quantities as possible of provisions, ammunition, and other supplies in the same direction. Inevitably, however, considerable amounts of stores and ammunition had to be abandoned, there being no time to take these into consideration. This also meant that much in the way of stores and munitions, particularly ammunition for the infantry, were in short supply. The King himself, accompanied by the Crown Prince, had arrived in Göttingen in the early morning of the 16th. After discussions with his senior officers, he appointed Major-General Alexander Ahrentsschildt as commander of his forces, with a promotion to the rank of Lieutenant-General.

A young Hanoverian infantry volunteer, 17 year old Friedrich Freudenthal, of the 2nd Battalion, 5th Infantry Regiment, described part of his own slow rail journey from Lüneburg, some 130 kilometres north of Hanover:

> The first, longer, interruption of our train journey happened on this evening at Ülzen. A number of old soldiers, workers, and countrymen from the town and the surroundings had gathered at the station, who greeted us, asked after friends and acquaintances in the regiment and served beer and other drinks. These people had not gotten call-up orders, but now that they were seeing that war was about to break out, they did not know how to act, whether they should act on their own initiative

Ahrentsschildt. (Fontane)

Hanoverian troops mobilise amidst scenes of confusion. (Cohn)

and follow the army, or stay at home with their wives and children and act as if the whole matter was of no concern. From their serious and thoughtful expressions, it could be seen that they did not take this issue light heartedly.[6]

The very able General Ahrentsschildt had immediately implemented a rapid organisation plan for the army, of necessity, based upon those troops which were to hand or, like Private Freudenthal, actually on their way. No time at all was available for any discussion or consideration. Of the existing force of around 20,500 men, about 4,400 were untrained recruits. The remaining 16,000 men were formed into five self-standing brigades, four of them mixed-arms, and the fifth, of cavalry. The mixed brigades were each composed of two infantry regiments (four battalions), one Jäger battalion, one cavalry regiment, and an artillery battery (two in the 4th Brigade).

The cavalry brigade comprised two regiments. There was also a small artillery reserve of three batteries, and a tiny artillery park of 10 guns. With little in the way of resources, and in very difficult circumstances, Ahrentsschildt had done his most commendable best.[7] The number of troops available would, of course, have been larger had the decision

---

6   Freudenthal, *Von Lüneburg bis Langensalza*, p.79. The underage Freudenthal had managed to talk his way into enlistment in April.

7   See Appendix II for further details.

to mobilise been taken earlier. This was not done, understandably, largely in case it prejudiced the then on-going negotiations with Prussia. This perceived diplomacy would, unfortunately, continue to bedevil Hanoverian plans. This is an easy mistake to observe with clear hindsight. No genuine negotiations were ever actually on offer from Prince Bismarck, at any time.

There had, as discussed, been precious little time for Hanover to react, and although the main part of the army was, for the moment, out of immediate danger, this was not universal. Several outlying forces of Hanoverian troops had no warning as to the Prussian moves, and were in most vulnerable situations. This was particularly true of the northern posts of the army, especially the important fortress of Stade.

Already impatient at any apparent delays, on the 16th, Count Moltke sent a curt telegram to General von Falckenstein, which read:

> General Beyer is moving from Wetzlar against Cassel. Hanoverian troops are extending towards Göttingen. Confirm receipt of this message.[8]

The Chief of Staff would continue to bombard von Falckenstein, as well as his subordinates, with messages to get to grips with the Hanoverians from this point on.

The 'Surprise' of the Fortress of Stade, June 17-18

The long neglected Hanoverian fortress of Stade lay on the west bank of the River Elbe, some 30 kilometres west of Hamburg. Stationed here was a depot, containing 150 older men, and also 200 recruits of the 4th Infantry Regiment, along with about 200 unassigned artillerymen of the 3rd Artillery Battalion, all under the command of the fortress governor, Major-General Rechtern. Also a not inconsiderable arsenal, Stade was a prime target for the invaders, completely unprepared for any conflict, and now ripe for the taking.

Until two days before, however, the fortress had also been the barracks of the Hanoverian 4th Infantry Regiment, and the 9th Foot Artillery Battery. After the Prussian ultimatum, on the 15th, both of these units were summoned in the general mobilisation. Both units duly arrived in the mustering point, Göttingen, overnight on the 16/17th.[9]

At twilight on the evening of June 17, two Prussian Naval vessels the *Cyclop* and the Paddle Steamer *Loreley*, in company with the privately locally chartered steamer *Harburg*, left the port of Harburg, south of Hamburg, on the 90 minute journey towards Stade. Embarked on these vessels was one infantry battalion, F/IR 25, Lieutenant-Colonel Cranach. Cranach's mission was simple; he was to take the fortress!

Accompanied by axe and hammer wielding sailors from the ships, von Cranach led his men ashore at Twielenfleth, some eight kilometres from the fortress. Although reported by mounted vedettes, the Prussians were able to force the gate, and enter the town. Shots were exchanged in the main square before General Rechtern sent an emissary to

---

8 *Korrespondenz*, Nr. 115, p.223.
9 Lettow-Vorbeck, pp.146-147 & Wyatt, p.22.

facilitate negotiations, which soon became a capitulation. The Hanoverian soldiers were sent home, and the officers released.[10]

This virtually bloodless 'coup de main' yielded not only the fortress, but also its considerable booty, including the following:

> All necessary equipment and armament to equip one six pounder battery
> Eight rifled twelve pounder cannon
> Seven rifled twenty-four pounder cannon
> 14,000 rifled muskets
> 110,000 kilos of powder
> One million rifle cartridges
> 11,600 woollen blankets

The six pounder battery was rapidly horsed and manned, and sent post-haste by road to Hanover. It was then attached to von Goeben's 13th Division.[11] Following this undoubted coup, there remained only a few small works remained in Hanoverian hands. On the 19th, the coastal batteries at the Weser were abandoned, as was the Ems battery, and the city of Emden, itself, was then also surrendered.[12] It had been immediately absolutely clear to both sides that the Kingdom's coastline was completely indefensible.

The Net closes on Hanover

Prussian Occupation of the City of Hanover

The first troops of the 13th Division entered Hanover itself, at around 18:00, on June 17, with Generals von Falckenstein and Goeben riding near the fore. Despite the herculean efforts of all ranks of the Hanoverian Army, and also those of the civil population, much materiel had to be left behind in and around Hanover due to the rapid escalation of the crisis. One of the first actions of the occupiers was an immediate suspension of the train service to Göttingen. No further munitions or supplies were now available from this source. This problem was particularly acute in regard to rifle ammunition. Of necessity abandoned to the Prussians in the area of the capital, included the following:

> Some 60 cannon, many not fit/appropriate for use
> 800 assorted vehicles and wagons
> One light bridging train
> Approximately 10,000 Minié-type rifles
> 200,000 kilogrammes of powder[13]

10 Ibid., pp.146-148.
11 See Appendix I. This battery, with its associated caissons, etc. arrived in Hanover on June 23. For Stade, see also Lettow-Vorbeck, Vol. I, pp.147-148, G.G.S., pp.52-53 & Rüstow, pp.99-100.
12 *Österreichs Kämpfe 1866*, Vol. I, p.172 (hereafter cited as Ö.K.).
13 Sichart, p.35.

Ahrentsschildt Pauses at Göttingen

By June 18, the Hanoverian Army in and around Göttingen was as ready to take the field in as far as was possible under the circumstances. In addition, hard work had been put in hand constructing defensive works there. The question over what to do next inevitably loomed large. After lengthy discussions amongst the senior commanders, a gloomy precursor of the next10 days, it was very sensibly agreed that the only realistic option was a southerly march, to link up with the VII and VIII Federal Corps'. Instructions were then given that the move would commence the next morning, and the orders then formulated. Fortunately, a firm decision had been made, but the dangerous spectre of possible protracted debate in times when urgency was of paramount importance had already raised its head.

The now existing March-Plan stipulated the following timetable and destinations:

	21 June	**22 June**	**23 June**
Headquarters	Heiligenstadt	Mühlhausen	Eisenach
Advance Guard	Via Heiligenstadt	Via Mühlhausen	Via Weberstedt
Brigade Bülow	to Dingelstädt	to Langula	to Mechterstedt
Brigade Knesebeck	Heiligenstadt	Mühlhausen	Eisenach
Brigade Bothmer	Via Jühnde and Manfried	Via Treffurt to Friedland to Heiligenstadt	Eisenach
Brigade de Bauer	Siemerode	Manfried	Kreuzburg
Reserve Cavalry	Kreuzber	Höngeda	Haina
Reserve Artillery	Heiligenstadt	Mühlhausen	Eisenach
Army Train	Bremke	Helmsdorf	Eisenach
Rearguard	Göttingen	Kreuzber	

Seven and a half kilometres behind & Army Train[14]

Also on the 21st, King George reiterated the situation of his forces to both Prince Karl and the Prince of Hesse by telegraph, once again requesting their assistance. The next day, although VIII Corps was still assembling, Prince Alexander did actually push a small force as far as Giessen.[15] Prince Karl also ordered the 4th Division, of Lieutenant-General Baron Zoller, towards Fulda the next morning.[16] Neither of these moves can be regarded as anything more than a gesture, at this point, though.

The Brigade of General Bülow, having crossed the River Werra at Heiligenstadt that morning, thus became the first hostile troops to 'invade' Prussian territory during the Wars of German Unification.

---

14   Sichart, pp.40-41.
15   Malet, pp.233-234.
16   *Antheil der Königlich Bayerischen Armee am Kriege des Jahre 1866*, p.17. Hereinafter, referred to as *Antheil*.

Skirmish at Witzenhausen, June 22

On the 22nd, the Hanoverian 2/Guard Hussars, Rittmeister von der Wense, were screening the right flank of Brigade Bothmer's advance towards Heiligenstadt, when the head of the squadron encountered a patrol of Prussian hussars near the village of Witzenhausen. In a brief bout of swordplay, von der Wense was wounded, and one Prussian hussar beheaded by a sabre stroke, with six of the latter's comrades being taken prisoner, along with seven horses.[17]

Hanoverian Uncertainty – The 'Zielberg Negotiations'

The next morning, the 23rd, a 'Prussian' officer, Captain von Zielberg, appeared at Hanoverian headquarters, purporting to be a peace emissary from Count Moltke himself. Von Zielberg's initial demand was for the immediate capitulation of the Hanoverian forces. As the Captain's credentials were open to some doubt, he was kept at headquarters, and, King George being once again unwilling to appear belligerent, a Hanoverian officer, Major von Jacobi, was sent to ascertain the true situation.[18]

The King's decision to halt on the 23rd was crucial. The supposed negotiations threw a blanket of confusion over the Hanoverian command. In stark contrast to the rapid and focussed action which followed the initial Prussian ultimatum, there was now considerable doubt and uncertainty appearing within the senior ranks. At a time when only unity and swift action could possibly benefit the Kingdom's continued existence, a mirage of self-deluding compromise appeared realistic to some senior Hanoverian officers. Chiefly responsible was the King, himself, who persisted not only in deluding himself that any compromise was possible, but also that he was dealing with men as good as their word, a truly naïve concept, at best, in the circumstances. The Hanoverian King, with his ingrained mediaeval sense of honour, allowed the Prussian concentration yet more time to develop. His own army, meanwhile, continued to allow precious time to slip way. The Prussian Staff History commented bluntly that:

> From the moment when, at the Hanoverian headquarters, diplomatic negotiations were entered upon, the fate of its army was decided.[19]

Further Hanoverian patrolling continued during the day, particularly in the direction of Gotha, aided by information from local inhabitants. Near Henningsleben, a troop of 4/Queen's Hussars, Premier-Lieutenant Meyer, after a brief clash, captured seven patrolling Prussian Landwehr dragoons, who were brought back to camp.[20]

---

17 Sichart, p.42 & Kunz, p.7. G.G.S. makes no mention of the incident. Wyatt, p.41, states that the prisoners were subsequently released by personal order of the Hanoverian King.

18 Von Zielberg was, in fact, an officer in the service of the Prussian ally, the Duke of Saxe-Coburg-Gotha, and not Prussia; hence the query!

19 G.G.S., p.69, and quoted in Wyatt, p.129.

20 Sichart, p.53 & Wyatt, p.45.

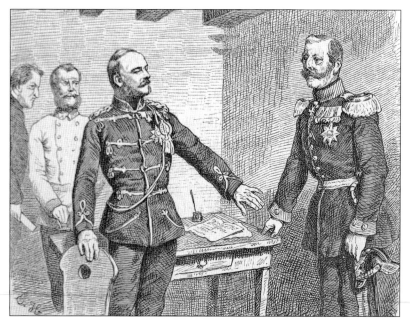

Negotiations between King George and the Hanoverian government, and the Prussians, continued as the net closed around the former's army. (Cohn)

Unfortunately, Major Jacobi's report had also caused the cancellation of the advance on Eisenach, by Brigade Bülow, which had already been ordered for the following day. The Hanoverians had lost yet more irreplaceable time.

That same day, the Hanoverian Rearguard, 2nd Brigade, detached two reconnaissance columns. The first consisted of three companies of the 1st Jäger Battalion, and the second comprised the remaining company of the battalion, along with two squadrons of the Cambridge Dragoons. The latter force, having scouted northwards towards Mühlhausen, then returned to Langensalza at about 14:00 the next afternoon, with nothing to report. The first column, commanded by the battalion's commanding officer, Colonel von der Decken, proceeded that evening to Langula, south of Mühlhausen, likewise finding no sign of the enemy, and then also returning to the main force.

That night, the Army was concentrated around Langensalza, apart from General Bülow's brigade, which was centred on Behringen, The following day was to prove both confusing and frustrating for all concerned.

Encounter at Mechterstedt, June 24

The next night, a reconnaissance pioneer detachment was sent out, under escort of 4/ Guard Cuirassier Regiment. During the operation, three Prussian prisoners were taken.[21]

---

21   Ibid., p.62. Three further Prussians were wounded.

Colonel Bülow was, by now, thoroughly convinced of the necessity of advancing on Eisenach. While awaiting instructions for such an operation, though, he despatched a force, led by General Staff Major Ahrentsschildt, towards Mechterstedt, with the objective of tearing up the rail and telegraph lines between there and Gotha. The column duly arrived, and work began. Fire was being exchanged, when a telegram was received, once again purporting to herald negotiations, and the action was quickly halted.[22]

King George's 'Last Hope' – Dr. Onno Klopp

That same evening, the Hanoverian King sent a trusted emissary from Langensalza to Prince Karl, at the latter's headquarters in Bamberg. This man was Doctor Onno Klopp, an academic, one of the key figures in the anti-Prussian movement in Hanover, and a very close confidant of the King.[23] The choice of a civilian envoy, no matter how loyal, was, however, to prove most unfortunate.

Klopp arrived at the town of Lichtenfels, some 40 kilometres north of Bamberg, on the next day. Before proceeding to Bamberg, he sent the following telegram to the Governments in Vienna, Munch, and Frankfurt, as well as to Prince Karl himself:

> The King of Hanover, with 19,000 men at Langensalza, on the 24th, proposes to break the Prussian lines between Gotha and Eisenach, and hopes that the Bavarians, who are believed to be at Coburg, will link up with him from the south. This information is assured. Ensure that it is passed on.

The reaction at Bavarian headquarters in Bamberg to this may well be imagined. It must also be noted that many telegrams were being both sent and received on both sides, sometimes out of order. In any case, having sent these messages, Dr. Klopp then left Lichtenfels at 13:45 that afternoon, on a train to Bamberg. From the railway station there, he went immediately to Prince Karl's headquarters.

Initially, Klopp met Lieutenant-General Baron von der Tann, Prince Karl's Chief of Staff, who extended him a courteous welcome, although it soon became clear that the two men had greatly differing reports and views of the actual situation. Commenting upon the fact that the Hanoverians had not pursued their own march plan to Fulda, as originally agreed, von der Tann also pointed out that circumstances had also very likely changed since the Doctor himself had left Langensalza, some 36 hours before. To this, Klopp voiced his own profound disagreement.

As a result, the two men went to the telegraph office to attempt to ascertain the current situation. Inevitably, further confusion ensued, although it did appear that Prussian troops had now occupied Eisenach. At this point, Prince Karl also joined the discussion, during which Klopp mentioned the Hanoverian strength as being some 19,000 men, to which the Prince answered, "Well, with 19,000 men, you can break through the enemy's

---

22 G.G.S., pp.62-67. It is refreshing to note that the G.G.S. is quite open about the fact that the 'negotiations' were being strung out, to give time for more Prussian reinforcements to arrive. King George's naivety is equally breathtaking.

23 Dr. Klopp was a prolific writer, penning, among other works, a volume on the overthrow of the House of Stuart.

line".[24] He did, however, also assure Dr. Klopp that he would do his utmost to support the Hanoverians.

For the Confederation forces, the most unfortunate result of all of the subterfuge and/or confusion arising out of the Zielberg-Jacobi affair was the complete immobility of the Hanoverians for the whole of the 25th, thus allowing von Falckenstein's forces to further extend their tentacles around them.

With hindsight, it is clear that the Hanoverian last army's chance of survival disappeared on this wasted day, during which it remained in place, to await the outcome of non-existent negotiations, and, at the same time, the Bavarian High Command once again made no effort at moving to support them. Their only hope was a joint effort, but neither force attempted one. For the second time, King George and his senior officers had allowed a possibility of escape to disappear.

The Prussian Net Closes around the Hanoverians

For the Prussians, speed remained of the essence. General Beyer's exhausted columns had continued their march towards Eisenach in the intense heat throughout the 24th and 25th, while other hastily gathered reinforcements also continued to be directed to join von Falckenstein's growing force.[25]

Following reports that Eisenach was only lightly held by the Prussians, on the morning of the 24th, Brigade Bülow advanced to attack it, to be subsequently followed by Bothmer and de Vaux, supported by the Reserve Artillery. Brigade Knesebeck was to provide a diversion. The entire operation ended in chaotic farce, however, involving Major Jacobi's supposed negotiations.[26] By the 26th, the Hanoverians were cut off to the south. Prussian troops were positioned in a southerly arc, as follows:

Gotha – Major-General Flies, with 13 battalions, three squadrons, and four artillery batteries (22 guns)

Eisenach – Lieutenant-General Goeben, with 12 battalions, four squadrons, and four and a half artillery batteries (28 guns)

Kreuzburg & Treffurt (east of Eisenach) – Major-General von Glümer, with eight battalions, two squadrons, one battery (six guns)

Further rumours of Hanoverian moves to the north, towards Mühlhausen, also arose overnight. Flies' decision to attack was due to this firm belief that a further telegram to him, containing orders to this effect, was imminent, and also his own certainty that the Hanoverians would, indeed, attempt to withdraw.[27]

---

24 Rüstow, p.286. For a slightly different version of this quote, see Chesney, p.69.
25 See Appendix II.
26 G.G.S., pp.64-66 & Wyatt, pp.47-53.
27 OK, Vol. I, pp.192-193 & G.G.S., pp.702-703. Both hold that Flies did, indeed, make the correct decision.

Hanover's Final Hurrah

The Battle of Langensalza, June 27

During the 26th, rumours circulated in the Hanoverian camps, as to an advance by the Bavarians. At about 22:00 that night, though, outposts of the Cambridge Dragoons beyond Hennigsleben, south of Langensalza, sent word to Hanoverian headquarters of a Prussian force approaching from that direction. Its composition was given as approximately two battalions, one squadron, and a battery. This was clearly more than a simple reconnaissance. This information was substantially correct. These were the advance elements of Prussian Detachment Flies. From around 03:00, intermittent small arms fire could be heard. Whatever the precise definition of his orders to remain 'close' to the

Flies. (Fontane)

enemy, Flies interpreted them in a robust manner – he would attack them![28] By 06:00, his columns, some 8,910 officers and men, with 22 guns (of which only six were rifled), were on the march from Gotha, towards Langensalza.[29]

Phase I -The Prussian Attack

For the reasons discussed, more than a reconnaissance was expected that morning. As suspected, near 08:30, Hanoverian pickets reported Prussian infantry columns approaching along the Gotha Road. Flies' troops had broken camp some time before, and commenced their advance. Soon after these sightings, Prussian artillery opened fire from the heights south of Hennigsleben.[30]

That morning, King George's Army numbered something over 16,500 officers and men, present on the field.[31] At this point, the Hanoverians were deployed thus:

3rd Brigade (Bülow)	Bivouacked in and east of Thamsbrück[32]
1st Brigade (Knesebeck)	Bivouacked north of Merxleben
2nd Brigade (de Vaux)	Bivouacked near Merxleben

---

28 G.G.S., p.73.

29 Lettow-Vorbeck, Vol. I, p.302. Kunz, p.29, gives a total of 8,320. Langensalza is some 18½ kilometres from Gotha, perhaps 20 by road.

30 Freudenthal, p.130 & Fontane, p.17.

31 See Appendix V.

32 I/3rd Regiment, Colonel Strube, of the same brigade, was posted in Langensalza, as a reserve.

| 4th Brigade (Bothmer) | Bivouacked on the left wing, near Nägelstadt |
| Cavalry Brigade (Geyso) | Bivouacked north of Merxleben[33] |

The two batteries of the Reserve Artillery were posted near Thamsbrück, while the Reserve Cavalry, along with Captain Röttiger's Horse Artillery battery were at Sundhausen, a little further to the north-east.

Significantly, though probably not deliberately, the Royal Entourage was quartered in Thamsbrück, while Army Headquarters was in Merxleben, about four kilometres away. Given King George's natural instinct to be involved in all decision-making, it is perhaps surprising.[34]

At about 08:30, a picket of the Duke of Cambridge Dragoons, under Premier-Lieutenant Stolzenberg, observed an enemy column approaching from direction of Gotha. Approximately an hour later, artillery fire was briefly opened from west of Langensalza. The dragoons then pulled back towards Merxleben.

As Stolzenberg withdrew, Colonel von Strube, in the town, swiftly assessed his situation. Judging that he had insufficient force to defend the dominant height, known as the Jüdenhügel, he posted a half-company about 500 paces outside the Gotha Gate, in skirmish order, and then occupied the gate itself, and the immediate area, with the rest of the battalion.

Lieutenant-Colonel Bock von Wülfingen, commanding the Hanoverian 3rd Jäger Battalion, was in Nägelstädt when the alarm came. He later wrote:

> The command over the infantry was given to me, for the time being. I formed it up immediately after leaving the village in columns of division at half distance, and I attached myself to Captain Barthold Wynecken, at the head, who was in charge of the brigade. Now the moment seemed to have come to enjoy the morning pipe that had been missed earlier. Soon I noticed that if we continued in the direction given by the Adjutant, marked by a factory chimney, we would have to march right between the enemy line and our own line. Still at first we had to continue in this direction by higher orders until an officer of the staff gave the order to change direction towards the left.
>
> The meadows that were visible at a distance were a sign that there had to be a stretch of water, so I rode ahead in order to confirm this and soon I found myself at the bank of the Unstrut River. At my return to the brigade the order was given to call all carpenters to the head of the column, in order to slope the banks to make the river crossing easier.[35]

The head of the Prussian column, I/Saxe-Coburg-Gotha Regiment, Colonel von Fabeck, appeared before Langensalza about 11:00, driving in von Strube's picket, and then forcing the south gate. Strube now endeavoured to retain possession of the

---

33 Two squadrons of the Garde du Corps were foraging on the 27th.

34 Wyatt, p.71.

35 Bock von Wülfingen, pp.45-46.

north-eastern access to the town. This effort though, also failed, whereupon he withdrew towards Merxleben.[36]

This setback provoked a strong, though confused Hanoverian counter-stroke. Brigade Knesebeck (1st) was immediately sent forward, and Brigade Bothmer (2nd) ordered, in the case of any further enemy incursion, to fall on its flank with his remaining five battalions. As he fell back on Merxleben, Colonel Strube encountered Knesebeck's command as it was crossing the Unstrut, in the opposite direction. There followed a period of confusion for 1st Brigade, culminating in it being posted in reserve north of Merxleben, its original position! This move was gallantly covered by the two battalions of Leib-Regiment, around the area of the Kallenberg Mill, fortunately only losing one man, before crossing the Unstrut.[37]

By 11:30, the Saxe-Coburgers had cleared both the town, and the Jüdenhügel. Flies' main column was then positioned in the south-east section of the town, and the reserve to the east, around a prominent building, the Siechenhof. There followed a protracted cannonade between the Prussian batteries now on the Jüdenhügel, covered by two companies, and the Hanoverians, in which the latter held the advantage. During this time, General Ahrentsschildt, and his staff occupied a height east of Merxleben, from which had good panorama of the field. In an increasingly difficult position, meanwhile, Flies opted for a further advance. One company and a squadron were despatched north, towards Thamsbrück, these then being followed there by two companies of Saxe-Coburgers. Although the town was unoccupied, the force exchanged fire with some Hanoverian troops beyond it.

Encounter at Merxleben

In the centre, Flies' main force advanced against Merxleben. Led by Colonel Hanstein, II/IR25 moved in company columns, supported by 3/Saxe-Coburg-Gotha on their left.

Upon hearing of the fresh Prussian advance, Ahrentsschildt sent word to Brigadier de Vaux to defend Merxleben and the adjoining heights to the utmost. At this stage, he had noted four enemy batteries in action on the Jüdenhügel, as well as two groups of infantry in sight. De Vaux deployed his troops thus:

First Line   I/2nd Infantry Regiment, Lieutenant-Colonel Engelbrechten
                    1st Jäger Battalion, Colonel von der Decken
Second Line   II/2nd Infantry Regiment, Colonel Flöcker
                    I/3rd Infantry Regiment, Colonel von Strube

The brigade's remaining battalion, II/3rd Infantry Regiment, Lieutenant-Colonel von Rettberg, was tasked to occupy Merxleben. Consequently, the battalion was responsible for some stretches of the Unstrut.

The Prussian infantry quickly moved to the banks of the Salza, and on their left, across it. Firing swiftly became general, the Hanoverian troops experiencing the rapid-fire

---

36   G.G.S., p.74. This unit was a two-battalion regiment. Note, too, that times sometimes given by
       both sides vary.
37   Wyatt, pp.74-75.

Prussian artillery on the Jüdenhügel, during the Battle of Langensalza. (Cohn)

capability of the enemy weapon. At about 12:30, two companies of Colonel Flöcker's battalion were pushed forward to strengthen the line against any enemy assault, as subsequently were two more under Major von Berger. Battery Blumenach was also forced to replenish its ammunition, before also returning to the line.

At roughly the same time, Flies committed I/GR11, Lieutenant-Colonel des Barres, and II/GR11, Major von Bonin, along with the Potsdam Landwehr Battalion, and a depot company.

Similarly, situated roughly halfway between Langensalza and Nägelstädt, lay the Erbsberg. This height now also appeared of some importance to the Prussian right flank. Consequently, the 1st Depot Company was posted there, to be joined by several other units. These measures were considered all that could be done to deter moves to cross the river by Hanoverian Brigade Bothmer.[38] This, though, was far from the whole story.

Phase II – Hanoverian Counterattack

Shortly before 13:00, Ahrentsschildt received a message from Bothmer that the latter was contemplating a crossing of the Unstrut. Thereupon, he realised that this was an opportunity for a larger operation. Consequently, the general sent Major Jacobi with orders orders to Bothmer to "Cross the Unstrut at Nägelstadt and advance upon the Prussian right flank."[39] Similar instructions to attack the Prussian left were also despatched to Bülow-Stolle and Knesebeck.

---

38   G.G.S., pp.76-77.
39   Bleibtreu, p.54 & Wyatt, p.81.

Bothmer had made his bid to cross in the vicinity of the Erbsberg. Here, several attempts failed, causing him losses of 14 officers and 119 men, and proving that some, at least, of the Prussian Landwehr would fight. Bothmer, for now, quickly withdrew to the hills north of the Unstrut.[40] Colonel Bock found himself wading the river here, on foot.

> The artillery fire, that had been steadily going on for a while in a more or less intense way, intensified again, and especially the speed with which the batteries on the heights of Merxleben were firing at the Prussians made a rather reassuring impression. This lively conversation with cannonballs was not dangerous to us as we were in the low-lying land of the Unstrut, and thus was taking place above our heads. Some time before, I had waded through the river which was reaching up to the middle of my thigh, having left my horse under the care of a Jäger, because the banks were too steep.[41]

Brigades Bülow (3rd) and Knesebeck (1st) both also commenced their march at much the same time, around 13:00. The former was directed south from Thamsbrück and the latter from Merxleben. At 14:00, Brigadier Bülow received orders to advance in the direction of the Langensalza Church on the market and cross the Unstrut on its way. Bülow himself was unable to ford the river on horseback, and so rode to Merxleben. Once there, he crossed the river as soon as the Kallenberg Mill had been cleared. Bülow's brigade crossed the Unstrut as mentioned before and then captured Graesers Fabrik, the brickworks and the Garrison Hospital, before advancing into the town.[42]

Private Freudenthal's unit, the 2nd Battalion of the 5th Regiment (Lüneburg) then advanced into Langensalza, by companies, at the double, with drums beating. He later wrote, "Without wasting any time to storm the buildings, many of which were fired from, the companies marched through the town in perfect order and occupied the southern exits of it".[43]

At about the same as Bülow's move, de Vaux (2nd) commenced his own advance. Moving through thick vineyards, against fierce resistance, his troops, joined by men of the 3rd Jäger Battalion (4th Brigade), were able to push across the Unstrut. With artillery support from three artillery batteries, this force was able to obtain the surrender of the Kallenberg Mill, along with some 100 prisoners, of IR25.[44]

Prussian Retreat

As the strongpoints in and around Langensalza fell, one after another, Flies realised that he must retreat, if this was still possible. General Seckendorff was directed to abandon the Erbsberg and pull back in the direction of the Siechenhof. The left wing had little choice other than to move south as and how possible. Flies assembled most of his wing south of Langensalza by about 16:00. Seckendorff subsequently joined him

40 Lettow-Vorbeck, Vol. I, p.310.
41 Bock, p.48.
42 Freudenthal, p.133.
43 Ibid.
44 Kunz, p.46 & Wyatt, p.89.

Prussian Landwehr at Langensalza. (Fontane)

Kanonier Rudloff defends his gun at Langensalza. (Cohn)

there. Three squadrons of the Hanoverian Cambridge Dragoons, led by Rittmeister von Einem, encountered the force. Von Einem, at the head of the 2nd Squadron, attacked the Prussian two gun 'sally battery'. The Rittmeister was killed, but both guns also had to be abandoned by the Prussians, in a hollow.[45] Both were captured.

As the Hanoverian advance continued, at about 15:30, Arendsschildt received a message that Langensalza would shortly be in his possession, and word that the Jüdenhügel, which the Prussian artillery had abandoned in the face of the relentless advance of Bülow and de Vaux. At this stage, the Reserve Cavalry, previously north of Merxleben, were trying to get across the Unstrut, through a 'traffic jam'. As they managed to clear this, the Hanoverian horse came upon a mixed force of Pussian troops, some having withdrawn from the Jüdenhügel, and others around the Bath Wood, east of that height.

These men were now attacked by the Hanoverian horse. A number of disjointed and unrelated actions now took place. In all, almost 17 Hanoverian squadrons were involved. Most of the action took place around two groups of Prussians. The first, under the commanded by Captain Rosenberg, of GR 11.This group, mainly from GR 11 and Potsdam Landwehr, repulsed an attack by the Hanoverian Garde du Corps.

Lieutenant-Colonel des Barres, of the same regiment, commanding the second group, formed square several times during his withdrawal. These troops were eventually able to escape to the west, towards Henningsleben. Colonel des Barres, himself, was taken prisoner.[46] The victors also had possession of two cannon, and some 1,500 rifles.[47] The victory, though, was to prove to be a hollow one.

Encirclement and Surrender of the Hanoverian Army

By 18:00, all firing had ceased. As King George settled into his quarters in Langensalza itself, General Ahrentsschildt issued a justifiably laudatory Order of the Day to the Army, a part of which read:

> You, My Brave Soldiers, with zeal never yet equalled, and promptitude unmatched in history, you assembled at my summons in the south of my Kingdom, and when, together with my son, the Crown Prince, I marched at your head to South Germany, you remained true to your colours, to the sacred rights of my throne, and to the freedom and independence of our beloved country. This day, combating with the valour of your forefathers, in the presence of myself and of my son and successor, in the battlefield of Langensalza, under the most gracious protection of the Almighty for our Holy cause, you have won a glorious victory.[48]

Information was soon disseminated as to the victory, and also, crucially, that the Hanoverian Army would now remain in position for eight days. How this news was

45 G.G.S., pp.81-82 & Wyatt, pp.95-96.
46 Prince Kraft zu Hohenlohe considers the square formed by II/IR 25 to literally be."…the only example in 1866 or 1870…" to have occurred. *Letters on Infantry*, Letter 5.
47 *Der Bundesfeldzug in Bayern im Jahr 1866*, p.19. Sichart, p.143, states the number of rifles as over 2,000.
48 Sichart, p.145.

The Hanoverian army lays down its arms. (Cohn)

received was felt to be of considerable importance, but in fact the presumption itself was illusory.

At the same time, Colonel Rudorff was despatched to the headquarters of General Flies, both proposing a cease-fire for the collection of casualties, and also to convey to the Prussian High Command an utterly unrealistic request for a free passage for the Hanoverian force, on condition of a cessation of hostilities. Flies readily accepted to forward both proposals to higher authority, of course being fully aware that King George's army was now surrounded by over 40,000 men. By 21:00, that evening, the reply inevitably came that no further discussion would be considered.

That night, in the Hanoverian camp, much time was spent considering the next move. The discussion regarding the remaining options was, to be sure, wide-ranging. Even the prospect of a counter-march to re-take Hanover was proposed. This clear atmosphere of unreality, though, merely served to highlight the true situation. Nothing, perhaps inevitably, was decided, and it was agreed to consider matters in the morning. Some time later, The Times newspaper acidly commented that, "Unfortunately for the Hanoverian dynasty, it contented itself with bivouacking round Langensalza, on the fields of its last victory."[49]

In Langensalza the next morning, perhaps equally inevitably, yet another conference was held by the senior Hanoverian commanders, in the presence of the King. Finally, though, a frank and realistic paper was now presented to His Majesty, outlining the

49   *The* (London) *Times*, October 19 1867.

complete hopelessness of the situation, not least due to the lack of provisions for both animals and men, and the fact that only enough small-arms ammunition remained for one further action. No choice other than capitulation on the Prussian terms was possible.

With every escape route now blocked, and, as discussed, almost without ammunition, the army was in no position to even offer another battle. The King, at last, was forced to make the bitter decision to capitulate. The proud Kingdom of Hanover, and its army, would both shortly cease to exist, by the stroke of a pen.

The tired troops of the Prussian Western Army were granted a well-earned rest day on the 30th. The operations against Hesse-Cassel and Hanover had lasted barely two weeks, although, inevitably, Moltke opined that they had taken longer than necessary. Vogel von Falckenstein's frequent wilfulness in his dealings with the Chief of Staff had certainly intensely annoyed the latter, and would not be forgotten by him.

Casualties

Statistics for the losses at the Battle of Langensalza come in all shapes and sizes, for both sides. Given the circumstances, much of this is comprehensible.[50]

	Prussians		Hanoverians	
	Officers	Men	Officers	Men
Killed	11	159	2	356
Wounded	30	613	80	1,409
Missing/prisoners	10	897	10	940

Movements of the Federal VII & VIII Corps' up to June 30

The mobilisation and assembly of both VII and VIII Corps' were painfully slow, an unfortunate precursor of what was to follow. Although the Federal high command was well aware of the danger to their Hanoverian and Electoral Hessian allies to the north, somehow, no sense of immediate urgency pervaded the proceedings. It was almost as if the matter at hand was, indeed, the summer manoeuvres.

Once the decision had been made that the Bavarian Army would actually be deployed in Western Germany, and not with the Austrians in the east, Prince Karl began preparations to deploy his forces along the Upper Main, anchored upon the cities of Bamberg and Schweinfurt. He placed his own headquarters in the latter.[51]

Prince Alexander, himself, arrived at Bavarian Headquarters in Schweinfurt on the 26th. That evening, and the next morning, he and Prince Karl discussed their plan of campaign. It was agreed that their operations would begin on June 30. Their two corps' were to converge near Bad Hersfeld, and from this point, move on either Cassel or

50 *Ö.M.Z.*, Vol. I, p.209. Lettow-Vorbeck, Vol. I, p.316, gives the Prussian killed and wounded as 41 and 805, respectively, and the Hanoverian as 102 and 1,327.
51 *Antheil*, pp.14-16.

Eisenach. As they finalised their plans that morning, about 110 kilometres to the north, a battle was being fought at the Thuringian town of Langensalza.

The Austrian Official History noted that:

> Perhaps it would have been advisable to continue the operations, to establish contact with the Prussian forces, and then to carry on depending upon the situation that was to be found.[52]

In the meanwhile, on June 29 the Bavarian army finally crossed the border and advanced to Coburg, Hildburghausen and Meiningen. The following day, the advance guard reached Suhl and Schmalkalden, but Prince Karl had also by now received word of the Hanoverian capitulation. Since any advance towards Gotha was now pointless, he opted instead to proceed northwest through the Werra Valley, to link up with Prince Alexander and check any Prussian advance upon Frankfurt.

How little hope was placed upon this movement, however, can be gleaned from the order which was sent at 20:00, on the 30th, to Prince Alexander which, contrary to the agreement of the 26th, was now of a defensive nature. The exact phrasing was:

> If I am to be compelled to retreat, it will be through Mellrichstadt and Neustadt and I hope, in this case, for the cooperation of the VIII Corps between Neustadt and Schweinfurt. I am thus returning to the plan your [princelyness] proposed in Schweinfurt,[53] while I urgently call upon your [Grand-Ducal Majesty] only to send some troops to my aid, setting aside all secondary aims, part upon the line Hanau-Fulda-Hünfeld, and, particularly, part by train upon the line Frankfurt-Gemünden and to set them in motion from there towards Kissingen.[54]

The issue of when Prince Karl knew the true state of affairs concerning the Hanoverian surrender, is a vexing one. A 37 year old Württemberg liaison officer on his headquarters staff, Major Albert von Suckow, on June 28, had received a telegram from the Württemberg Foreign Minister, Baron von Warnbüler. This message announced that, "The Hanoverians have surrendered to the Prussians at Langensalza." Suckow, naturally reported this information, but was told that information had been received, via telegrams from Munich and Vienna, as well as Hanoverian sources, that King George's army could hold its position for some days. This latter information was, unfortunately, widely accepted.[55]

---

52 Ö.K., Vol. V, pp 15-16, and also quoted in Lettow-Vorbeck, Vol. 3, p.37.
53 Biebrach notes that this was actually originally General von der Tann's plan, which had already been rejected by the Württembergers.
54 Ibid., pp.13-14.
55 *Rückschau des Königl. Württembergischen Generals der Infanterie und Kriegsministers Albert von Suckow*, pp.86-87, *Antheil*, p.86 & G.G.S., pp.571-572. *Antheil* gives the time possible as eight days.

6

The Campaign of the Main, July 1-9

Consolidation of the Prussian forces

On July 1, Vogel von Falckenstein's force was now formally designated as The Army of the Main, after the river of that name. It numbered, on this date, some 44,000 men.[1] That same day, the whole force was concentrated around the town of Eisenach, some 25 kilometres south-west of Langensalza.[2]

Events around the Rivers Werra and Fulda

On the 2nd, Falckenstein began his march towards Fulda, further to the south-west, in the direction of Frankfurt.[3] The divisions of Beyer and Goeben descended into the Werra Valley, with Beyer on the right, to cross the river at Vacha, and then to advance on Hünfeld. Goeben, to his left, moved on Salzungen. Manteuffel followed at a distance, both to act as a rearguard, and also ready to support the others, as necessary.

First Contact: Skirmish of Immelborn, July 2

At the same time, the Bavarians were also active, Lieutenant-General Hartmann having ordered Colonel Aldosser to send a reconnaissance to the area of Salzungen. When this was carried out without result, Hartmann ordered a further probe for the evening of the 2nd. This time, Colonel Aldosser would himself lead the expedition, which consisted of one and a half companies of his own 9th Infantry Regiment, transported in 17 wagons, and one squadron of the 9th Chevauleger Regiment. At about 22:00, a patrol of Prussian hussars exchanged shots with Aldosser's force, before withdrawing past a platoon of Prussian infantry of 3/IR13, commanded by Second-Lieutenant von Tabouillot, 66 men. As they pulled back, one of the hussar troopers called out, "The enemy is about 800 paces away, and is composed of three companies and one squadron!"[4] With this cheery news, the platoon prepared for action. Some 15 minutes later, Tabouillot came into contact with the Bavarian force at a distance of some 150 paces. Tabouillot's company

---

1 65 Hiltl, p.100. See Appendix to Tabouillot, *Die Dreizehner in Feindesland*, p.12 & Hausser, pp.65-66.
2 Lecomte, p.199, particularly highlights this point.
3 See also Biebrach, pp.14-15.
4 Tabouillot, p.12.

commander, Captain Wichmann, also soon appeared, shouting, "Rapid fire, people, rapid fire!"[5] The Bavarian force, having now established the undoubted presence of enemy infantry, then swiftly withdrew, though not before Aldosser had received a wound in his right hand. The talented colonel was out of the campaign in the first act; he would be sorely missed.[6]

Prussian losses in this skirmish were four men wounded. The Bavarian casualties were three men killed, and four officers (including Colonel Aldosser) and seven men wounded. One of the officers, Second-Lieutenant Baron von Massenbach, was actually hit by six bullets.[7] Prince Karl could now be certain that the Prussians were no longer concentrated in the vicinity of Eisenach. Their offensive had begun.

Beyer. (*Illustrirte Kriegs-Chronik*)

That same night, a small Prussian probe was also made by General Beyer's division, in the direction of Dermbach, south of Salzungen. A platoon of IR Nr.32, 30 men, along with a half-troop of hussars advanced south from Lengsfeld. Nearing Dermbach, the force encountered a Bavarian outpost of two men. Perceiving that larger numbers of Bavarian troops were present in the area than anticipated, the reconnaissance was terminated by the platoon commander, and the troops withdrew. One Bavarian soldier, of the 5th Regiment, was killed. There were no Prussian casualties.[8]

On the same day, came the first minor incident involving VIII Corps. That morning, pickets of the 7th Württemberg Infantry Regiment exchanged scattered shots with Prussian vedettes at Offenbach, a mere seven kilometres from Frankfurt, on the east bank of the Main.[9] Although an unimportant incident, nerves in the city and Parliament were jangled by it. As a result, fears of a Prussian advance on Frankfurt added to the already considerable pressure on Prince Alexander to protect the city.

Biebrach outlines the Bavarian intentions for the following day:

---

5   Ibid., p.13.

6   *Antheil*, p.31.

7   Ibid., wherein the Bavarian losses are also stated. The Prussian Staff History (G.G.S.) gives the Bavarian loss as two men killed, and three officers and 17 men wounded, p.393. Lettow-Vorbeck, p.62 & Tabouillot, pp.11-13.

8   Lettow-Vorbeck, p.62 & Ö.K., p.25. This second probe is not mentioned in the G.G.S. (Prussian Staff History).

9   Marx, *Geschichte des Infanterie-Regiments Kaiser Friedrich, König von Preussen (7. Württembergischen)*, p.58.

As far as the Bavarian movements on the 3rd were concerned, the reconnaissance which had been carried out on the night of the 2nd-3rd convinced General Hartmann that he had nothing to fear from the east. Accordingly, in the course of the day he had concentrated his division around Roßdorf and only weakly occupied the Werra crossings. Because of the poor weather, he only left the 8th Brigade along with two squadrons and half a twelve pounder battery bivouacked at Roßdorf, while the 7th Brigade was in cantonments stretching for about a mile. The 3rd Division marched towards Neidhartshausen and Zella where they moved into cantonments. The 1st Division advanced to the vicinity of Herpf, Ober-Katza, and Mehmels, and the 2nd Division to the area of Helmershausen, Battenhausen and Unter-Maasfeld.

Thus the four Bavarian infantry divisions still remained echeloned in a depth of 1½-4 miles.[10]

Bavarian reconnaissance towards Dermbach, July 3

Following reports that Prussian hussars had been encountered in the area of Neidhartshausen, on the morning of July 3, Lieutenant-General Zoller ordered that a force be sent to probe towards Dermbach, in the meanwhile halting his own division's march. Commanded by his divisional Chief of Staff, Major Heckel, this force consisted of 1st Schützen/14th Infantry Regiment, and 2/2nd Chevaulegers. Heckel's command, under the impression that only a few cavalry pickets were ahead, actually encountered the Prussian rearguard, 12/IR 13, Captain Stockhausen and 4/8th Hussars, Rittmeister von Grodzki.

Heckel's infantry, in open order, advanced on both sides of the road, until, some paces from the village, they came under sustained rifle fire. In a half-hour engagement, Heckel's men were driven back, and withdrew, the main body of the supporting battalion having already done so. The withdrawal is described in the Bavarian report as being made in, 'the best of order …'[11]

Bavarian casualties in this sharp encounter were six men killed, four wounded, and 38 missing. Of the latter, 20 men were taken prisoner. Stockhausen's troops suffered no loss.[12] This relatively minor action caused a considerable stir amongst the Bavarian high command. General Zoller was now convinced that a major enemy offensive was underway, as was indeed the case.

The Advance of the Bavarian Cavalry

The Bavarian Reserve Cavalry had meanwhile independently advanced with the two light brigades towards Hünfeld, but, after receiving reports that the Prussians had succeeded in reaching Rasdorf (near Fulda), they drew back to the area of Bieber (somewhat over 11 kilometres northeast of Fulda). The Heavy Brigade was in Fulda.[13] The impatient and

---

10   Roughly 11 by 30 kilometres.
11   *Die Gefechte der bayrischen Armee mit der preussischen Main-Armee am 2, 3, und 4 Juli 1866*, p.267.
12   *Antheil*, Appendix III, Table III & Tabouillot, p.14.
13   Biebrach, p.16.

aggressive old Prince Thurn and Taxis, however, would not be denied his chance to come to grips with the enemy.

He now requested infantry support from VIII Corps, for the next proposed move northwards by his own advance guard the next day. During the course of the night of the 3rd/4th, two Bavarian couriers arrived at VIII Corps headquarters. First came Oberlieutenant von Krafft, at about 01:30 (July 4), and Oberlieutenant Baron Andrian followed some three hours later. Both officers had the same request – infantry support for the Bavarian horse.

Unfortunately, the 4th had already been designated as a rest day for VIII Corps, as demanded by all four divisional commanders, their troops having been slogging along poor, muddy roads in the bad weather. In any case, the only unit anywhere close to Taxis was the 1st Württemberg Jäger Battalion, which, along with one squadron, was at Lauterbach, some 20 kilometres north-west of Fulda. This force was not considered, probably accurately, by itself to be strong enough for the purpose. Prince Thurn and Taxis was duly informed that support would be available on the following day, as Prince Alexander noted in his Journal:

> A rest day for the most exhausted troops. Received a request from General of Cavalry, Prince Taxis, who is moving, with the entire Bavarian cavalry, into the Fulda Valley, while the Haun and Ulster valleys are completely vacant, to assist him with infantry support. Tomorrow night, that is possible.[14]

The rough strength of the Prince Karl's force, at this point, was some 41,640 men, of which 33,360 were infantry, and 5,280 cavalry, with 136 guns. As yet, the Bavarian Infantry Reserve Brigade had not been constituted, and four other battalions were also still on the march to the 'Mobile Army'. Vogel von Falckenstein, at the same time, had on hand 45,580 infantry and approximately 3,400 cavalry, with 94 guns.[15] Both armies now knew that they were in close proximity.

For both sides, of course, the weather in the early days of July was largely unpredictable, with pouring rain, and strong winds, contrasting with periods of sunshine. The conditions of roads were found, as might be expected, to be most variable.

Engagements near Dermbach, July 4

On the night of July 3, Goeben concentrated the Brigade of Kummer around Dermbach, and that of Wrangel at Oechsen, four kilometres to the west. The following morning, Kummer was directed south, towards Zella and Neidhartshausen, while Wrangel advanced, covering Kummer's left flank to the west, towards Wiesenthal. The two brigades were somewhat intermixed for the coming operation, each flank comprising the following:

---

14   Baur-Breitenfeld, pp.26-27 & *Feldzugs-Journal*, p.6. Note the justifiably implied criticism of Thurn und Taxis.
15   Förster, Brix, *Der Feldzug von 1866 in Südwest-Deutschland*, p.2.

Kummer. (Fontane)

Left Flank – Major-General Wrangel
I/IR 13, II/IR 13
II/IR 15
I/IR 55, II/IR 55
1/8th Hussars, 2/8th Hussars, 3/8th Hussars,
Battery Coester, Battery Eynatten I

Right Flank – Major-General Kummer
I/IR 53, II/IR 53, F/IR 53
F/IR 13
F/IR 55
4/8th Hussars, 5/8th Hussars
Battery Eynatten II, Battery Weigelt
4th Cuirassier Regiment
Horse Battery Metting

In Dermbach, Goeben retained a reserve of four battalions, I/IR 15, F/IR 15, II/IR 19, and F/IR 19. The remaining battalion of IR 19, Major Wangenheim's Second Battalion, was in Gehaus.[16]

Actions of Zella and Neidhartshausen

A contemporary Bavarian source described the position in and around the village of Zella:

> The narrow and sharp cut defile of Kaltennordheim extends at Fischbach to the 1600 paces wide valley of Diedorf which is enclosed by steep hills to the right, with a side valley west of the village towards Empfertshausen. At the bottom of the

16 Note that IR 19 was actually a component of Major-General Beyer's Division.

valley, about 300 paces east of the road leading towards Vacha, is the Felde river, a small river between 6-20 ' wide and 4' deep with muddy banks, engulfed by meadows and crossed by light ridges.

The bottom of the valley and the lighter slopes were grown with grain or freshly ploughed – the ground was thoroughly soaked, due to the constant rain.

In the middle of the valley, a road led through the village of Diedorf, which was irregularly built, mostly with stone buildings. 15 minutes to the north-west of Diedorf lies Zella, and 10 minutes to the southeast of the aforementioned village, stands the village of Fischbach through which the river Felde flows.[17]

The village of Zella is situated on steep slopes, and represented a strong position. Within the village, the walled Monastery (Cloister) of Zella also increased this natural strength.

Defending the area around Zella that morning were Bavarian troops of Lieutenant-General Zoller's 3rd Division, specifically those of Major-General Walther's 6th Brigade. Baron Zoller himself, had, in fact, been making alterations to the brigade's dispositions up until just before the appearance of the enemy. The defenders here were deployed as follows:

Northern area of Neidhartshausen – 1/1st Jäger Battalion with pickets posted in the north of the village, as far as the river. 3/1st Jäger, was posted in the west and south of the village. 4/1st was held in reserve on the heights behind the village. Finally, 2/1st, initially guarding the bridge, after a personal inspection by Baron Zoller, was also placed in reserve, and another company, from another regiment, 1st Schutzen Company/6th Regiment, was brought up from Zella, as well.

In the north-east part of Zella, stood two guns, under the command of Second-Lieutenant zu Rhein, while in the village itself, were posted II/14th Regiment, commanded by Major Dichtel, along with 1/6th Regiment, Captain König. In addition, the 4th Schützen Company was placed in the main garden of town. Finally, 5/14th, and 3rd Schützen Companies were held in reserve.[18]

To the east of Zella, where the slopes rose immediately from the side of the road, were posted three squadrons of Lieutenant-Colonel Horadam's 2nd Chevaulegers, with I/14th Regiment, Major Täuffenbach, deployed in cover, some 800 paces further south. The 2nd Schützen Company stood between the road and the Seemuhle, while 3 and 4/14th formed the reserve, deployed on another height, again further south.[19] Further south still, Major-General Ribaupierre had his 5th Brigade deployed across the road, in front of the village of Fischbach. This settlement itself stood about a kilometre further south, along the road from Diedorf.

At 08:00, General Goeben ordered Kummer's brigade forward from Dermbach, south against Zella. Four battalions, two squadrons, and one battery, duly moved along the valley towards that village. At the same time, he sent Brigade Wrangel towards Wiesenthal, accompanied by the remaining three squadrons of the 8th Hussars. As the

---

17 *Geschichte des Königlich bayerischen 15. Infanterie-Regiment*, p.8.

18 *Die Gefechte der bayrischen Armee mit der preussischen Main-Armee am 2, 3, und 4 Juli 1866*, p.268.

19 His other two companies present were detached as artillery escort, *Antheil*, p.49.

Brigade Wrangel advances. (Cohn)

first troops of Kummer's troops had approached Neidhartshausen, at around 09:00, they were fired upon by two Bavarian guns.[20]

The cannonade prefacing the action could be clearly heard several kilometres to the north, by thousands of men of the Prussian Reserve, and also by Wrangel's troops, including Lieutenant Tabouillot, and his men:

> It did not take long, as muffled cannon thunder was heard from Zella, the rattling of distant rifle fire was adding more and more, which could be clearly differentiated from the twitching sound of the salvoes and the rolling of our Schnellfeuer (rapid fire); on that side the fighting was in good progress.[21]

The Prussian brigade battery, 3rd Six Pounder Battery, Captain Eynatten I, was then sent forward, and supported the advance effectively, enabling the infantry to assault the Bavarian positions at Neidhartshausen, those in the woods to the east of there, and at Zella.[22]

F/IR 53, Major von Rosenzweig was directed towards Neidhartshausen, I/IR 53, Major von Frankenberg, on his left, against the eastern heights, and II/IR 53, Major Gontard, directly on Zella itself. Both of the flanking moves were successful, after brief engagements with the defenders.

---

20 G.G.S., p.579. *Antheil*, p.50, however, is equally clear that the first rounds were fired by the Prussian guns.
21 Tabouillot, p.16.
22 Hamm, pp.169-171. The battery fired a total of 110 rounds, and had two men wounded, one seriously.

The attack on Zella was specifically directed against the Monastery, located in the front of Zella on a wall-like outcrop. The village was also taken in the first rush, though not without a struggle. Major Gontard's battalion forcing its way in from the west, while the Fusiliers of IR 13 scrambled over the walls to the north, losing a man of 10th Company bayoneted, and had several others wounded.[23] In the struggle for the village, Major Gontard was shot from his horse, shortly after he had ordered 8th Company to 'swarm' (skirmishers). Captain von Kerssenbrock immediately took command of the battalion, Gontard dying shortly afterwards.[24]

As the Prussians gained the upper hand, the defenders, of necessity, began to fall back. Both Captain König and Lieutenant Brunner were killed, attempting to evacuate Zella. The gallant zu Rhein fought his guns as long as possible, and was somehow able to get them away. Major Dichtel, at about 11:00, judging that the time had come to withdraw, as his orders allowed, proceeded to do so.[25] Of the men in Captain König's company, only one officer and 19 men were able to escape from the village.

Major-General Walther's brigade was now pulling back on the position of Ribaupierre's 5th Brigade, the latter posted here in the case of such an eventuality. From about 11:00, the action degenerated into a cannonade, since General Kummer did not consider further advance advisable under the circumstances. He did, though bring up his reserve battery, 4th Four Pounder Battery, Captain Weigelt, and the horse artillery battery.

Weigelt's battery duly unlimbered on the main road east of Zella, and entered the action. There was no space, however, for the horse battery to do so, and it, and the 4th Cuirassier Regiment, Colonel von Schmidt, were both forced to hang back. A partial move on Diedorf by Prussian skirmishers resulted in inconclusive exchanges of small-arms fire on the northern fringes of that village. From this point, the action stagnated into a cannonade, which itself petered out between 14:30 and 15:00.

Prince Karl had arrived on the field at around Noon, and proceeded to observe the action. As the fire gradually died away, he judged that no more Prussian offensive moves would be made here, and gave orders for a concentration of the army between Kalten-Nordheim and Kalten-Sundheim, some 15 kilometres to the south.[26] In similar vein, Major-General Kummer was also recalled to Dermbach, by orders from General Goeben.

Losses in this series of encounters were as follows:

Bavarian
Killed: 3 officers and 7 men
Wounded: 3 officers and 69 men
Prisoners or missing: 1 officer and 46 men
Total: 7 officers and 122 men[27]

---

23 Blume, p.168.
24 *M.W.B.*, vol. 55, pp.434-438.
25 *Antheil*, pp.53-54.
26 This was described as a 'strong position', by Biebrach, p.21.
27 Ibid., Appendix III, pp.4-5. G.G.S., p.581, gives Bavarian losses as seven officers, and 157 men.

Brigade Kummer at Zella, drawing by Hoffmann. (Regensberg/*Mainfeldzug*)

Bavarian infantry during the actions around Dermbach, July 4, drawing by Hoffmann.
(Regensberg/*Mainfeldzug*)

Prussian

Killed: 1 officer and 10 men

Wounded: 3 officers and 58 men

Prisoners or missing: 2 men

Total: 4 officers and 70 men

Despite the care with which Baron Zoller had personally supervised the dispositions around Zella, the defence here and at Neidhartshausen had been neither prolonged, nor successful. For the Prussians, a successful action had been followed by a frustrating, and for the men, inexplicable withdrawal. The total Prussian ammunition expenditure in the actions around Zella-Neidhartshausen had been some 10,000 rounds of small arms, and 186 shells.[28]

Actions of Wiesenthal-Roßdorf

As General Kummer's attack on developed to the west at Neidhartshausen began, the advancing brigade of 53 year old Baron Wrangel also came into contact with Bavarian troops to the west of the village of Wiesenthal. With cannon fire clearly audible from the south, Wrangel initially directed 3/8th Hussars, Rittmeister Wolter, towards the town, followed by II/IR 15, Major Rüstow, the latter advancing in company columns.

After initial probing, at about 09:00, Wrangel initiated his attack here. Major Rüstow's battalion was initially directed along the main road against Wiesenthal, but then moved to the left, with II/IR55, Major Gotskow in the centre, and II/IR13, Major Dürre, on the right. Captain Cöster's four pounder battery provided prompt and accurate fire support throughout the action. The advance initially took place in a heavy rain shower.[29]

Wiesenthal, at this point, was defended by two Bavarian battalions, these being the 6th Jäger Battalion, Major Baron von Guttenberg, the senior officer present, and III/9th Infantry Regiment, Major Dietrich. The forward posts of Guttenberg's battalion lay on the heights to the west of the town, which itself lay in a dip among these, further east. Supporting the defence from then north-east of the conical height of the Nebelberg, were two twelve pounders, commanded by Oberlieutenant von Lutz, with a squadron of chevaulegers, also some 1800 paces from the town.[30] Dietrich, at this point, was in Roßdorf. Also present, and subject to Guttenberg's immediate control, was I/6th Regiment, Major Sebus, in Wiesenthal.[31]

About 08:00, pickets of Guttenberg's battalion, posted west of Wiesenthal reported the approach of Prussian columns. This, Guttenberg duly reported to the brigade commander, Major-General Cella, in Rossdorf. After some observation and probing on the part of the Prussians, about half an hour later, firing broke out. A defence of Wiesenthal, situated in a deep hollow, in these circumstances was considered unrealistic, and, as the rain eased, Guttenberg withdrew both battalions from the town, and then pulled back to the heights to the east.

---

28   Kunz, p.72.

29   Fontane, p.73. Note again, that rain came and went during this period.

30   *Antheil*, p.38.

31   Sebus' battalion was actually a unit of Baron Zoller's 3rd Division.

Major Rüstow leads II/IR 15 against the Nebelberg during the actions at Wiesenthal-Roßdorf. (Cohn)

As this took place, Major Dietrich's III/9th Regiment advanced from Rossdorf to take up a position on the north-east elevation of the Nebelberg, a most prominent height near the road. They were joined on this feature by two twelve pounder guns, under the command of Oberlieutenant Baron von Lurz, who then began to bombard the enemy infantry, lacking the range to duel with the Prussian guns.[32]

Additionally, following on from Rossdorf, came General Cella with the main body of his 8th Brigade infantry. Under the misapprehension that the Prussian artillery fire was coming from Dermbach, he directed his troops in that direction. Consequently, III/4th Regiment, Major von Leoprechting, moved along the main Dermbach road, with Lieutenant-Colonel Bösmuller's II/4th on his right, with I/9th, Major O. Guttenberg, following at a distance. III/9th, Major Dietrich, was intended to link with the other units, while on the march.[33] Advancing 'blind', and under artillery fire, this force gravitated towards the Nebelberg, Major Guttenberg being mortally wounded as they did so. Approaching from the opposite direction, Prussian Major Rüstow was hit by two bullets, falling from his horse. While being attended the battalion surgeon, he was struck a third time, and killed.[34]

---

32 *Antheil*, p.38. The Nebelberg had a height of some 125 metres.
33 Ibid., p.39.
34 Krieg, *Kriegstagebuch des 2. Westfälischen Infanterie-Regiments Nr.15*, p.34.

This vital feature was also the focus of the Prussian attack, as Captain Krieg later described in his 'War Diary' of IR 15:

> The dense swarms of skirmishers followed the enemy to the eastern edge of the wooded hill and sent their bullets after the fleeing Bavarians into Roßdorf. Here there was a prepared strong fall-back position covered by artillery, and the 6th Company had to abort the attempt to cross the valley, because a well positioned Bavarian battery heavily shelled it with grenades, and forced it to fall back inside the wood.
>
> In order to cover the right flank the 1st half platoon, under Second-Lieutenant Beckhaus II, was sent down the south-eastern slope of the Nebelberg, and to set up a good position from which it exchanged fire with the enemy infantry placed on the opposite heights.
>
> On the north side of the Nebelberg, Captain Weissich had sent forward a couple of sections under Second- Lieutenant von Ditfurth, Second-Lieutenant Hülsen, and Feldwebel Pepersack, in pursuit towards Roßdorf. They were successful in capturing several prisoners, as well as about 1,000 backpacks of the enemy, which had been laid down on the eastern edge of the mountain. A large number of wounded, among them several officers, fell into the hands of the 8th Company, and Captain Weissich allowed these to be brought back to Wiesenthal.[35]

Lieutenant Tabouillot was also present that day, though further to the right of II/IR15, and his battalion, too, was in the midst of the action:

> Formed up in half battalions, the 6th and 7th Company deployed as advanced guard, the battalion advanced through Wiesenthal towards the Nebelberg, 15 minutes from the town. 400' high, very steep and gradual, the hill presented no cover: just the top was heavily wooded. The rain had softened the ground, and made it slippery, making the way up nearly impossible.
>
> This hill was occupied by the Bavarians and about two battalions were deployed on the top. They had to be driven out of this dominating position. Led by Lieutenant-Colonel v. Dürre the advanced guard advanced along the road at the foot of the hill, while the (other) half-battalion, the 5th and 8th Companies, (advanced) to the right of the road. Advanced skirmishers lightly returned the sharp enemy fire at the columns. Soon several men were falling on our side.
>
> Captain von Lederer fell dead at the head of his company. Nothing could stop us! Lieutenant von Rudorf took his place, and forced the companies up the centre of the hill. Here, the general exhaustion demanded a brief halt. Under such fire such fire, how it now on that heads our showering, nevertheless, is to be held more than one of somebody, only one life to lose, may expect to, and can. "Forward", furrowed the leader, "Slog, slog!" sounded from every man in the entire column. A new hurtled hammer appeared. All stormed forward with new heart, and rapid fire decimated the enemy column. Captain Ledebur and Lieutenant Hesse killed,

---

35 Ibid., p.36 *& Antheil*, p.42.

Lieutenant-Colonel Dürre and Lieutenant von Wagenhoff, badly wounded. Colonel von Gellhorn and Captain von Mayer had their horses shot from under them. 17 men were killed and 81 wounded, in the II/13th. (The) Battalion (was) reduced to 950-960 men.[36]

The Bavarian Major-General von Hartmann, 4th Division's commander, arrived on the field at about 11:30. Riding up to the Nebelberg, he appeared amongst the foremost of his skirmishers. Encouraging and cajoling troops along the way, himself organising and leading a new assault, shouting to the men of the 9th Infantry Regiment, "(Men of the) Ninth, you must retake those heights! Forward!"[37] Hartmann's efforts, along with those of General Cella, and their officers, somehow succeeded in instilling a new spirit amongst the men, and the 'tired' troops of II/9th once again went forward, up the slope.[38] The attack, however, was a complete failure. The Nebelberg remained firmly in Prussian hands.[39] After the repulse of General Hartmann's assault, the Prussian encroachment continued on the Bavarian right. Intrepid elements of II/IR 15 pushed on, forcing the withdrawal of Captain Hang's Bavarian twelve pounder battery.

Hartmann. (Fontane)

As the various Bavarian formations fell back towards Roßdorf, and defences were hastily prepared, Major-General Faust appeared on the field, at the head of Major Schwalb's I/5th Regiment, the vanguard of Faust's brigade. The General accompanied the battalion in an immediate counter-attack against the encroaching Prussians. This move failed, both Faust and his aide being killed, with Schwalb's battalion suffering over 50 casualties, and falling back.[40] By 12:15, Roßdorf itself was under attack, with Prussians of II/IR15 being particularly close to the town.

At about 13:00, with the Bavarian units reorganising both in and east of the town, a very welcome asset appeared on the scene, in the form of Captain Königer's rifled six pounder battery. The battery had been sent to the sound of the guns, from Oepfershausen. After an exhausting three-hour march, on arrival at Roßdorf, Königer was assigned a position on a hill, just south of the main Roßdorf road. The battery rapidly proved its

36   Tabouillot, pp.16-18.
37   Käuffer, *Geschichte des königlich bayerischen 9.Infanterie-Regiments Wrede*, p.68.
38   *Antheil*, p.41, agrees that the troops were tired.
39   Käuffer, as above.
40   *Antheil*, Appendix III, p.III.

worth by engaging the battery of Captain Eynatten, at a distance of a little under two kilometres, and forcing it from the Nebelberg.[41]

In the event, however, no assault on Roßdorf actually took place. General Wrangel had been in the process of formulating his instructions for this task, when he, himself received a brief peremptory instruction of his own, from General Goeben. He, like Kummer to the west, was to break off the action, and return to Dermbach. This was duly undertaken.[42]

As the Prussians withdrew, the Bavarians followed up, re-occupying the Nebelberg. Despite the fatigue of his men, General Hartmann made preparations to pursue Wrangel towards Wiesenthal, but he, too was prevented from doing so. Instead, he received instructions to move to Oberkatza, some 10 kilometres south of Roßdorf, and to bivouac there. These orders were duly executed. July 4 had proven to be a frustratingly inconclusive day for both sides.[43]

Casualties[44]

| | Prussian | | Bavarian | |
	Officers	Men	Officers	Men
Killed	5	32	9	43
Wounded	5	208	18	274
Missing/prisoners	–	20	–	59
Total	10	260	27	376

That night, at his headquarters, Prince Karl encountered the Württemberg liaison officer, Major Suckow. In the presence of his entourage, the Field Marshal took Suckow's hand, and, referring to the Hanoverian debacle, said simply, "You were the only one to tell me the truth; I made a huge mistake, for which I now have to pay." It was a decent gesture, though one which could not alter the situation.[45]

Prince Thurn and Taxis, and the Bavarian Cavalry Stampede

Encounter at Hünfeld

As these moves developed to the east, the Bavarian cavalry commander, Prince Thurn and Taxis continued his own independent advance northwards, through this heavily forested, and, for cavalry, most restricting terrain (see map). Despite the refusal of immediate infantry support from VIII Corps, as noted, Prince Taxis, having previously

---

41   Ibid., pp.44-45.
42   G.G.S., p.584. Falckenstein's original order to Goeben was sent at 12:15, Regensberg, p.33.
43   *Antheil*, pp.46-47.
44   Losses as given by Prussians.
45   Rückschau, p.92.

pushed forward an advance guard comprising the 1st and 2nd Cuirassier Regiments and a horse artillery battery, decided that he would nevertheless continue his advance from Fulda with the troops at hand. He commenced his further move from about 04:00, on the 4th, once again moving north, towards Hünfeld.[46] The march took place under a gloomy overcast sky, and was accompanied by rain showers.

Two hours later, the advance guard of Major-General Beyer's Prussian division left Rasdorf, 15 kilometres north-east of Fulda, and marching towards that same village, also unknowingly heading directly for Prince Taxis' on-coming force. Beyer's foremost unit was one troop of 4/9th Hussars. Following these came, in turn, I/FR 39, Major Cederstolpe, Four Pounder Battery Schmidts, the other three troops of 4/9th Hussars, II/FR 39, Major Kruse, and finally, III/FR 39, Major Kurth, all of these being elements of Major-General Glümer's Combined Infantry Brigade.

At approximately 07:00, as the leading elements of Prince Taxis' advance guard column, headed by the 1st Cuirassier Regiment, approached the edge of the forest on the road between Rasdorf and Hünfeld. Here, some 1,600 paces east of a hostelry named the New Inn, it most unexpectedly came face to face with the tip of Glümer's Brigade, which, as noted, was advancing from the opposite direction. The surprise was, indeed, mutual![47]

After his initial probing patrols came under small arms fire from skirmishers of Major Cederstolpe's battalion, Taxis quickly ordered a gun of Captain Massenbach's horse artillery into action against them. As this took place, he then instructed the leading 1st Cuirassier Regiment to deploy, and also to send a squadron to patrol the woods from where the firing had come.

Glümer, however, had also reacted instantly, ordering a section of Captain Schmidts' Four Pounder Battery to the head of his own column, Schmidts himself in the lead. These two rifled guns rapidly unlimbered, and engaged the enemy. The first round, fired by Unteroffizier (NCO) Schwartz, landed in the middle of the deploying horsemen, and was followed by several more. The result was utter chaos. The panic stricken 1st Cuirassiers were thrown into complete disorder, and swept backwards into the oncoming 2nd Regiment, then also carrying that regiment away in their flight.

Captain Massenbach's horse battery attempted a brief resistance, but this soon faded, with the captain retreating with three of his four guns. The remaining cannon had to be abandoned to the Prussians, as a shell had smashed its limber. Massenbach then followed the disorderly progress of the main column.

The Prussian force subsequently followed up Taxis' withdrawal. Major-General Beyer marched south along the main road, pushing the Bavarians beyond Fulda. Here, his main force then spent the night with his advance guard bivouacked at Rückers, about 20 kilometres further south.

Casualties in this affair were very light, with no Prussian casualties at all being recorded. The Bavarian losses are given as:

---

46   108 G.G.S., p.587 & Lettow-Vorbeck, p.82. *Antheil*, p.65 & Kunz, p.81, however, both say 'near 06:00'.
47   109 Rintelen, pp.189-190.

1st Cuirassier Regiment: 1 officer and 7 men killed, and 11 men wounded
3rd Cuirassier Regiment: 1 man killed, and 2 men wounded
Battery Massenbach: 1 man killed, and 2 men wounded
Total: 1 officer and 9 men killed, and 15 men wounded[48]

As related, one of Captain Massenbach's cannon was also lost.

Bavarian Cavalry Panic at Gersfeld

After this setback, Prince Taxis began the withdrawal of bulk of the cavalry north-east-wards, towards the town of Bischofsheim, on the evening of the 4th, while the 1st Light Brigade remained at Lütter, some nine kilometres to the east-southeast. On this march, the column encountered a staff officer returning from Bavarian Headquarters to Prince Alexander, the Württemberg Colonel Triebig. The Colonel, along with reports on the outcome of the fighting at Zella and Roßdorf, had brought orders for the Cavalry Corps to now withdraw to Brückenau, a move to the southwest. Accordingly, the force turned around to gain the road to Brückenau. As this march began to develop, a few shots, probably accidental or nervous discharges, caused another panic, as Biebrach relates:[49]

> The experiences of the day, the changing directions of march, the hurrying back and forth of the officers, the influence of the night; all of these had placed the troops in such an excitedly nervous state that suddenly, upon an accidental signal, the cavalry – to the smallest unit – scattered in wild flight in all directions. Only by day was it possible to assemble the mass at Bischofsheim. Individual horsemen had fled as far as the Main, and were only returned to their units from there. The cuirassiers were assembled and reorganised at Brückenau, and the 2nd Light Brigade at Kissingen. For the time being, neither brigade was useable.

Biebrach's clinical description does not downplay the chaotic state of most of the Bavarian horse. The following morning, Colonel Pechmann, the commanding officer of the 5th Chevaulegers, the first unit to disintegrate, shot himself. The next day a squadron commander in the same regiment, Captain Strommer, also committed suicide, after being strongly criticised by a senior officer.

The Bavarian horsemen had been scattered far and wide, not only in the Rhön, but with numbers of fugitives fleeing as far as Schweinfurt and Würzburg. Considerable effort was needed in rounding them up. British Captain Chesney, in Würzburg at this time, was scathing in regard to the behaviour of the Bavarian cavalry, some of which he witnessed:

---

48 *Antheil*, Appendix III, pp.4-5. A Prussian assistant-surgeon attempted to save the officer, Second-Lieutenant von Grafenstein, but was unable to do so.

49 Biebrach, p.19. Lecomte, pp.202-203, is more scathing, and considers that the shots actually came from poachers. Bischofsheim should not be confused with Tauberbischofsheim, on the River Tauber.

Bavarian cuirassiers under fire at Hünfeld, drawing by Hoffmann.
(Regensberg/*Mainfeldzug*)

It was the evening of the 5th before the bulk of them collected at a rendezvous near Kissingen; whilst fugitives, still missing by the score; spread alarm on every road leading to the Main. Not satisfied with riding 40 miles (approximately 64 kilometres) to the rear at Schweinfurt, some of these stragglers went thence by train to Würzburg, and threw that city into such dire alarm by the reports they spread, that the authorities gave all up as lost, and telegraphed to the King for his permission to yield an entry to the Prussians unresistingly.

Chesney also saw, pasted on a wall in the city, a notice stating that Prince Karl and the whole of his staff had been taken prisoner![50] Not until the army had moved east of the Saale, was the Cavalry Corps again placed back in any tolerable state of order.

Prince Karl Withdraws to the River Saale

After the actions on the 4th, Prince Karl was now certain that he was facing the whole of von Falckenstein's force. The partial battles on the 4th had likewise convinced General von Falckenstein that he had probably encountered the complete Bavarian army, and most certainly at least the greater part of it. This was the most agreeable thing which

---

50   Chesney, p.77. Note that the captain refers to English miles in his account.

could happen for the Prussian commander, since it gave him the hope that he could defeat the most integrated portion of the enemy's forces, and thus prevent a combination with the other main body. Who could say what the VIII Corps would do if the 'heart' of the coalition, the Bavarian army, was to be neutralised?[51] Thus, although the scope of the clashes on the previous day had been limited, the Field Marshal made the decision to withdraw behind the River Saale. VII Corps' withdrawal towards the Saale began on the afternoon of the 5th, described by him as taking place, "with the intention of extending a hand to VIII Corps", which was also expected to act in accordance with the move.[52]

For his part, at 08:40 that morning, Prince Karl had sent the following telegram from Kissingen to Prince Alexander:

> Because of the general advance of Prussian columns across the Werra on all sides, it is no longer possible to achieve a union of the 7th and 8th Army Corps' north of the Rhön. I therefore propose to withdraw to the line of Neustadt-Bischofsheim, and require that VIII Corps remain at the same height as myself, and, as quickly as possible, to reopen communications by way of Brückenau and Kissingen. It is impossible to undertake any further measures at present. On the 7th, I will be on the Heights of Neustadt.[53]

This instruction was very difficult for Prince Alexander to accommodate. Firstly, his own corps was still far from fullly assembled, and had twice the distance to traverse, over difficult terrain to achieve it. In addition, sketchy reports were coming in to him of the rout of the Bavarian Cavalry. In the circumstances, therefore, Alexander agreed to endeavour to assemble a force at Schlüchtern, some 35 kilometres south-east of Fulda, as a link with the Bavarians.

Very rapidly, though, these circumstances were to alter again. Discussion of possible pending diplomatic negotiations suddenly muddied matters.[54] Alexander's earlier concerns for Frankfurt once more came to the fore. He, literally, again changed direction.

Having already decided upon his own retreat to Frankfurt, Alexander then informed Prince Karl of this fact in two reports on July 6 and 7 respectively. He advised the Field Marshal that the enemy was in Fulda, and suggested that the line of the River Main was now the priority to be held, rather than that of the Rhön; he further suggested that the VIII Corps withdraw on Hochst, Friedberg, and Hanau, and the Bavarians upon Aschaffenburg and Gemünden.

Word of VIII Corps' retreat reached the Field Marshal at the village of Ostheim, some 20 kilometres south-west of Meiningen, on the morning of the 7th, as VII Corps itself prepared to pull back to the Saale. Having done so, he immediately issued counter-orders for this move to be stopped. It was certainly an inauspicious beginning to Karl's own71st birthday.[55] Ironically, Vogel von Falckenstein, from his own headquarters in

---

51 Biebrach, p.20.
52 *Antheil*, p.73.
53 Baur-Breitenfeld, p.28.
54 Prince Alexander was also by now aware of heavy Austrian defeats in Bohemia, and consequent possible negotiations. This news would have increased his concern for the defence of Frankfurt.
55 *Antheil*, p.71.

Fulda, had granted the Prussian troops a rest day, on the 7th. From there, via the main roads through Brückenau and Schlüchtern, he could turn either towards the Saale or towards Frankfurt. In normal circumstances, it was most probable that he would choose the first option, to avoid having a stronger force in his flanks and rear. That is what Bavarian headquarters supposedly expected.[56] Thus, as both Federal forces marched away from one another, the Prussians rested.

Unfortunately, Prince Karl's recall to VIII Corps was not delivered until the next day, by which time the latter's march was completed. Meanwhile, the Bavarian withdrawal towards the Saale, on the morning of the 7th, as planned, took place.

On July 8 and 9 Prince Alexander had reached the line of Frankfurt-Hanau, and he then granted his troops a rest day on the 10th, the day of the fighting on the Saale. A Bavarian telegram, received early in the morning, brought the news of the Prussian advance through Brückenau, and the order to mount a thrust from Hanau towards Schlüchtern.[57] During the 8th, main body of the Bavarians reached Neustadt, with the advance guard at Münnerstadt. The main columns began to arrive along the Saale from the early morning of the 9th. That same day, the Prussian division of Beyer reached Schlüchtern, that of Manteuffel, Brückenau, and that of Goeben, Geroda.[58]

Along the Saale, at first nothing was done in the way of anticipating an enemy attack. The plan was to offer a trip-wire defence of this small river, but then to fight with all forces united in the defensive position of Poppenhausen, a day's march behind its centre, near the junction of the two main roads from Fulda through Kissingen to Schweinfurt, and that from Meiningen through Neustadt and Munnerstadt to Wurzburg. Indeed, no measures whatsoever were taken to prepare for that defence or that battle. For reasons the logic of which cannot easily be seen the Prussians were not expected to reach the Saale before the 11th, and the army was left strangely dislocated, until it was surprised strategically and chased from its positions.[59]

Prussian Moves towards the River Saale[60]

As thoroughly as Prince Karl had been convinced by the battle on the 4th that he was facing the whole Prussian army, just as thoroughly was General von Falckenstein convinced thereby, that he had either encountered the whole Bavarian army, or at least the greater part thereof. This was the most agreeable thing which could happen to the Prussian commander, since it gave the hope that he could defeat the most integrated portion of the enemy's forces, and also prevent a combination with the other main body. Who could say what the VIII Corps would do if the 'heart' of the coalition, the Bavarian army, was neutralised?

For these reasons, von Falckenstein ordered the narrow concentration of his army for July 5. Therefore, General von Goeben assembled his troops between Oexsen and

---

56 Booms, p.17.
57 Ibid., p.13.
58 *Antheil*, pp.73-74 & G.G.S., p.406.
59 Booms, pp.15-16.
60 There are two German rivers named the Saale. The Franconian Saale is the one which concerns this study – see Map 1.

Lengsfeld, General von Manteuffel was ordered to Lengsfeld itself, and General von Beyer was forced to quickly turn back to Geisa, leaving his advance guard of three battalions, one squadron, and one battery at Hünfeld. However, on the 5th, when the Prussians sought to come to grips with the enemy, they found that the Bavarians were no longer there.

Prince Karl had successfully disengaged, without any sign of where or when. What options were open to the Prussians? A direct pursuit of the Bavarian Army from Dermbach was not possible for three reasons:

1. It had to be assumed that they had a headstart of 12 hours and, owing to the paucity of Prussian cavalry and artillery, it would be most difficult to bring them to a halt.
2. In the case that the Bavarians had marched to Fulda, such an attack would strike nothing and would not prevent a junction.
3. In the case that the Bavarians persisted in their retreat, the danger also existed that the VIII Corps could soon appear on the flanks and rear of the Prussians.

As a result of these conditions, von Falckenstein then ordered that von Beyer's division once again move to Geisa, with an advance Guard at Hünfeld, von Goeben's division between Oechsen and Lengsfeld, and Manteuffel at Lengsfeld itself. A further advance on the 5th was not possible, as only one road ran from Geisa to Fulda, and this was completely occupied by Beyer's division. It also took a day to disentangle the troops from their previous concentration.

Let us summarise the strategic situation of the Prussian Main-Army as it was on the morning of the 5th, when the report arrived that the Bavarians had disappeared. It was as follows:

The Army of the Main, which had orders to first paralyse the Bavarian army, and which to this end had been concentrated between Geisa and Lengsfeld on a line some 15 kilometres long, found, on the morning of July 5 that the enemy had retreated. The reason for this was naturally not known; however, it might be assumed that, since the Prussian Headquarters had received reports of the VIII Corps advance north of the Rhön, the Bavarians had continued their advance to the left, and that Prince Carl was seeking to affect a junction with the VIII Corps via Fulda.[61]

If the Prussian army therefore reached this place before the Bavarians, or at the same time as them, the possibility existed that the enemy VII Corps could still be defeated in isolation and driven away south from the VIII corps, thus giving the Prussians control of the interior lines. The possibility thereof was suggested by the fact that the vanguard of the Prussian army was 1 to 1½ miles closer to Fulda than the Bavarians, and could use a good road, while the latter could only reach it by means of transverse ways.

If the Bavarian army had, on the other hand, marched to the south – which was actually not to be assumed – a march to Fulda would at least provide the advantage of placing the Prussians between the two enemy masses, after which they would (be able to) respond to circumstances.

---

61   Biebrach, pp.20-21.

In fact, as seen, the Bavarians had begun their withdrawal to the Saale on the 5th and this was largely complete by the 8th.

It had been known at Bavarian headquarters, that the Prussians were at a distance of ten hours march, at Fulda, because on the 6th, Vogel von Falckenstein had resumed his march in that direction, in search of VIII Corps, when the reconnaissance parties he had sent out on the 5th brought back news of the previous surprisingly lengthy retreat of the Bavarians. On the 7th, then, he allowed his men a day of rest in his quarters around Fulda

Despite continuing overt political moves, once again orchestrated by the Prussian Chancellor, by the evening of July 9, the Army of the Main was still facing the Bavarians, in the following positions:

> Division Beyer – Bad Brückenau
> Division Goeben – Geroda
> Division Manteuffel – Bad Brückenau

The route across the Rhön Mountains from Fulda to Brückenau, approximately 40 kilometres, was a very exerting for the troops, because the mountain roads were steep, and the Prussians had to drag along a large wagon train, having had to provide themselves with supplies to last for several days. The crossing was achieved without any interference by the enemy, however, and thus, by July 10, Beyer and Goeben were at their assigned positions: the first stood before Hammelburg, the second in front of Kissingen.[62]

The following morning, as previously instructed by General Vogel von Falckenstein, the main body broke camp at 06:00, with the division of Beyer moving on Hammelburg, and that of Goeben, further east, towards Kissingen. Both would very soon encounter the enemy along the line of the River Saale.

---

62 Rietstrap, p.63.

7

The Struggle along the Franconian Saale – July 10

The bulk of the Bavarian army had, in a series of short daily marches, arrived on the east bank of the Saale on July 7 and 8. The Reserve Cavalry had preceded the main force, much of it, as seen, in unfortunate circumstances. Many of the other troops were also somewhat vexed by their retreat, considering that they had done well in the fighting on the 4th, and not understanding the need for it.

At first, it was not considered that the line of the Saale should be defended, and certainly no measures were taken to do so, the crossing points being weakly held. However, the Bavarian army was now in a position behind a minor river, having taken no measures to defend it, with a major river, The Main, to its rear.[1]

However the political situation had developed for the Prussians, by the morning of July 10, as the action developed to the south around Hammelburg, the division of Goeben, followed by that of Manteuffel, moved against Kissingen. The forces assembled for the coming battle along the Saale totalled some 26,700 infantry, and 2,060 cavalry for the Prussians, with 73 guns. Prince Karl commanded a slightly smaller force, of 20,715 infantry and 2,220 cavalry, with 81 guns.[2]

The Combat of Hammelburg

The far left of the Bavarian deployment lay anchored in the town of Hammelburg, a little over 16 kilometres south-west of Kissingen. In this isolated position, in a loop on the west bank of the Saale, commanded by Prince Thurn and Taxis, stood the five battalions of the 3rd Division's 6th Brigade, Colonel Schweizer, and one foot artillery battery, along with the 20 squadrons and the two horse artillery batteries of the Heavy and 1st Light Cavalry Brigades respectively.

Hammelburg was the objective of the southern-most Prussian push against the River Saale. During the course of the 9th, information had been received by Thurn, as to the approach of a Prussian force,(Waldfenster) and patrols of the 1st Uhlans had been pushed along the valley of the River Thulba, past the village of Unter Erthal, towards Ober-Erthal, an hour's march beyond. These patrols had found the latter settlement, "unoccupied by the Prussians, and only on the edge of the woods beyond had observed

---

1 Booms, pp.16-17, considers this a serious violation Clausewitz' theory on the defence of small river lines.
2 Hoenig, p.79, quoting Kunz.

a few lonely enemy units, consisting of both infantry and cavalry, which however, soon disappeared in the direction of Kissingen."[3]

This incurious reconnaissance had actually discovered the advance elements of the Prussian force destined for Hammelburg, and the sighting of infantry should have sounded immediate alarm bells. In fact, moving towards Thurn was the bulk of Major-General Beyer's Division, 13 battalions, five squadrons, and 30 guns. At about 07:30, on the 10th, Beyer had broken camp, and began his advance from Bad Bruckenau towards Hammelburg, his columns personally accompanied by the army commander, General von Falckenstein.

Lieutenant Emil Jentsch, commanding a platoon in IR 20, like many others, uneasily awaited the day's events, as he later wrote:

> Our dewy coats were rolled in great haste and the drill cloth shoved into our packs and everyone sought to hurry to end his morning toilet, in order to slip into his correct spot in the company, under the strict eyes of our captain.
>
> The sergeant hurried back and forth the length of the company, counting off the files, dividing up the sections, and, smiling to himself contentedly because no man was missing, reported to his company commander, who was indignantly walking up and down the Platz: " The company is in order!" Just as the rooster at the manner in which we had spent the night called out his "cockadoodledoo" as a morning greeting, as though he wished to send us a farewell. In a short time we were united with the rest of the companies of the 2nd Battalion in the Regiment and proceeded in a merry march tempo down the wide, pretty, main street through the shadowy woods of the gorgeous Bavarian lands. Suddenly a disturbance was noticeable at the head of the advanced guard. The speedy march faltered and soon came the command; "Halt, (Face) Front!" The adjutants moved back and forth and then the order passed from mouth to mouth: "The artillery should advance!"[4]

On the night of the 9th, Thurn's main force had been posted north of Unter Erthal, actually facing the oncoming enemy. As the Prussians approached in the early morning, however, the Bavarian force was undertaking a relief of the forward units, and a consolidation of positions, apparently expecting any possible attack to come on their right. The majority of troops were pulled back closer to Hammelburg. About 10:00, the 1st Uhlans received orders to pull back across the Saale, to Fuchsstadt, to feed their horses. Half the regiment immediately complied, while the other half awaited the return of some patrolling elements. Once these reappeared, Colonel Korb, the regiment's commander, led the two squadrons back across the Thulba Bridge, to then withdraw through the 1st Jäger Battalion. As they did so, there came the sound of cannon fire.

Major-General Schachtmeyer's lead units reached the heights north of Unter-Erthal a little before 11:00, reporting that both enemy horse and foot were visible, to the south of that settlement. The General swiftly ordered Captain Schmidts' 1st Four Pounder

---

3   *Antheil*, p.134. This information doubtless 'confirmed' Prince Thurn and Taxis' apparent belief that any threat would come from the north. The Prince was also directly responsible for the area to the north, around Kissingen. He had delegated this to Baron Zoller.

4   Jentsch, p.159.

Battery forward to a height west of the village, from where Schmidts opened fire upon the Bavarian troops around the Thulba Bridge. As had been the case at Hünfeld, six days earlier, the initial rounds were on target, and Colonel Korb's uhlans were scattered in flight towards Hammelburg, and stampeding into the 1st Jäger Battalion, Major von Göriz, causing that unit also to disintegrate and flee. Neither formation could be rallied north of Hammelburg.

Two guns of Six Pounder Battery Lottersburg, commanded by Oberlieutenant Tauscheck, now engaged Schmidts' battery in support, in a vain attempt to cover their fleeing comrades. Tauscheck's own guns were then themselves instantly targeted, with he himself being mortally wounded by the second return shot! Immediately after this, the section limbered up, and withdrew to Hammelburg, taking no further part in the action.[5]

In the meanwhile, 7/FR39, Captain Tellenbach, had entered Unter Erthal, as had the leading troop of 4/9th Hussars, Lieutenant von Hagen. As von Hagen's men moved through the village, they captured two Bavarian Jäger. Tellenbach's men also exchanged some shots with Bavarian troops on heights south of the village, the Graslerberg.[6]

Lieutenant Jentsch and his men had also now moved into harm's way:

"Aha," said the man next to me, who had been conquered by his 'cannon fever' at Hünfeld, and now wished to demonstrate that he was a real man and soldier, " … today there is work and I will show now that I know no fear!"

The Magdeburg Light Battery came whistling by like a whirlwind, followed quickly by two others. As soon as the rifles were loaded and we were broken down into sections, we proceeded forward in a hurried march tempo, without music. Finally the woods came to an end, at the edge of which there were scattered remains of Bavarian newspapers, and the trampled down grass showed that Bavarian troops had camped here. Hardly had the half of my regiment stepped out of the woods when a cannon shot boomed across the area towards us, which was soon followed by a second and third. Now it was clear to us that we had the enemy before us and we were in for a hot fight.

The hostile Bavarian artillery, which was positioned on a dominating height on the other side of the town of Hammelburg, sent its well-aimed shots towards us; these would have torn great holes in our ranks if, instead of the timed fuses then in use by the Bavarians, they had used the percussion fuses used by our artillery. Loudly and ever more loudly roared the cannons' thunder, the road was already blocked with wagons and guns – Only look! There, up in the sky appear strange little grey clouds – They crackle, – suddenly a yellow lightening springs from these little clouds.

"Aha," says the man next to me, "shells!"[7]

---

5   *Antheil*, pp.134-135. Also see Booms, pp.81-82, for his scathing comments upon the Bavarian performance.
6   Von Bredow, p.100 & Rintelen, p.193.
7   Jentsch, pp.159-160.

By a little before 12:00, Captain Schmidts' Prussian battery was positioned west of the Hammelburg road, from here then being engaged with the Bavarian Battery Lottersberg, now positioned on the height of Schloss Saalech, south of the Saale, above Altstadt. A lively cannonade took place for some time, but with little effect on either side, due to the range, roughly, some 2,400 metres. Two Prussian guns of Schmidts' battery did, however, fire a few rounds with telling effect on the 3rd Cuirassier Regiment, Colonel von Mayer, posted at Diebach, on the Bavarian left flank, driving it back in some confusion.[8]

At approximately 12:15, Major-General Schachtmeyer, up alongside the firing line of FR 39, having already lost his horse, was also wounded in the hand, as well as being hit by several spent rounds, and was forced to quit the field. For roughly the next two hours, the conflict continued in a desultory manner, with little direction or energy on either side. Schachtmeyer's absence was already sorely felt on the Prussian side.

Beyer's slow advance continued, with the ranges of the various firefights mostly between some 300 to 600 metres. The Prussian infantry finally entered Hammelburg itself, by then on fire, at around 15:00, as the Bavarians abandoned it. By this time, Vogel von Falckenstein had received word of the fighting further north, around Kissingen. Leaving Beyer with instructions that his division remain concentrated in the vicinity of Hammelburg, he and his suite then hurried towards the scene of the new conflict.[9]

Thurn and Taxis subsequently withdrew his force to Arnstein, in the direction of Würzburg, over 15 kilometres away.[10] He, himself, would shortly be replaced, on an interim basis, by Major-General, Duke Ludwig of Bavaria.

Casualties

Losses in this scrappy engagement were, perhaps surprisingly, low. They were as follows:

Prussian
Staff Major-General Schachtmeyer, wounded
IR 20: 1 officer and 6 men wounded
IR 32: 2 officers and 1 man killed, 1 officer and 9 men wounded.
FR 39: 1 officer and 16 men killed, 43 men wounded, and 1 man missing
Total: 3 officers and 17 men killed, 3 officers and 58 men wounded, (1 officer and 8 men of these subsequently died of wounds), and 1 man missing[11]

Bavarian[12]
1st Jäger Battalion: 11 men wounded, and 7 men missing
I/6th Infantry Regiment: 3 men killed, and 2 officers and 20 men wounded
III/6th Infantry Regiment: 2 men wounded, and 1 man missing

---

8   Hoenig, p.236 & G.G.S., p.597.
9   Hoenig, p.241.
10   Rüstow, p.303.
11   G.G.S., p.599, gives the Prussian loss as six officers and 76 men. Förster, and regimental sources, are as given in the text.
12   *Antheil*, Table IX. Förster, p.13, gives figures of five men wounded and 11 missing for the1st Jäger Battalion.

I/14th Infantry Regiment: 15 men wounded, and 10 men missing
3rd Cuirassier Regiment: 1 man killed, 1 officer and 3 men wounded
1st Uhlan Regiment: 4 men killed, 7 men wounded, and 1 man missing
Six Pounder Battery Lottersberg: 1 officer killed, 1 officer and 6 men wounded, and
3 men missing
Horse Artillery Battery Massenbach: 1 man killed

Total: 10 men killed, 4 officers and 64 men wounded, and 22 men missing

The Battle of Kissingen

Prince Taxis, who was in command at Hammelburg, was also, as noted, overall commander at Kissingen, to the north. He had entrusted the defence of the area around the latter place and further north to Waldaschach, however, to Baron von Zoller, the commander of the 3rd Division. It was here that the primary Prussian blow would fall.

Colonel Booms offers a detailed picture of the town of Kissingen, and its immediate vicinity, soon to be a battleground:

> The un-navigable Franconian Saale flows towards the Main at Gemünden through a rather narrow valley, mostly consisting of pasture with little vegetation, and near Kissingen, is 500 to 800 paces wide. At that point it is bordered on the right bank by the Staffels and Altenberg, rather steep and wooded on the side turned to the river, hills of 1200 and 800 feet, while the hills on the left bank: the Sinnberg and the Stationsberg, the Bodenlaube, crowned by the ruins of the castle of the former counts of Hennenberg, and the Finsterberg, reach the same height, but descend towards the river with gentler slopes and are more open. At the foot of the Sinnberg and the Stationsberg, at the junction of the valley of the Saale with the narrower vale from Garitz to Winkels, is Kissingen, an open town of 3,500-4,000 inhabitants, contrasting a centre dating partly from the 9th Century, with a surrounding girdle of modern hotels and villas, already spreading to the far bank of the Saale. The Saale is a gently meandering mountain stream, incised some two to four feet, in summer averaging a width of between sixteen and thirty feet, with a current widely varying in speed and depth, fordable in several places, in others presenting dangerous gullies with muddy or slimy bottoms, but on average not a very serious obstacle to infantry. The Prussians found the river within its bed. In the wet season, the Saale easily overflows its banks and floods the valley. That is why the stone bridges are very long in relation to the water levels in summer; that at Kissingen numbers six arches with a combined length of more than 100 paces, with a further dam on the side of the town of 150 paces. The bridges of Hausen, Kleinbrach and Waldaschach, villages half an hour to more than an hour upstream, are not as long, however. Besides these permanent bridges, for use during the summer one finds, between Hausen and Kissingen, a wooden trestle bridge just above, and one for pedestrians at the baths and saltworks of Friedrichshall; at Kissingen, a wooden footbridge opposite the Schweizer and Bayerische hotels, and an iron one at the Kursaal; finally, just below the town another wooden footbridge near the

Lindenmühle. In this picturesque but rather isolated rolling part of Franconia one finds nonetheless many good roads, mostly gravel. Thus, the main road from Brückenau through Kissingen to Schweinfurt, branches off there twice more shortly before it reaches Kissingen; once via Stralsbach and Waldaschach, once from the Claushof via the Seehof and Garitz, the latter (running) past Winkels and through Nüdlingen, reaching the main road from Münnerstadt to Poppenhausen; a little more to the south, near the Schwartze Pfütze – a lonely homestead in a dark little gully – another road connects to this, winding its way from Kissingen up to the saddle ridge between Finsterberg and Bodenlaube, and from there descending once again to Reiterswiesen. Furthermore, the connecting road between Kissingen and Gemünden through Euersdorf and Hammelburg should be mentioned, with the undulations of which the bather must make his acquaintance on arriving by rail at Gemünden from the northwest. This also grants him the opportunity to become acquainted with the gullible and *gemütliche* country folk that so often provides the *Fliegende Blätter* the material for caricature and caption. The dwellings in these parts are mostly constructed from stone, and among them are many spacious and sturdy buildings.[13]

View of Kissingen from the east bank of the River Saale, 1867.
Key: 1. Sinnberg, 2. Winkels Heights, 3. Stationsberg, 4. Maria Chapel,
5. Ludwigstrasse. (Author's collection)

13   Booms, pp.22-25. The *Fliegende Blätter* was a popular contemporary satirical journal.

View of Kissingen, from the Sinnberg, 1867. Key: 1. Altenberg, 2. Garitz, 3. Staffels. (Author's collection)

View of area where the Prussians first crossed the Saale, seen in September 1867. Key: 1. Stationsberg, 2. Bodenlaube, 3. Finsterberg, 4.Location of initial Prussian crossing. (Author's collection)

Many in the town, who had naively counted on neutrality on account of its status as a spa, were by now in a considerable state of commotion. The bathers and many inhabitants of the far bank sought refuge on the east bank, and on the Stationsberg, and many young men had also left Kissingen for fear of Prussian conscription. The shops were largely closed, as goods and chattels were moved to safety.

Present in Kissingen that morning, was an American traveller, John Sherwood, who was there, of course, to take the waters. He, like many visitors, was completely unaware of the coming events, and had spent much of the afternoon of July 9 catching up with his correspondence. He then, as he later narrated, went to post the items, encountering Bavarian troops in the streets, and being most unimpressed by their bearing:

> On going out to the post-office, I found the streets filled with armed men, heavy beer-logged Bavarians, awkward and unsoldierly in appearance, movement and discipline. Big, ungainly horses, bestraddled by officers whose figures were as unequestrian as well filled bags of flour, were walking about with true German phlegm, or slowly dog-trotting in different directions in what they call a hurry.

Including some reinforcements which he had received the previous day, Lieutenant-General Zoller had under his command eight battalions, 12 squadrons, and 16 guns. In and around Kissingen itself, where Brigadier-General von Ribaupierre held immediate command, stood five battalions (II and III/15th Regiment, III/ 11th, III/9th, and the 6th Jäger Battalion), 12 guns (four twelve pounders from Captain Schuster's battery and the eight of the 6th Battery, Captain Redenbacher), and the 2nd Chevaulegers belonging to 3rd Division.

Major-General Count zu Pappenheim, commanding officer of the 2nd Light Cavalry Brigade, had overall responsibility for the Friedrichshall-Hausen-Waldaschach area, to the north. Each of these villages was occupied by one battalion, respectively the 5th Jäger Battalion, II/11th Regiment, and I/15th Regiment. Count Pappenheim also had the other half of Battery Schuster at his disposal (four twelve pounders), and his own two cavalry regiments, the 5th Chevaulegers, and 3rd Uhlans.

As has already been seen, it was only towards the evening of the 9th, when the foremost troops of Goeben's division had already reached Albertshausen, Poppenroth, and Stralsbach, that certain defensive measures were undertaken by the Bavarians. Nevertheless, in Kissingen, Major-General Ribaupierre, whose 5th Infantry Brigade was responsible for the defence of the town, as noted, had largely completed some defensive measures by 09:00, on the 10th. Five companies of his two immediately available battalions, II/15th, and III/11th Regiments, were deployed in the first line along the east bank of the Saale. These troops were posted in open order behind the young chestnut trees overshadowing the river path north, to the Friedrichshall saltworks, as well as in hastily barricaded houses on the town's outskirts to the north of the bridge, and behind the row of wooden stalls stored in the meadow in front of the houses there, during the summer. A half-platoon of 4/Schützen Company, 15th Infantry Regiment, was allocated the defence of the bridge itself. Behind these were placed a section of twelve pounders, under Lieutenant Halder. At the western end of the bridge, an ad hoc barricade had been put together, assembled around three water carts.[14]

Men of 5/15th Regiment were also posted in the Heilmann and Collard Houses, immediately to the south of the bridge, and in the Kurgarten, next to it, as well. Somewhat to the rear of the bridge, in the side streets to the right and the left, were two companies acting as supports, while four companies III/11th Regiment took up position in and around the Maria Cemetery, which was near the outskirts of Kissingen on the road to Nüdlingen, This walled and barricaded position was intended as the key point in the defence of the town. All told, some 900 men were in the town. Ribaupierre certainly appears to have expected a direct assault.

The remaining infantry company, 3/11th Regiment, had been detached to Euerdorf, some 10 kilometres down river, where a detachment from Hammelburg was also posted, guarding the bridge there, and another at Aura, linking the two forces. In reserve, Ribaupierre had concentrated three battalions in reserve at Winkels, two kilometres behind Kissingen. In addition to these units, III/15th, and III/9th Regiments, and the 6th Jäger Battalion, he had assembled a further ten guns, a section of smoothbore twelve pounders (Lieutenant Gossner), and the eight rifled six pounders of 6th Battery, Captain Redenbacher. These were placed, in two groups, on the lower slopes of the Sinnberg, covering the main road (500 paces away). These guns had a close escort of one and a half squadrons of the 2nd Chevaulegers, with the main body of the regiment being held close by.

Finally, the Bavarian baggage train had been hurriedly put in readiness, during the previous evening. This work was finally completed around midnight. In the early hours of the 10th, the wagons and pack animals were directed towards Schweinfurt.

Although matters on the east bank of the Saale had been addressed, it will be noted that no such arrangements had been undertaken on the west bank. Not only the village of Garitz, but also the Staffelsberg and the Altenberg heights were completely unoccupied. Not even a few vedettes were posted in these areas, a most serious, indeed almost amazing, omission.

South of Kissingen, near the Lindenmühle, was another bridge, in any case unsuitable for use by any troops other than infantry. Almost certainly due to time constraints, the decking of this structure had been removed, but leaving the supports completely intact. Whether by accident, design, or lack of time, this omission was a potentially serious flaw in the defensive line.

Upriver, some defensive measures had also been undertaken. The wooden bridges at Friedrichshall and at the Steinhof were both pulled down; the infantry posted there being partly ensconced in the massive stone buildings and behind the heavy wooden racks, with galleries, of the saltworks, and partly remained in support. The four twelve pounders here, commanded by Premierlieutenant zu Rhein, were positioned some 800 paces to the rear, at the foot of the Sinnberg, opposite the entrance to the valley of the Cascade; the cavalry was close by.[15]

---

14   Easily found in a spa town, especially in the summer.
15   *Antheil*, p.76.

At Hausen, the stone bridge was barricaded, and the battalion there took up position behind it. That at Waldaschach remained clear, and each of the three roads leading up to it was occupied by a company, while the other half of the battalion held the left bank.[16]

The Assault on Kissingen

Early on the morning of the 10th, the landlord of an inn on the north-eastern spur of the Altenberg came into Kissingen to report the presence of Prussian cavalry patrols on the fringes of the Clauswood.[17] Upon receipt of this information, a Bavarian patrol of a corporal and six men of the 15th Regiment, led by Oberlieutenant Schoberth, was sent out to recconoitre.[18] The Bavarian *Antheil* merely comments that"…a patrol of about 12 men was sent out from the Kissingen bridge, which then established itself on the Altenberg, near Garitz,"[19] and there made themselves comfortable. This detachment later exchanged a few shots with the next mounted Prussian vedettes to appear, but then withdrew to the left bank when, between 08:30 and 09:00, enemy infantry also appeared from the direction of Garitz.

Wrangel in Kissingen. (Cohn)

These troops belonged to Goeben's division, numbering 16 battalions, nine squadrons and 31 guns. During his march from Waldfenster to Kissingen, Goeben had, near Schlimpfhof, received the information that Kissingen remained occupied by the

---

16 Booms, pp.27-28.
17 Ibid., p.32. He times this at about 07:00. Hoenig, p.98, though, places the initial Bavarian patrol sighting at 08:00.
18 *Geschichte des Königlich bayerischen 15. Infanterie-Regiments*, p.22.
19 *Antheil*, p.80, which also places this at around 08:00.

Bavarians in force. At this point, he directed his leading brigade, that of Kummer, (five battalions, 1 squadron, 12 guns), to the right through Albertshausen to Garitz. Kummer was followed by Wrangel's brigade (five battalions, four squadrons, 13 guns), and Wrangel, in his turn by a reserve (three battalions, four squadrons, 6 guns). To the right, was pushed a flank guard of one battalion. In addition, Goeben placed a battalion in Aura, and on his left, II and F/IR 15, under Colonel von der Goltz, were pushed to the left, through the Claushof. Goltz was instructed to deploy against Kissingen via the Cascade Valley opposite Friedrichshall. Thus, the Prussians did not make the mistake of a direct assault on the town, as Zoller seems to have expected.

The vanguard battalion of Kummer's brigade, F/IR 53, Major von Rosenzweig, advanced from the village of Garitz in open order against the Altenberg and the southern outskirts of Kissingen, where it occupied the nearest buildings without opposition. Kummer's other four battalions marched out of Garitz between 09:00 and 09:30, then deploying in two lines to follow the vanguard, which had, by then moved on. While these had already been met by rifle fire from the Bavarian companies and the twelve pounders deployed along the river, at this point, the eight rifled six pounder guns of Battery Redenbacher, posted on the Sinnberg also opened fire, at a distance of some 2,200 metres and with some effect on the manoeuvring Prussian company columns, which then advanced at the double to take cover behind the buildings and the Altenberg itself. One shell hit directly amidst 11/IR 53.[20]

To counter this shelling, Kummer brought forward Captain Weigelt's four pounder battery to the Staffels, an area of open slopes north-east of Garitz (see illustration), immediately followed by Captain Eynatten I's rifled six pounders, as described in the regiment's history:

> Turning to the left in marchcolumn in front of Garitz, they climbed the rather steep southern slope of the Staffelberg, the with the Four Pounder Battery. In the lead, and established a firing line at some distance from the wooded crest of the hill. As soon as they marched up, they received heavy fire by the enemy artillery deployed north of Kissingen: namely the 3rd Six Pounder Battery suffered severe losses in a matter of minutes. Soon, the counter-battery fire could be opened up with visible success.[21]

Rapidly, however, the cannonade would become more general. As with the artillery, the Prussian infantry here presently held no particular advantage. Their vanguard had now occupied all of the west bank suburb of Kissingen and occupied most of the Altenberg with skirmishers, but when the former attempted to cross the major bridge and the footbridge near the Kursaal, a few rounds of canister from Lieutenant Halder's two twelve pounders, supported by rifle fire from the infantry lying there in cover, forced them once more to take shelter in the woods and buildings on the west bank. Cleverly,

---

20 Hoenig, p.99, places this just after 09:30. He further states that Goeben, initially, would not allow a bombardment of the town, p.100.

21 Hamm & Moewes, p.181 & Hoenig, pp.99-100. Eynatten I's battery lost two men killed, and four wounded, along with seven horses killed and another injured, Hoenig, Appendix 5. The Staffelberg was also known as the Staffels.

Halder loaded his pieces out of enemy sight, and had them pushed forward to actually fire, thereafter repeating the process.

About 10:30 the designated 'main body' of Goeben's division, Brigade Wrangel, had arrived on the field, at Garitz. Weltzien's brigade, following on, was halted at Albertshausen. Wrangel was directed to Kummer's right, towards the south side of the Altenberg, now seeking a point to cross the river here. Captain Coester's seven four pounders, of Wrangel's brigade battery, were deployed on the northern spur of the Altenberg, and, together with the two batteries already on the Staffelsberg, redoubled the duel with the Bavarian guns across the river.[22]

The Prussian bombardment initially made little progress, despite its superiority in numbers. The Bavarian infantry along the river were, for the most part under cover, and the position of Captain Coester's battery was such that his plunging fire was ineffective, and Coester also had to be wary of hostile small arms fire. Similarly, the Prussian infantry facing them were forced to remain in cover, and by around Noon, the firing here had largely petered out. General von Zoller must have begun to hope for a success, especially since he had been promised further reinforcements.[23] With the Bavarian troops under cover, the effect of the needle-gun had been demonstrably less effective than in the open. Lieutenant Halder's two guns, at the same time, had heavily shelled the Bayerische Hof, a large hotel on the west bank of the river, north of the principal bridge, from which came heavy rifle fire. Though the building was badly damaged, the defenders, of Lieutenant-Colonel von Henning's IR 19, a largely Polish regiment, were not driven out.[24]

In the meanwhile, reinforcements were on their way to Baron Zoller. From Münnerstadt, about 10 kilometres to the north-east, Lieutenant-General Feder had despatched three battalions, one squadron, and six guns from his 2nd Division. These troops successively arrived near the village of Winkels between 10:00 and around 10:45.

The guns were deployed, as they arrived, on the Sinnberg, at the same level as the village itself, and then opened fire against Kummer's batteries on the Staffelsberg. Unfortunately, these guns lacked the range to reach those positions, although in their turn, they could not be reached by Captain Coester's Prussian four pounder battery, on the Staffelsberg. On the other hand, Coester's guns could reach the Bavarian battery behind Kissingen, low on the Sinnberg, forcing Captain Redenbacher, and the two supporting twelve pounders back, initially some 1,200 paces, and subsequently, behind Winkels, leaving only the gallant section of Lieutenant Halder, in Kissingen, now providing close support to the Bavarian infantry here.

---

22   Colonel Booms, p.33, alludes to the temporary withdrawal of Eynatten I's battery, in the initial stage of the action. However, Prussian sources do not mention this.

23   Ibid., p.36, from *Antheil*; he also rightly criticises G.G.S., p.600, for placing the start of the action that day an hour later than it actually did. Note also that Captain Coester's battery had seven guns. This is because an extra four pounder had been 'acquired' the previous month, in Hanover. No one appears to have queried this (Hoenig, p.100).

24   Ibid., p.100. Men of the regiment did avail themselves of the hotel wine cellar, along with other items, see Heinemann, pp.18-19!

Prince Karl, himself, had arrived on the Kissingen battlefield at about 11:00, accompanied by General Von der Tann. By this time, there could be no illusions whatever as to the Prussian intentions, as even the Bavarian official history acknowledges:

> Soon after 10 AM, the enemy had received reinforcements with the arrival of Wrangel's Brigade, and it became more and more clear that his main thrust would be directed against Kissingen. This presumption was further confirmed by a report from the companies of the 15th Regiment sent towards Reitersweisen, which, from the lower eastern slopes of the Bodenlaube, had sent out scouting parties towards the ruins and the Finsterberg; since the last-mentioned could clearly observe there that numerous masses of enemy infantry stood drawn up behind Garitz, while cavalry and artillery were moving against the Saale. [25]

Neither Prince Karl nor Von der Tann made any changes, simply ordering Zoller to defend himself stubbornly, in expectation of further reinforcements, which would be sent from 4th Division. The Prince then rode north to Friedrichshall spending some time there. General Von der Tann remained at Kissingen, but instead of assessing the overall situation and checking the dispositions in general, he concerned himself with details, meddled somewhat with the fighting itself, and rode rather aimlessly to and fro, in equal measure. Unfortunately, his normally sharp instinct, on this occasion, did nothing to lift the general paralysis hanging over the defence of the town. This state of affairs was about to change much for the worse.

Prussian Brigade Wrangel crosses the Saale south of Kissingen

South of the town, as the Altenberg was occupied, and the Bavarian pickets there were pushed in, at around 11:30, the small partially dismantled bridge was discovered just north of a mill, the Lindesmühle, by Prussian troops of Major Kaweczynski's I/IR 15, which had been assisting in the clearing of the Altenberg. About a kilometre south of the main Kissingen bridge, this structure was still standing, although, as related, the surface planking had been removed. Captain von dem Bussche, the company commander of the leading unit, 2/IR 15, was ordered, by his battalion commander, Major Kaweczynski, to, "Lead your company over there and have a look if you can get across here! ". Von dem Bussche immediately put his men to work, under fire from the opposite bank, to make it possible to use. This was undertaken with any materials at hand from the immediate vicinity, including local dwellings, and tables from the nearby guest house, the Villa Vay. Remarkably, this feat was successful to the extent that troops were able to move along it in single file, and cross the river, von dem Bussche's men being most deservedly the first to do so.[26] Before 12:30, troops were crossing the improvised structure. The key to the Kissingen position had been found, and the lock opened.

This flanking movement, however, did not go completely unnoticed. It was first reported to two Bavarian officers at the Maria Cemetery, by a local inhabitant. One,

---

25 *Antheil*, p.85.
26 Lettow-Vorbeck, p.152, Goeben, p.20 & Regensberg, *Der Mainfeldzug*, p.67.

apparently, stated that he could not leave his position, a not unreasonable point. A second officer sent an NCO with the man, but by this time, the situation was beyond redemption.[27]

Although there were no substantial Bavarian forces covering the east bank of the Saale, south of the town, there were units charged with watching the area. Specifically, a chevauleger picket had been left to scout the roads south of the Stationsberg. More importantly, though, two companies of the 15th Infantry Regiment, 5th Schützen, Captain Kohlermann, and 9th Fusilier, Captain Correck, were supposed to be posted in the area specifically to, "… guard against any enemy attempts at crossing (the river) in that direction." Certainly, some of these troops were present here, as when the Prussians crossed the river, as the latter certainly came under considerable small arms fire.[28]

Subsequently, two Bavarian more companies, 4/6th Jäger, and 10/11th Regiment, made a stand on the southern edge of Kissingen, but the increasing flow of Prussian reinforcements crossing the makeshift 18 metre long bridge, supported by fire of the units across the river soon made this stand untenable.[29] The three companies of Major Kaweczynski's I/IR 15, which had already crossed the bridge, were swiftly followed by two companies of Major Rohdewald's Lippe-Detmold Battalion, and then I/IR 55, Lieutenant-Colonel Böcking.[30] The trickle had become a flood.

As these events developed south of the town, a number of Bavarian units in Kissingen were replaced in the line with fresh troops. Partly these changes were due to growing ammunition shortages, and some as a consequence of the growing threat on the southern flank, initially as the Prussians extended their line southwards, and subsequently, of course, as they actually began to cross the river, as related. One by one, the units brought up from Winkels were fed into the line, from about 10:30 onwards.

First to be pulled back were II/15th Regiment, Major von Brückner, followed by III/11th Regiment, Major Dietrich, being replaced by the units originally held in reserve III/15th, Major Pöllath, III/9th, Major Dietrich, along with the spread out 6th and 7th Jäger Battalions. As the fighting continued to escalate both in the south, and along the river, the Bavarian line was strengthened, and extended along the left.

This wing now encompassed the promenade, in front of the Kursaal. Along the river, there were now six and a half companies in action, with four more in support, from the 2nd, 3rd, 9th, 11th, and 15th regiments, and the 7th Jäger. Behind these units, stood II/15th Regiment, and at this point out of ammunition, together with three companies of III/15th. Two of the latter were on the Zimmerplatz, and the third near the foot of the Sinnberg. Just east of the town, two and a half companies of the 9th Regiment held the fortified Cemetery.

On the western slopes of the Sinnberg, the remaining one and a half companies of III/9th Regiment, having withdrawn from the town, had mustered, together with three companies of the 6th Jäger Battalion, at the Stationsweg. The remaining company was still in the town, as noted. Major Ysenberg's 7th Jäger Battalion also withdrew from the

---

27 Booms, p.41.
28 G.G.S., p.601, states that the crossing took place under 'heavy' fire.
29 *Antheil*, pp.88-89.
30 Hoenig, *Entscheidungskämpfe*, p.119. Kaweczynski's last company subsequently followed.

town, and also took up a position on the Stationsweg, between the units of the 9th and 15th, presenting a heavy skirmish line.

In front of Kissingen, the Prussian batteries had advanced as closely as possible, and their cannon balls found their victims both in and across the houses. To the front, the second half of the Lippe battalion now pressed on towards the iron footbridge of the Kursaal, and F/IR 53, Major Rosenzwig, to the main bridge. Here, the gallant Bavarian Lieutenant Halder and his two twelve pounders had held on as long as possible, but had withdrawn to the back of the Ludwigstrasse when threatened to be cut off on his left flank; from that position he fired two more rounds at the advancing skirmishers of IR/53, before, at about 12:30, continuing his retreat behind Kissingen, to the south of Winkels.[31]

Of the Bavarian troops cut off in buildings by the Prussian advance, many were captured, especially those north of the main bridge. The chances of escape from the lower town were better, and many men were able to do so, including General Ribaupierre himself! Others fought to the end, most notably Corporal Schmitt, who was killed in Room 11 of the Sanner Hotel, in the south of the town, after refusing to surrender.[32] Most of his comrades there were made prisoners. In the same hotel, Prussian troops also found guests sheltering in the dining room, as well as in their rooms. By 13:30, the whole of Kissingen was firmly in Prussian hands. This left only the 'Redoubt', the Maria Cemetery, to be dealt with, on the edge of town.

At about the same time as these events took place, the Stationsberg, too, fell into Prussian hands. The majority of the two and a half battalions which had made the flanking move from the south, had advanced against the heights, taking full advantage of the protruding wooded slopes of the Bodenlaube to outflank the Bavarian skirmishers' left, while these were already being engaged in front.[33] As the withdrawal took place, Major Ysenburg, the commander of the 7th Bavarian Jäger Battalion, was killed.

Prussian Assault of the Maria Cemetery

Booms described this strongpoint thus:

> Sited upon a low spur of the Sinnberg, in a bend in the road, and therefore covering it, is the Maria-Cemetery, which include a chapel and a house. The complex, some 200 paces in length and 50 wide, is surrounded with a wall which can only be scaled without a ladder at the rearmost part along the south- or road -side. The main entrance, overlooking the town, is reached by a rather high staircase; the first two doors on the side are a couple of stairs above this, and the last two, level with the road on the side of the fields the wall is highest. In front, one finds a picturesque miniature lake, the Liebfrauen-See, which is fed by water from the mountains, a

---

31 Booms, p.45 & Kunz, p.95.
32 Booms, p.44 & Hoenig, footnote, p.122.
33 These, it will be recalled, were I/IR 15, I/IR 55, and half (two companies) of the Lippe-Detmold Battalion.

Bavarian infantry near the Sanner Hotel at Kissingen. (Fontane)

mill that floats and discharges into the Saale. After this, are a couple of houses with gardens on both sides of the road.[34]

The land behind the cemetery is generally open. Up on the cultivated mountain slopes, were some folds in the ground, some more or less sunken country roads, and here and there, a fruit tree or a very transparent screen of low woods; the hilltops themselves, however, are wooded.

A more convenient strongpoint than this cemetery could hardly be imagined. The garrison of the 'redoubt' consisted of two companies, and one platoon of the III/9th Regiment. These were 9th, Captain Thoma, 10th, Captain von Ausin, and the one platoon of the 5th Schützen Company, Oberlieutenant Reis, a total of some 300 officers and men.[35]

These troops had made some loopholes in the surrounding wall and also barricaded the entrance with gravestones. This strongpoint, along with a walled garden on the opposite side of the road, which was occupied by a company of III/15th Regiment, could have made this road a veritable shooting gallery, and would have prevented the Prussians from deploying for some considerable time, had it not been turned by their flanking move along the Stationsberg. Even so, it held them back for a while, and thus served its purpose.

For some time, the Prussian infantry made no attempt to assault the stronghold, merely keeping up a steady fire against it. Around 13:30, however, the Prussian attackers became more aggressive, and some 15 minutes or so later, an assault began, led by Major

---

34 Booms, p.52 & Hausser, p.70.
35 Häusser, p.70.

Böcking, with two companies of his of his own II/IR55 and two more of I/IR15. In the event, no spectacular struggle for the strongpoint actually took place. Captain Thoma, possibly just in the nick of time, ordered a withdrawal from the position. The gate was cleared, and the Bavarian troops rapidly withdrew as best they could, Thoma being killed in the process. Of the 300 or so officers and men in the 'redoubt' before the attack, Captain Thoma, Sergeant Straub, and three men were killed, another 20 men wounded, and some 20 or more taken prisoner.[36]

Although troops were available to continue the struggle here, specifically I and II/12th Infantry Regiment, which had been pushed forward by 2nd Division, these were not used for this purpose. I/12th, Major Hugenpoet, was inexplicably left behind in Winkels, while Major Kohlermann's battalion, directed towards Reiterswiesen, upon leaving the cover of the woods, came under fire from Prussian skirmishers on the Bodenlaube. Kohlermann swiftly pulled back, leaving patrols to observe.[37]

Thus faced with the complete loss of Kissingen itself, at about 14:00, Lieutenant-General von Zoller also ordered the withdrawal of the Bavarian units around Friedrichshall and Hausen, all in the direction of the formations deployed around Nüdlingen. These troops had already seen their own trials and tribulations.

As the Prussians now pushed forward all along the entire front, General Zoller was killed by shrapnel beside the main road at Winkels, a horse having been shot from under him earlier. General Von der Tann also received a painful grazing wound to his neck, which fortunately, however incapacitated him only for a short time. During this withdrawal, four horses pulling a gun of Battery Zeller were killed at a stroke, and without the assistance of a handful of the covering infantry, which made it possible to cut the harness, the gun would have been taken.

At about that time, around 14:30, Prince Karl now sent orders to the 4th Division, from which he had yet to hear, to hasten "immediately" to the battlefield with all available forces.[38] General Ribaupierre, who had again assumed local command, attempted to make a stand, at the village of Winkels, "… which, in its dark frame of fir-topped crests hints of a Swiss landscape".[39] However, Batteries Zeller and Redenbacher, along with their attendant cavalry escorts, having reached the main road, then continued the retreat towards Nüdlingen, as had the two twelve pounder sections of Lieutenants Gossner and Halder. The former batteries withdrew to the north of the Sinnberg, and the latter sections to the south of Winkels, These unfortunate, but probably unavoidable withdrawals, left the infantry without any artillery support.

Nevertheless, they put up resistance. North of the road, on the Sinnberg, I/12th Regiment, and II and III/15th Regiment, were joined by elements of the 3rd Battalion. South of these, were other elements of the same units, together with some Jäger and men from the 9th and 11th Regiments. These efforts were, however, unsuccessful, although Colonel Booms paid the Bavarian troops the following compliment:

---

36 Ibid., p.71 & Hoenig, pp.128-129.
37 *Antheil*, pp.95-96.
38 Ibid. pp.99 & 113
39 Booms, p.59.

With a final effort these troops now ascended the rather steep slope that raises itself between Winkels and Nüdlingen, continually pursued, and getting more into the line of fire because of the landscape. This caused their tactical order, which had already suffered considerably, to be lost completely; and a final attempt to stop them again at those heights, where the support by fresh troops so very necessary was lacking entirely, failed. Nüdlingen showed itself at a short distance from them in the valley, and the retreat towards it also sheltered them from their pursuers' fire for a while.

Where they had made a stand, however, was shown to me by the remnants of cartridges drawing curved lines in the ground here and there, and that they made a stand at all proves that these infantry were tough, virtuous troops.[40]

Bavarian infantry at Kissingen, drawing by Hoffmann. (Regensberg/*Mainfeldzug*)

The Prussian Advance Continues: Nüdlingen

Although the crossing of the Saale at Kissingen had now been achieved, and the position there made safe, there was as yet still no let up in the Prussian pressure. While IR 53 and F/IR 13 were mustered in and to the east of Kissingen, General Goeben ordered von Henning's IR Nr. 19, across the river, from the area in and around the hotel Bayerische Hof. This regiment was to advance upon the heights above the village of Winkels, and was duly committed there, at around 14:30.

Somewhat later, a little after 15:00, troops of I/IR55, Major Böcking, and the Lippe-Detmold Battalion, Major Rohdewald, which had earlier crossed the river on the 'makeshift' bridge, were climbing the Schlegelsberg, the height behind Winkels. Skirmishers of I/ IR 55, commanded by Lieutenant von Papen, surprised the Bavarian Battery Zeller. Von Papen almost overran the battery, but a combination of a quick

---

40 Booms, p.60.

reaction by two Bavarian schützen companies (1 and 2/ 12th Regiment) sent forward from Winkels, and the battery's close escort squadron of the 5th Chevaulegers, led by Rittmeister Egloffsheim, swept away the Prussians, capturing the wounded von Papen, and a number of others. The overall situation did not allow any further exploitation of the situation, however, and this position, too, soon had to be given up in the face of the general Prussian advance.[41]

While these actions were in progress, as related, at about 14:30, Prince Karl sent urgent orders to Lieutenant-General Ritter von Hartmann, to hasten immediately to the battlefield with all available forces.[42] With little immediate else in the way of other options, the Prince then once again shuffled his weary men. A little over half an hour later, General Ribaupierre's withdrawing force had arrived in the vicinity of Nüdlingen, along with troops who had marched from Hausen and Friedrichshall. These latter had been most fortunate that the Prussian advance from the direction of the Sinnberg was weak, at this point, and that of Wrangel's troops was greatly impeded by both the Calvarienberg and the Schlegelsberg.

These two lucky circumstances were greatly to the immediate favour to the Bavarians. The retreating columns moving through the narrow streets of Nüdlingen were especially burdened, and vehicles and artillery caused more considerable difficulties. Lieutenant Halder's two guns both fell into a ditch, and it was only with enormous effort that both were somehow rescued, the second one being pulled out under fire! It was only possible for infantry to cross the Calvarienberg.

At Nüdlingen, the left wing of the retreating Bavarian infantry initially attempted a stand on the western slopes of this height. There being little in the way of cover here, the fire from the Prussians on the Schlegelsberg, immediately south of Nüdlingen, soon drove them off. Now, a position was taken behind the crest of the Calvarienberg, the units here being reinforced by II/ 12th Regiment, a relatively fresh battalion, while detachments from 7th Jäger Battalion, III/15th Regiment and II/11th Regiment occupy the outer Nüdlingen perimeter area, including the cemetery on the heights in between.

In addition Captain Kirchhoffer's four twelve pounders were also deployed, having been relieved at Bischofsheim, and sent here. In addition, two companies of 10th Regiment, marching through, left behind two companies to assist; finally, a reserve was formed at the Schlossberg, from several companies of the 15th, I/12th Regiment and III/4th Regiment from 4th Division, which appear to have been waiting here, idle and without purpose, since early morning. Major-General Schumacher had, by this time, taken over from Ribaupierre.[43]

At this point, the action here appeared to be slipping into a somewhat desultory cannonade. Certainly, Major-General Wrangel considered that his own objectives had been achieved, in that he had occupied Winkels and its surrounding heights. At this point, too, he also received orders from General Goeben, instructing him to picket the area around Nüdlingen, and also placing the three battalions of IR 19 under his direct

---

41 Goeben, p.26, gives the number as one officer and 30 men. *Antheil*, pp.97-98 is not specific. G.G.S., p.603 says the number of prisoners was 'about six', as does Hoenig, pp.154-155.The latter's list for men missing from this battalion for the whole day is one officer and 13 men (Appendix V).

42 *Antheil*, pp.99 & 113.

43 Booms, pp.67-68.

command.[44] However, without the fateful event happening now, these measures probably would have all but stopped the weakened pursuit; it had already largely come to a halt, and was confined to an exchange of fire, in which two Prussian batteries from the Sinnberg also took part, while a third, along with the cuirassier regiment (Westphalian Cuirassier Regiment, Nr.4 Colonel von Schmidt) were called up from the reserve, but not then committed to to any further action.

Also about this time, the Bavarian 1st Horse Artillery Battery of Captain Lepel, which had been posted all day on the slopes north-east of Nüdlingen, about 700 paces east of the village, at the junction of the Kissingen and Münnerstadt roads, suddenly galloped forward, deployed, and opened fire. Unfortunately, the battery's target proved to be their own II/12th Regiment, Major Kohlermann, on the Calvarienberg. The effect of this completely disordered Kohlermann's battalion, while at the same time re-igniting the combat. A pair of guns of Battery Kirchhoffer were also pushed forward on to the height to support Lepel, but this merely accentuated the general confusion One of these guns was overrun, after five of its horses were wounded. An ad-hoc group of Kohlermann's men then attempted to regain the gun, but were repelled by Prussians of 1 and 4/IR 15, commanded by Captain Amelunren.[45]

Around 16:30, Prussian patrols were sent forward towards Nüdlingen, as the occupation of the Calvarienberg also took place. The Prussians, too, had been under arms since the early morning, and had also undergone hard marching in the past few days. Von Wrangel received orders to establish pickets and pitch camp behind Winkels. In the meantime, the Reserve, Lieutenant-Colonel Henning's IR/19, which, as noted, had earlier been assigned to him, and had been involved in the most recent fighting, remained in the front line just mentioned. Now, at last, the main battle finally appeared to be over.

Combats along the Upper Saale, July 10

As the struggle at Kissingen had taken place, as noted, other, though to an extent unrelated, actions had taken place on the Upper Saale at Friedrichshall, Hausen and Waldaschach.[46]

Between 14:15 and 14:30, General Goeben, himself then still in Kissingen, suddenly heard heavy and continuous artillery fire coming from the north, in the direction of Friedrichshall and Waldaschach. This occurrence was potentially especially relevant now, since he had not recently advised Vogel von Falckenstein of the local situation.[47]

---

44 G.G.S., p.604 & *Antheil*, p.114. Note that IR 19 was committed to action having already marched some 30 kilometres wearing packs.
45 Booms, p.69 & *Antheil*, p.108. G.G.S., p.603, gives the distinct impression that this was a formal, organised assault. It was, in fact, very much ad hoc.
46 These combats, are generally, as noted, considered as part of the 'Battle of Kissingen', as is the later one of Nüdlingen-Winkels.
47 Hoenig, p.160.

Friedrichshall

As seen, General Goeben, on his march towards Kissingen, had, before approaching the town, already detached a number of formations for other duties. One of these columns, two battalions, II and F/IR 15, under the command of the regiment's colonel, was to cover the advance on the left, and support the attack upon Kissingen itself. However, as Colonel von der Goltz' s column, having passed through the village of Claushof, at about 10:15, was approaching the Saale, when it unexpectedly came under fire from Bavarian troops occupying two salt mills near the road.

The area around Friedrichshall was, in fact, occupied by the Bavarian 5th Jäger Battalion, under temporary command of Staff Captain Königstall, some 750 men, supported by four smoothbore twelve pounders, of Battery Schuster. In reserve stood the 3rd Uhlan Regiment, the 5th Chevauleger Regiment, and a half squadron of the 2nd Chevaulegers, 565 horsemen altogether. The cannon were posted on a terrace, to the east, at the foot of the Sinnberg. For the most part, the defenders occupied sturdy buildings, and the galleries of the salt mills.

Von der Goltz quickly deployed F/IR 15 in company columns, with 9 and 12/IR 15 lining the woods on the east bank of the river, and 10 and 11/IR 15 respectively covering the left and right flanks. 8th Company was posted in support of the 10th, and the three remaining companies of I/IR 15 held in reserve. After some time, finding that he could make little headway, von der Goltz was forced to accept that no more could be achieved without further support, and a brisk firefight continued as the Colonel awaited help.[48]

Somewhere between 11:15 and 11:30, General Manteuffel himself arrived, at the head of a squadron and a battery, under the impression that Goltz was engaged in a major action. The General now discovered that the cavalry was useless here, and that in the narrow road defile, only two guns could be brought to bear. These duly fired a few rounds, but soon had to withdraw before the fire of the concealed Bavarian Jäger.

Thus, so, too, the almost simultaneous attempt by von der Goltz's column upriver to move up from the Cascade Valley was thwarted by artillery and rifle fire from Friedrichshall, also keeping that column at a disadvantage. The stalemate here was finally to be broken by the defenders.

Somewhere around 14:00, the order had arrived at Friedrichshall for the Bavarian force to retreat to Nüdlingen. Captain von Lacher's company was assigned to cover the retreat here, while the rest of the 5th Jäger withdrew. Booms notes that the withdrawal was less than orderly, although he concedes that Deßloch's battalion was very low on ammunition.[49] General Staff Captain Schlagintwert was killed here, General zu Pappenheim having been wounded earlier. Fortunately, the Prussian pursuit at this moment was not very energetic. As Hausen, to the north was being cleared, so too Colonel von der Goltz pushed 6 and 7/IR 15 across the Saale covered by artillery fire. Any further pursuit here was rendered impossible by the destruction of the bridge, although work on repairing this was swiftly put in hand.[50]

---

48 G.G.S., pp.607-8.

49 Booms, p.63. Major Deßloch was temporarily absent.

50 G.G.S., p.609. The reader will recall that *Antheil*, p.76, described the bridge here as having been 'pulled down'. Perhaps this was done in the same manner as applied to the bridge partially pulled

Hausen

As General Freyhold finally took possession of Friedrichshall, Colonel von der Goltz now also made his move on Hausen. This small village, about a kilometre north of Friedrichshall, was defended by four companies of the Bavarian II/11th Regiment, Major Mühlbaur, some 520 officers and men.[51] At around 14:00, this force was probed by Prussian skirmishers, and had its own outposts engaging those that the Prussians brought into action along the steep and wooded hillsides on both sides of the defile.

Events here, however, were also overtaken by greater priorities. Shortly before his own death, General Zoller himself had also ordered the abandonment of Hausen. This order was received some time after 13:45, whereupon a withdrawal on Nüdlingen took place. This proceeded well enough until four Prussian four pounder guns of the 4th Battery, and the six six pounders of Battery Hellingrath opened fire on the withdrawing columns, prompting a mutual cannonade. At this point, General Freyhold, now ordered the three battalions of IR 59, Colonel von Kessler, forward. The latter's advance prompted a further Bavarian withdrawal, which had been intended, in any case.[52]

Waldaschach

The northernmost anchor of the Bavarian line was the village of Waldaschach, some two kilometres north of Hausen, and actually on the west bank of the Saale. Posted here was Major Moor's I/15th Regiment. Moor had three companies in the village itself. With the other three respectively, he covered the roads to Premich, Stralsbach, and Claushof, in an arc to the west.[53]

Major Moor and his command remained in their assigned position throughout the day, listening to the sound of battle. No orders reached him, and finally, at about 17:00, having heard unfavourable accounts of the fighting to the south, he decided to withdraw. There, late in the afternoon, he was reinforced by the III/8th Regiment and four six pounders from Battery Hutten, sent there by 1st Division from Münnerstadt. Soon, though, he also observed hostile columns on the east bank of the Saale, actually behind him, and severing his line of retreat via Nüdlingen. With little choice, and with his artillery needing decent roads, Moor chose to retreat to the north, and then east. His boldness was rewarded with eventual success, though one company was mauled by the encroaching Prussians.

Prussian cavalry probes had reported the presence of enemy troops in and around Waldaschach. This information caused Colonel von Hanstein, acting commander of Manteuffel's Main Body, ordered F/IR Nr, 25, Lieutenant-Colonel von Cranach, to be sent against the village. Although most of Major Moor's battalion, as noted, was able to evade the enemy, 1st Schützen Company, Captain von Sauer, was not so lucky. By some mischance, the Captain did not receive word to pull back, and stayed in his assigned position at the hamlet of Kleinbrach, on the road to Claushof, about a kilometre south of

---

down to the south of Kissingen.
51   *Antheil*, p.101.
52   Ibid. pp.105-106. Also see Hoenig, pp.144-145 & Booms, pp.65-66.
53   *Antheil*, p.76.

Waldaschach itself. Assailed by overwhelming numbers, von Sauer's command lost three men killed, one officer and eight men wounded, and a further 29 men missing, before escaping. The Prussian loss was only two men wounded.[54]

Bavarian Counter-Attack at Nüdlingen – Winkels, Evening of July 10

Although the Prussian commanders now considered the day's combat to be at an end, there was, in fact, a further act to play. It will be recalled that Prince Karl had earlier that afternoon sent orders to Major-General Stephan's 1st Division, then bivouacked around Münnerstadt, theoretically about an hour's march to the north-east, to join him. Stephan commenced his move at about 13:00, leaving II/8th Regiment, as a link. The remaining force, nine battalions, four squadrons, and 10 guns, found their progress considerably slowed by the withdrawal of both troops and wagons, of other formations, moving in the opposite direction.[55]

Not until after 17:00, was Stephan actually able to assemble most of his force, east of Nüdlingen, whereupon Prince Karl, who was also still confidently expecting the additional support of the 4th Division, instructed him to proceed with his attack. To this end, Stephan's ten guns (six twelve pounders of Battery Mussinan, and four six pounders from Battery Hutten), reinforced by Lepel's and Schuster's batteries, advanced left and right of the Schlossberg road. Three battalions formed the first line, deployed in company columns preceded by skirmishers. Five more were in the second line, of which one was close behind the right wing of the first line. Another battalion, and the 3rd Chevaulegers remained in reserve, as did, for the time being, four of the battalions that had already fought along the Saale that day.[56]

At approximately 17:30, the assembled Bavarian artillery commenced a brisk cannonade of both Nüdlingen and the Calvarienberg, which was rapidly followed by an assault by Stephan's infantry. The Prussians were completely surprised, with four companies of IR 19, under the immediate command of Lieutenant-Colonel von Henning, being caught flat-footed, with five companies (including 10/IR 19) around the western road between the Sinnberg and the Schlegelsberg, and the remainder milling about below the eastern slopes of these heights.[57]

Immediately prior to General Stephan's counterattack, the Prussian II/IR 55, Major Gotskow, had been in the process of relieving the forward outposts of IR 19, in anticipation of the force assembling, and then bivouacking for the night. With his own twelve pounder battery already heavily engaged by the Bavarian artillery, Captain Eynatten II

---

54   Ibid., pp.123-124 & Appendix VII, Booms, p.66 & Hoenig, pp.220-221. Ö.K., Vol. V, p.67, gives the Bavarian loss as about 40. Colonel Booms considers that von Sauer's withdrawal was carelessly undertaken.

55   *Antheil*, pp.110-111.

56   Booms, p.71. Rietstrap, p.64, gives the time here as 19:00, surely much too late, though all times are variable for this action.

57   Reichenau, pp.267-268. It will be recalled that earlier men of this regiment had paid particular interest in the wine cellar of the Hotel Bayerische Hof, in Kissingen. Booms, p.72, considers that without this preliminary bombardment, the surprise would actually have been even more effective.

swiftly despatched a courier to General Wrangel reporting the strength of the enemy assault. Upon receiving this information, the irascible general blurted out, "Bah; Impossible! How can any enemy be there?!"[58]

Despite the General's scathing scepticism, there indeed, were the enemy. As if to mock him, a short time later, a Bavarian shell exploded near Wrangel, killing his horse, which partially fell on him, and knocking him unconscious. IR 55's Colonel Stoltz immediately took temporary command of the rapidly deteriorating situation, handling it with great skill and nerve.

On the Prussian left, the swift Bavarian assault might well have completely over-whelmed the defenders in and around Nüdlingen, had they not first been 'warned' by the shelling. As it was, three Bavarian battalions, II/1st, Major Ysenburg, II/2nd, Major Duntze, and III/1st, Major Schultheis, moved into the village, only to find that most of the defenders had pulled back shortly before. A lunge by accompanying cavalry was also just too late, and was met by rifle fire. As it was, these three battalions advanced to the right (north) of the village, continued past the Hainmühle, and occupied a wooded posi-tion on the eastern slopes of the Sinnberg. As noted, the north and east of the Sinnberg itself was then occupied only by the Prussian10/IR19, Captain Wlosto, who could do little more than try to slow the enemy advance.

Surprised, but at least alerted by the bombardment, the Prussian detachment occu-pying Nüdlingen itself, a platoon of IR15, Lieutenant von Riedel, had the time to evacuate that village, and thus 2nd and 3rd Battalions, Bavarian Leib-Regiment, which were the first to enter it along the main road, found it virtually abandoned, and the cavalry detachment, attempting to cut off the retreat of the withdrawing troops on the left flank, was during its pursuit immediately met with rifle-fire from the far bank of the stream. Three other battalions, as noted (II/1st Reg., II/2nd Reg., III/1st Reg.), had largely circumvented the village on the right, and then, passing the Hainmühle, reached the eastern slopes of the Sinnberg, and established themselves there in the woods there.

The infantry here were followed by Baron Lepel's battery, which now once again occu-pied its former position to the north-east of Nüdlingen. So, too, the centre was followed by Captain Mussinan's battery, taking up a position near the cemetery to the south.[59]

On the Bavarian left wing, six companies from two different battalions (III/2nd Regiment and 2nd Jäger Battalion) had climbed the Calvarienberg, while the other four remained in support on heights further east. The two remaining battalions (I/2nd and I/8th Regiments), and the remaining batteries were held in reserve behind Nüdlingen, as were the cavalry, other than one troop which, having driven off some Prussian skirmishers north of Nüdlingen, then remained there. This lack of aggression on the Bavarian left was proving instrumental in aiding the Prussian defence, which might otherwise well have been stretched and overwhelmed here.

While Lieutenant-Colonel Henning's regiment was receiving its unexpected battering, the unit that had been expecting to relieve IR 19 in the outpost line equally found itself engaged in the middle of a major action. Major Gotskow's II/IR 55, supported by the hussar squadron of Oberlieutenant von Cranach, and the twelve pounder battery

58 Bleibtreu, p.17.
59 Booms, p.72.

of Captain Eynatten II, were pushed forward straight towards Nüdlingen, personally accompanied by a now recovered, though somewhat bruised and battered, General Wrangel.

This force, having attained a position with Nüdlingen in sight, the battery then deployed south of the road and attempted to engage the advancing Bavarians. This proved unworkable, however, due both to the unfavourable undulations of the slopes here, and the battery itself now coming under small arms fire from the Sinnberg.[60]

Unable to maintain this location, Eynatten was forced to limber, and pull back. Gotskow's battalion, however, had occupied a ravine running between the road and the foot of the Schlegelsberg. At around 18:30, its rapid fire brought the Bavarian infantry, already descending from the Sinnberg, to a halt, and also covered the retreat of the battery, which had been in danger of being overrun, also by elements of the 3rd Battalion, Leib-Regiment, which had simultaneously approached it at the double from the low ground south of the road. Crucially, IR 55's senior officer, Lieutenant-Colonel von Rex, was also able to link his troops with the elements of IR 19 still on the Schlegelsberg.

The Bavarian left wing, having by now descended from Calvarienberg, then allowed itself to become bogged down in a skirmish, probably just when it was vital to seize the heights ahead as soon as possible with the united forces. Thus, the left wing lagged behind the right. Only on the far left wing, two companies of Major Baron von Treuberg's 2nd Jäger Battalion had gained some ground. These troops worked themselves into a wooded position between the Schlegelsberg and the Osterberg, near Winkels. They had then established themselves in the wooded heights here, south of Winkels, from where they continued firing on the outflanked Prussian skirmishers. Unfortunately, von Treuberg's other two companies were already assigned to the protection of Battery M|ussinan, and no other units were moved to support these two companies, a push which could have posed a serious threat to Wrangel's weak right flank.[61] Indeed, when Captain Lepel's Bavarian battery was moved to a new position to the north-west of Nüdlingen, and its two escort companies also complied, the left flank was left without any further offensive capability.

Even after these moves, two further battalions remained, which could, perhaps, have been moved to the left. These units, I/8th Regiment, Major Lachemair, and I/2nd, Major Duntze (three companies) were held in reserve, along with the cavalry, on the road east of Nüdlingen. On this shortage of troops, Colonel Bothmer later stated that, "Had we had a few battalions in reserve, that same evening we might have been able to obtain a firm foothold beyond Nüdlingen, and might perhaps have thrown the Prussians out of Kissingen. We did not have any troops left; we sought them in vain".[62] The time for taking advantage of any such weaknesses was, however, past. General Wrangel now had a surprise of his own to spring.

---

60 Ibid., p.73 & Hoenig, pp.220-221.
61 Von Treuberg's battalion, a unit of 1st Division, lost a total of one officer and two men wounded, that day; see *Antheil*, Appendix III, p.7.
62 Zander Trial, p.22.

Wrangel's Counter-attack – The end of the Battle

By now, some time around 19:30, General Wrangel had gathered his forces for a counter-attack, and was also aware of the presence of Manteuffel's force in his support. Accordingly, he had earlier had Captain Coester's four pounder battery advance to the right of Winkels, and Eynatten II's twelve pounder battery to the left, together with the two battalions immediately at his disposal F/IR55, Lieutenant-Colonel von Rex, and the Lippe Fusilier Battalion, Major Rohdewald.

Now, he directed six companies (II/55, Major Gotskow, and two companies, Lippe Fusiliers) against the wooded area south of the main road, and also to the north, six more (I /IR19, Major Drygalski, and the other two Lippe companies).[63] He then followed himself with the rest of his force in the centre, as soon as these wings had made some progress. With drums beating, all now stormed forward, and although the defenders' fire caused many casualties – amongst whom were Major Rohdewald, of the Lippe Battalion, killed while riding well forward, in the skirmish line, and Major Drygalski badly wounded – the heights around Winkels were fully retaken, and the Bavarians once again thrown back to Nüdlingen.

The Prussians did not, however, this time descend from the edge of the woods. Equally, Prince Karl, who also now knew for certain that Hartmann's 4th Division would not now arrive, and who very likely had concerns for his own right flank because of some enemy demonstrations around Haard, then ordered 1st Division to give up Nüdlingen and to move back to the Münnerstadt Road, and there pitch camp. By this time, probably about 20:30, down in the valley, the twilight had obscured all difference between friend and foe. Firing gradually petered out, and soon the echo of the last shots fired finally died away.[64]

Now, also finally, the Sinnberg and all of the adjoining heights on the right were firmly in Prussian hands.[65] After some 12 hours, what would come to be called the Battle of Kissingen was over. An anonymous wounded Prussian NCO, of IR 19, later related his feelings on the action thus: "God damn those Bavarians; they shredded us quite a bit with their 'shooting irons'. In return, though, we took quite a splendid revenge as well!"[66]

Casualties

Losses in the string of actions known as the Battle of Kissingen were reported by the Prussians as being 36 officers and 863 men, and those of the Bavarians as 52 officers, and 1,205 men. These were further tabulated as follows:[67]

---

63 It will be recalled that the Lippe Battalion was composed of four companies, in the Prussian manner. Note also that many formations were inter-mixed and/or ad-hoc at this stage of the action, sometimes confusing narrative. Major Drygalski's 'battalion', for example, at this point had only two of its own companies, together with two others – Drygalski, himself, as noted, was also severely wounded during the action.

64 Booms, p.78-79.

65 Schmidt, p.36. As noted, reports of times vary greatly amongst tired participants.

66 Schmitt, p.24.

67 G.G.S., p.610 & *Antheil*, Appendix III, pp.6 -7. The Prussian IR 19, alone, had total casualties of 10 officers and 313 men, the highest loss of an individual regiment.

| | Prussian | | Bavarian | |
	Officers	Men	Officers	Men
Killed	10	133	9	92
Wounded	25	673	37	554
Missing/prisoners	1	57	6	559

The most senior fatality was the commander of the Bavarian 3rd Division, Lieutenant-General Baron Zoller, his place being taken by Prince Luitpold. In addition, one Bavarian cannon, a smoothbore twelve pounder, was lost during the action near Nüdlingen, during the afternoon combat there. Colonel Booms, however, in his research the following year came to the conclusion that Prussian losses may perhaps have been somewhat heavier, in that he concluded that about 920 Prussian troops had been treated in the field hospitals in the town alone. It may be, though, that some of these men were actually sick.[68]

One interesting aspect to the actions of July 10, was the sheer volume of small arms ammunition that the individual Prussian soldier was now capable of loosing against his foe. The Prussian rate of small arms ammunition use, on July 10, was prodigious. At Kissingen and Friedrichshall, 14 of General Goeben's battalions had fired almost 110,000 rounds amongst them. Major Kühne's F/IR 19, alone, expended nearly 18,000 of these, and three other battalions fired more than 10,000 each! Only one battalion, Captain von Kerssenbrock's II/IR 13, had remained unengaged.[69]

Tourists

Kissingen had always enjoyed a high reputation as a spa town, amongst the well to do, and the summer of 1866 was no exception. The rude awakening of a battle occurring outside the hotel window understandably must have come as a considerable shock to many, to put it mildly.

An anonymous British visitor to Kissingen that summer, arrived shortly before the battle, and declared himself surprised that only 500 guests were in the town, instead of the 3,000 odd that might be expected in the summer! This gentleman remained in Kissingen during the battle, and that evening found himself in a dining room with numerous Prussian officers, including a table at which Generals von Falckenstein, Manteuffel, and Goeben were all seated![70]

Mr. Sherwood, who was also still in the town, but now somewhat humbled by his experiences, subsequently offered a fitting epitaph to the fallen of these actions:

> Immediately around the spring are many dead; one lying directly in its bubbling mouth, shot, doubtless, as he stopped to drink its enticingly cool waters – waters I can never drink there again.

---

68 Booms, pp.78-79.
69 See Appendix VIII.
70 *Macmillan's Magazine*, Vol. XVI, May-October 1867, p.222.

Looting

Looting had always been a part of war, and so it remained in this conflict. The inevitable emptying of wine cellars has been briefly discussed, but other items of all sorts, were also considered fair game. Many windows had been broken during the actual fighting, and doubtless many more subsequently. Occasionally, though, missing items even reappeared! Such was the case with three articles that found their way back to Kissingen, two months later.

On September 10 1866, an officer of the Prussian 4/8th Hussars, Second-Lieutenant August Schrumpf, sent three items to the Kissingen city authorities. He explained, in a note, that these items, a spoon, a fork, and a coffee-filter, had been 'found' by one of his men, in Kissingen, on July 10. The lieutenant then expressed the hope that the items, presumably of silver, could be returned to their rightful owner(s).[71]

Kissingen – Postscript: The 'Non-Appearance' of the Bavarian 4th Division & Reserve Artillery

4th Division

Ever since his order that morning to General Hartmann, commanding the 4th Division, to march to the battlefield, Prince Karl had anxiously awaited the latter's compliance with this clear instruction. Indeed, the Nüdlingen – Winkels counter-attack by 1st Division had been largely predicated upon the additional support of the 4th, and this support would undoubtedly have been of considerable importance. What, then, had happened?

The 4th Division had begun the day marching to its designated assembly areas, in the vicinity of Pfersdorf, near Poppenhaausen. Around 09:30, Prince Karl ordered the main body towards Euerdorf, to prevent the Prussians from slipping between his forces at Hammelburg and those around Kissingen. Amazingly, this order, however, did not reach the 4th Division until just before Noon.[72]

Compounding this already serious delay, not until 14:00, did General Hartmann actually respond, by sending three battalions, one squadron, and an artillery section towards Euerdorf, then following along with the main body. Towards Kissingen, the general sent one battalion, the 8th Jäger, Major Rudolf, and the 6th Chevauleger Regiment, Colonel von Tausch. Neither move was made with alacrity or thoroughness, the latter formation going as far as the 'edge of the woods'.

Prior to Hartmann reaching Oerlenbach, however, reports came to him that Euerdorf was already actually occupied by the enemy, and also that Prussian infantry were advancing against him from Kissingen.[73] Neither of these eventualities were actually the case, but they were sufficient to cause the general to abandon his advance, and concentrate around the road junction at Oerlenbach. It was stated, at the Zander Trial, that

---

71 With special thanks to Oliver Heyn. (Kissingen Archives – Stadt A Bad Kissingen, A 210, 10.09.1866, fol. 1r.)

72 *Antheil*, p.87. This appears an excessive time.

73 Ibid., p.113.

some men had stamped their rifles on the ground, in frustration at their own inaction.[74] Uncertainty prevailed here, as *Antheil* noted:

> Even before this movement had been completed – the vanguard, having advanced along the Ramsthal road, received the order to return only at 17:00 – the division commander (at about 17:30 in the afternoon) received the Field-Marshal's order to hasten with all available troops (immediately) to the battlefield.

This is the order that Prince Charles had despatched from the Deputy Chief of Staff, also in the name of the Commander-in-Chief, which requested holding on to Poppenhausen.[75]

In the end, General Hartmann, confronted with contradictory orders, taking account of the lateness of the hour of the day, the great distance from the battlefield, the extensive area over which the division itself was dispersed, and finally the fatigue of his troops, then decided that his intervention was no longer possible. Certainly, by then, that was true. Hartmann's division almost appears to have been in a state of paralysis.

Reserve Artillery

The slightly less problematic issue of the handling of the Bavarian Reserve Artillery at Kissingen was also matter of contention. As we have seen, on the morning of the 11th, the four twelve pounder batteries of this artillery reserve were initially halted at Schwartze-Pfütze. From 10:00, they were left standing there waiting for orders, but received none at all until late in the evening, then being told to rejoin 4th Division in its bivouac area near Poppenhausen.

The fact that they were there was well-known, and public opinion subsequently turned the conscious idleness of those 32 guns into another accusation against the army High Command. It was frequently asserted that these batteries could easily have been deployed on the Finsterberg, within half an hour, since the distance from their position from there to the Schwartze-Pfütze being just over an hour. Colonel Bothmer, also at the Zander Trial, stated that there would have been considerable difficulty in moving the Artillery Reserve to these heights. At this, a witness, in the form of the Kissingen District Treasurer, then testified that there was a 'very passable' road available! Colonel Bothmer, and the Army, were once more made to look foolish.[76]

It certainly appears that Prince Karl had allowed an important opportunity to escape him. The opportunity to fully concentrate at Kissingen was certainly missed, though this is easily said with hindsight. The Prussian General Staff consider that the Bavarians themselves probably should have attacked with three divisions, from Neustadt and Münnerstadt, towards Waldaschach.[77]

---

74   Zander Trial, p.51.
75   *Antheil*, p.113.
76   Zander Trial, p.50.
77   *Antheil*, p.140 & Rüstow, p.303.

Bavarian withdrawal to the east

In addition to the immediate factors at hand, reports had by now also arrived at Bavarian Headquarters from Hammelburg, where, as seen, Beyer had also forced the Saale, thus threatening the army's left flank. Prince Karl now lost no time in ordering a general withdrawal, to begin at 05:00, on the 11th, and also stipulated a rapid subsequent concentration on the heights around Schweinfurt, across the River Main, some 20 kilometres to the south-east of Kissingen.[78] However, the Prince's orders for a complete concentration were once again not destined to be completely executed. Late that evening, Lieutenant-General von der Tann sent a singularly curt and uninformative telegram to Prince Alexander. It read:

Von der Tann. (Fontane)

> Münnerstadt, July 10, 11:30 PM.
> Following several heated actions, the Bavarian army will, in the morning, withdraw to Schweinfurt.[79]

Immediately upon receiving the report of the results of the battle at Kissingen, Prince Alexander had himself telegraphed Prince Karl:

> We have learned via Baron Kübeck that the Royal Bavarian troops (have) suffered a setback at Kissingen. Please send information on your Royal Highness' further intentions by the fastest possible means, in order (for me) to know precisely whether and where a union with the VII corps is possible.[80]

A subsequent message stated:

> Despite the collective demands of Württemberg, Bavaria and Hesse, and despite the demands of the Bundestag to not give up Frankfurt or the Main River Line before any armistice, on July 11 at 7 pm, as no response had arrived to the missive

---

78   Prince Alexander, *Feldzugs-Journal*, p.11.
79   Ibid.
80   Biebrach, pp.43-44.

above, to Fieldmarshal-Lieutenant Count Huyn, given full power (to make decisions) in the Bavarian headquarters:

> I request that you most urgently to obtain from Prince Karl a response to my telegram of this evening concerning our concentration.

As no answer followed from this, the Austrian Colonel von Schönfeld was actually dispatched to the Bavarian Headquarters on the 12th, in order to bring back a response.[81] By then, though, the issue was largely irrelevant.

In the meantime, Prince Alexander had been looking to his own potential situation with regard to the Prussian 'about-face', and ordered the First Hessian Brigade to be detached to Aschaffenburg to guard the defiles of the Spessart passes and this important crossing point over the Main, which was followed by the Second Brigade on the 12th, after a scouting report of the appearance of the heads of Prussian columns in the woods of the Spessart.

Once again, the Federal forces had failed to link up, and continued to operate separately, greatly to the benefit of the Prussians. On schedule, Prince Karl had wasted no time in putting his own withdrawal into motion. Allied cooperation, for now, would again have to wait. The Bavarian retreat itself began largely on schedule.

In fact, Prince Karl's main body, which had camped in the vicinity of Münnerstadt, actually withdrew via Poppenlauer, Massbach, and Ballingshausen, with a flank guard on either side, as the initially planned route was judged as being too close to a potential Prussian line of advance. Hartmann's 4th Division was to provide the rearguard. Consequently, that General kept his force concentrated around Poppenhausen until news of the Prussian advance. Prince Luitpold, now commanding 3rd Division, was to make his way to Schweinfurt, and assume command there for the present, which would include the newly arrived Infantry Reserve, six battalions.

The Prince was naturally anxious for a rapid withdrawal, followed by an equally speedy concentration around Schweinfurt, which he then resolved to hold at all cost, defending the heights around the city. The retreat itself, with two exceptions, was to be largely a success.[82]

Firstly, not all units of the 2nd and 3rd Divisions, which had been engaged in and around Kissingen, were directed to Poppenhausen on the evening of the battle. Only three battalions, and the 2nd Chevauleger Regiment, were marched towards Poppenhausen, and the rest in the opposite direction, to Münnerstadt. These, in accordance with the previous orders broke camp on the 11th, to try and reach Schweinfurt by a deviation through Poppelauer. Upon hearing that the Prussians were also on their way there, General Von der Tann, having initially remained at Münnerstadt, thought it expedient not to march with these troops to Schweinfurt where Prince Charles was waiting for him, and led them, except for a small body that was already out of his reach, marched to

---

81 Ibid.
82 *Antheil*, p.140. G.G.S., p.647, compliments Prince Karl with the resolve to do so. Rietstrap, p.64, comments that the Prussians would, in any case, been unable to cross the Main for the lack of a bridging train.

Schweinfurt, along a roundabout way through Lauringen to Hofheim and Aidhausen, in order to cross the Main at Hassfurt, the next day.

Bavarian Rearguard encounter at Oerlenbach

As noted, the withdrawal of the main Bavarian force proceeded, for the most part, reasonably smoothly. The first had concerned the withdrawal of units of 2nd and 3rd Divisions just noted. The second involved Ritter von Hartmann's 4th Division.

At a wood, the Kirchhofholze, near the village of Oerlenbach, about six and a half kilometres south-east of Kissingen, stood the division's rearguard of Ritter von Hartmann's 4th Division, comprising two schützen companies the 9th Infantry Regiment, commanded by Captain Stark, a total of four officers and 249 men. Stark did not receive any orders, either to move or otherwise. Instructions to withdraw had, indeed, been despatched to the captain, but the chevauleger courier had been unable to locate Stark's command to deliver them![83]

At about 11:00, Lieutenant Beyer and 19 men, at this point separated from Captain Stark's main body, were fired upon by the encroaching Prussian advance-guard of Manteuffel's division, four battalions, commanded by Baron von Hanstein. After a heavy exchange of small arms fire, Stark was able, perhaps surprisingly, to withdraw the majority of his command, and follow the retreating army, with a loss of only one officer and 47 men.[84] No further clashes marred the movement.

In the meanwhile, the force of Prince Taxis also withdrew independently. Having been driven across the Saale from Hammelburg on the 10th, he proceeded to move directly south from there to Arnstein, some 20 kilometres further south. From here, he then moved directly on to Würzburg, another 20 kilometres further south, on the east bank of the Main. At this point, the Bavarian army now covered a front of a nine to 10 hour march, from Würzburg to Hassfurt.[85]

With, perhaps, a little luck, the withdrawal had been largely successful, if not entirely as planned. On the evening of the 11th, the Bavarian forces were disposed as follows:[86]

Schweinfurt:
1st Brigade, 1st Division – six battalions, three squadrons, four guns
2nd Brigade, 1st Division – two battalions
5th Brigade, 3rd Division – six battalions, two squadrons
4th Division – 11 battalions, four squadrons, 16 guns
Reserve Infantry Brigade – four battalions, eight guns
2nd Light Cavalry Brigade – eight squadrons
Reserve Artillery – 32 guns

---

83   *Antheil*, p.142.These were 1st and 2nd Schützen companies.
84   Kunz, p.121. *Antheil*, Appendix III, pp.7-8 gives the loss as two wounded, and one officer and 47 men missing. Manteuffel's initial account (Lettow-Vorbeck, p.182) stated the companies simply as 'captured'!
85   Booms, p.98.
86   Biebrach, p.40.

Between Nidhausen and Hersfeld:
(Part) 2nd Brigade – three battalions, one squadron, 10 guns

Haßfurt:
(Part) 2nd Brigade – one battalion, 28 guns

Maßbach:
2nd Division – 11 battalions, four squadrons, 16 guns
Reserve Artillery – eight guns

Hofheim:
2nd Division – one battalion

Würzburg:
6th Infantry Brigade – five battalions, eight guns
Reserve Cavalry – 20 squadrons, 12 guns

Once again, the Federal forces had failed to link up, and the Bavarians had also been firmly pushed onto the east bank of the Franconian Saale, most then moving towards the Main, and some subsequently to Schweinfurt, and as seen, in some cases, even beyond. A Prussian officer, Lieutenant Wiese, of Grenadier Regiment Nr. 11, later noted that July 11 was the first day, since June 29, that there had been no rainfall.[87] Not only the weather, though, was about to change!

The following morning, Captain Fleschuez, of the Bavarian General Staff, set off on a reconnaissance ride, with an escort of five chevaulegers. The captain was tasked with an extensive scouting mission as far west as Sömmersdorf, re-tracing some of the route of the army's recent withdrawal, in reverse. Fleschuez returned with six prisoners, and the news that the Prussians had gone![88]

There was, however, no discernible concern at Prince Karl's headquarters on the 12th. An Austrian liaison officer there, Oberlieutenant Moritz von Klingenstein, of the 13th Hussar Regiment, recently attached to the Prince's staff, noted that, "When, by mid-day on the 12th, no sign of the enemy had been seen, Headquarters was moved from Schweinfurt to Gerolzhofen". This was a move of some 18 kilometres to the south-east.[89]

Despite Prince Karl's apparent lack of apparent worry, the' big-picture' had already dramatically intruded on to centre stage. The same day that the Prince pulled back from the Saale, an urgent telegram had been sent to the headquarters of General von Falckenstein, directly from Prince Bismarck, and despatched from the Prussian King's Headquarters in Bohemia. Count Moltke was neither mentioned, nor appeared to have been sent a copy. Its key passage flatly stated:

87 Wiese, p.93.
88 *Antheil*, pp.146-147 & Lettow-Vorbeck, Vol. III, p.265. Fleschuez had attacked a patrol of 17 men.
89 Kunz, p.121.

It is now of political importance to be in actual possession of the districts north of the Main, for the sake of negotiations which will probably take place on the basis of the (then) status quo.

A rapid rethink as to how to address this instruction; one outside the realms of 'simple' strategy was required. On July 11, too, Prince Alexander received entreaties from the Governments of Württemberg, Baden and Hesse, not to give up Frankfurt, and the line of the Main before any impending Armistice.[90] In addition, minor matters such as the Prussian Chief of Staff, and the Bavarian Army also remained to be dealt with. At the same time, on the other side of the fence, concerns at VIII Corps headquarters also grew as to the situation and intentions of the Bavarian army. Although Prince Karl may have previously offered battle around Schweinfurt, circumstances had altered considerably since then.

On the next day, the13th, too, under the instructions of the Bavarian government, Prince Karl opened channels for possible negotiations with the Prussians. Most fortunately for the Federal forces, any such possible occurrence rapidly vanished when the Prussians proposed talks with only Bavaria. The Prince, to his great credit, then immediately cut off contact, and hostilities continued.[91]

Finally, on July 13, the Austrian Colonel von Schönfeld, who had been sent to Bavarian Headquarters to help facilitate a link-up with the Bavarians, telegraphed back:

… that the VIII Corps should immediately set out towards Franconia, and seek a unification with the VII Corps at Uffenheim.

In the Colonel's absence, however, the situation had, of course, again changed! The plans at VIII Corps had altered completely; what could possibly have happened on the 11th, and perhaps even on July 12, was now no longer achievable.

On July 12, meanwhile, the Prussian army had continued its own advance further west, in what had suddenly become stifling heat. During the day, Goeben's division arrived at Lohr, followed by Manteuffel's. Beyer was directed towards Hanau via the Sinn and Kinzig Valleys. At the same time, General von Falckenstein, himself, had directed a request to the acting commander in Coblenz to make a demonstration against Mainz and Nassau, in order to thereby keep as many Federal troops occupied as possible. As a result, General von Röder was therefore sent with five fortress battalions, one fortress squadron, four four pounder cannon, four twelve pounders, and one fortress squadron, roughly 4,000 men, from Coblenz towards Nassau.

For the moment, then, on the Lower Main, the 3rd and 4th Divisions of VIII Corps remained covering Frankfurt, with the Hessian Division being just north of Offenbach, and the Austrian/Nassau at Bockenheim, immediately west of the city, with the Corps' Reserve Artillery south of the Main. The Württemberg (1st) Division was deployed along the Fulda Road north-east of Offenbach, and the Baden (2nd) Division stood north-east of Frankfurt along the line of a minor river, the Nidda, which originates in the Vogelberg

90 *Feldzugs-Journal*, p.12.
91 *Antheil*, p.147.

heights, west of Fulda. Many of these troops were still engaged in the construction of field works.

Prussian Incursion into Nassau

As authorised by von Falckenstein some days earlier, upon instructions from the Prussian Military Governor of the Rhineland and Westphalian Provinces, Prince Hohenzollern, on July 7, a Prussian force, consisting of five Landwehr battalions and eight guns, commanded by Major-General Julius von Röder, advanced from Coblenz, in the Prussian Rhineland, and crossed into the Duchy of Nassau, occupying a number of towns.[92] This ruse, actually specifically requested by Vogel von Falckenstein, was intended to act as a diversion, and, on that basis, succeeded admirably in its purpose, the Parliament in Frankfurt being in absolute uproar at this sudden perceived threat to itself.[93] General von Röder himself, however, was also in for a surprise. His hastily mounted expedition had succeeded rather too well for its own good.

As an immediate consequence of the Prussian incursion, Prince Alexander received an urgent message directly from Duke Adolph of Nassau that his realm was under immediate direct threat by a fresh Prussian invasion. Though the Prince could not, of course, ignore the Duke's plea, his solution was a considerable over-reaction. Overnight on the 10/11th, the whole of Major-General Roth's Nassau Brigade, apart from the two squadrons of Kur-Hessian hussars, was ordered towards Wiesbaden, to deal with this 'invasion' threat.[94]

Skirmish at Zorn, July 12

Major-General von Röder's 'occupation' force had moved east from Coblenz, occupying Emms and Nassau itself, and, further south, also Holzhausen and Diethardt, thus holding a string of villages north-west of Wiesbaden. The 'occupation' would, however, prove very short-lived.

Prussian Battalion Trier II, of Landwehr Infantry Regiment Nr. 30, was positioned in and around the village of Zorn, south of Holzhausen, along with a section of two guns of the Brandenburg Artillery Regiment. Unknown to them, approaching this village, on the afternoon of July 12, came the advance guard of the Federal Nassau Brigade, I/1st Nassau Infantry Regiment, Lieutenant-Colonel Schwab, and four guns of Battery Nauroth. The head of the column soon came into contact with Prussian pickets, and their two guns. A brief skirmish took place, in which the Prussian guns fired seven rounds, and ended with the Prussian posts being driven in, with a loss of eight men wounded, and two others captured.[95]

---

92   These were II./Landwehr Infantry Regiment Nr. 25 (Jülich), Colonel Caemmerer, III./LIR Nr. 25 (Malmedy): Major Baron von Schaumberg, III./LIR Nr. 28 (Siegburg): Major Halter, I./LIR Nr. 30 (1st Trier), Lieutenant-Colonel Steneberg, and III/LIR Nr. 30 (2nd Trier), Lieutenant-Colonel Ekensteen.

93   Biebrach, p.44.

94   Baur-Breitenfeld, p.44.

95   Pulkowski, *Kurzegefasste Geschichte des Fußartillerie-Regiments General-Feldzeugmeister (Brandenburgischen) Nr.3*, p.28.

A further clash took place that evening, near Holzhausen, in which a Prussian NCO and 16 men were taken prisoner. One Nassauer died of his wounds the next day, 27 year old Private Philipp Peter Ludwig, of 5/1st Nassau Regiment. This strong reaction caused the Prussians to rapidly abandon their incursion, and swiftly withdraw to Coblenz. The prisoners taken by the Nassauers were taken to the fortress of Mainz, and incarcerated there. The brigade having completed its task, it was now returned to direct VIII Corps control. This was not a moment too soon. This Prussian diversion certainly diverted a substantial Federal force, but probably not for the length of time hoped for.

8

Vogel von Falckenstein turns west

After Kissingen, with the Bavarian Army now back behind the line of the Saale, Vogel von Falckenstein had then proceeded to turn his back upon it. As discussed, his instructions from higher command had often been inconsistent, quite apart from his noticeably less than cordial relations with the Army Chief of Staff, General von Moltke. This unfortunate circumstance even now continued.

After the actions on the 10th, Falckenstein had initially nominally pursued the Bavarians towards Schweinfurt, in accordance with his previous orders from Moltke. The next day, however, he received the previously discussed telegram directly from Count Bismarck, who was then with the King's Headquarters in Bohemia. This message had advised him that it was now necessary to occupy as much territory north of the Main as possible, and no doubt most especially the city of Frankfurt itself.

Accordingly, the general having then halted his advance against the badly shaken force of Prince Karl, and would now move, instead, on the home of the Confederation's Parliament. Most unwisely, especially considering his previous dealings with the Chief of Staff, he did not seek any confirmation from Moltke, before doing so.

Falckenhayn was still at his headquarters in Kissingen on July 11, when he received this telegram, at about 13:00. Immediately, he altered the axis of his march away from the Bavarian Army, to the south, and instead re-routed it towards Gemünden, some 40 kilometres south-west of Kissingen, on the road to Frankfurt! Orders to this effect did not reach Manteuffel until after 17:00, the general then altering his march back towards Poppenhausen. Beyer thereupon halted his own force near Oerlenbach, ready to support his colleague, if need be. Goeben also began to retrace his steps towards the Saale, heading for Hammelburg.[1]

Events in the Spessart

Over the next two days, Falckenhayn's troops marched west, towards the Lower Main, with Goeben's division in the lead. Goeben's orders were to occupy Laufach, on the road to Aschaffenburg, on the 13th. The previous day, on the way to Lohr, they had enjoyed a well-earned rest, as the Prussian Lieutenant Tabouillot later recalled:

> At 5 AM, the next morning, we marched over Gemünden towards Lohr. About half way there, we had a long halt, and meat, apples, beer, and bread were issued

---

1 G.G.S., p.614.

and delicately cooked. The food, but in particular the good Felsenbier of the town of Gemünden, worked wonders in the sticky heat on that day.

After a four hour rest, we moved on, but left behind, to the greatest delight of the men, were the backpacks, which were then sent to us by boat. Late that evening, we arrived in Lohr.[2]

Meanwhile, telegraphic notice of the Bavarian withdrawal towards Schweinfurt after Kissingen, had also been received at VIII Corps Headquarters, then in Bornheim, some four kilometres north-east of Frankfurt, on the morning of July 12. This news caused great concern that the Prussians might now move on Lohr, and perhaps even threaten Würzburg.[3] The abrupt Prussian about face following on from the Bavarian retreat naturally caused consternation in Frankfurt, as well as at Corps Headquarters. Although, because of rumours of a possible ceasefire, the smaller states were firmly against the abandonment of the line of the River Main, Prince Alexander now perceived this setback as an opportunity to finally link up with the Bavarians, as was, of course, also Prince Karl's wish.[4]

The concerns expressed as to Prussian intentions were well founded, as noted, although their political nature doubtless was not. In any case, Prince Alexander again now foresaw a possible concentration with Prince Karl in the vicinity of Würzburg, his previous preoccupation with the protection of Frankfurt seemingly completely forgotten. Once again, though, his attention would swiftly be returned to it.

Action of Laufach and Frohnhofen, July 13

Despite the collective demands of Württemberg, Bavaria, and Hesse, and despite the demands of the Bundestag to not give up either Frankfurt or the Main River Line before any possible armistice, on July 11 at 7 pm, as no response had arrived to the missive above, to Fieldmarshal-Lieutenant Count Huyn, for now given full authority in dealing with Bavarian headquarters signalled:

> I request you most urgently to obtain from Prince Karl a response to my telegram of this evening concerning (a concentration of our forces).[5]

As this also elicited no reply, the Austrian Colonel v. Schönfeld was dispatched to the Bavarian Headquarters on July 12 in order to bring back a response. Any possible link with the Bavarians at Würzburg required control of the railway bridge at Aschaffenburg.

As these deliberations took place, the 1st Hessian Brigade had been detached to the town of Aschaffenburg, both to guard the defiles of the Spessart passes and also this important crossing point over the Main. This formation was then followed by the 2nd

---

2 Tabouillot, p.27.
3 Baur-Breitenfeld, p.46.
4 G.G.S., p.617, pointedly comments that Alexander had shown little interest in doing so previously.
5 Biebrach, p.44. The confused nature of communications between VII and VIII Corps' is self-evident. Not until the 15th was a semblance of reasonable cooperation achieved.

Brigade, on the 12th, after the receipt of scouting reports of the appearance of the heads of the Prussian columns which were by then already pushing through the Spessart.

Finally, on July 13, Colonel von Schönfeld telegraphed that the VIII Corps should immediately set out towards Franconia, and seek a rendezvous with the VII Corps at Uffenheim. Meanwhile, the situation at VIII Corps had changed completely; what could possibly have happened on the 11th, and perhaps even on July 12, was now no longer achievable.

At midday on July 12, the Hessian Grand Duchy's Division headquarters, then in Hanau, received the message by telegram direct from the Bavarian Headquarters, then at Aschaffenburg, that the Prussians, on their westward march, had just occupied the town of Gemünden. This was promptly relayed to the VIII Corps High Command at Bornheim at 12.30. At 14.30, from there, the following telegram was received by the Hessian Division:

> Message: The brigade at Hanau is to be ready for a march to Aschaffenburg. I will bring a written order with me. At 2:45 PM, the first infantry train will be ready for embarkation at the railway station of Hanau. The materiel for further infantry trains will follow immediately thereafter, so that the trains can follow on at intervals of one hour. The Train materiel for the brigade battery will follow at the end. I request that strength reports for men, horses, and wagons shall be made available at the station.[6]
> (By order) Ober-Lieutenant Oberhoffer

On the 13th, Prince Alexander also received reports of the presence of large groups of the enemy in the Spessart (mountains). He therefore ordered that:

> A Württemberg Brigade should march from Rücklingen, the Austrian Hahn brigade by train, through Darmstadt to Aschaffenburg, and, on the 15th the entire division will follow. The division's command [namely the Hessians] should therefore not allow itself to be drawn into any serious engagements, although they should keep the road and railway towards Lohr under most careful observation, and protect Aschaffenburg by means of an appropriate position in front of that place.
>   The Hahn brigade is, of course, to be supported by the 3rd Division, and only it should be used primarily to protect the crossing at Aschaffenburg.[7]

Before his departure from Bornheim, the Hessian divisional commander, Lieutenant-General Perglas verbally instructed General Frey that he was to, " … advance with his brigade, the 2nd Foot Battery, and the cavalry on Laufach-Hain, and with the spearhead, consisting of some cavalry, two guns, and one battalion, to take position opposite Hain."[8]

Frey's 1st Brigade began its march from Aschaffenburg towards Laufach at 10:00, his column arranged in the following order:

6   Zimmermann, *Antheil der Großherzoglich hessischen Armee-Division am Kriege von 1866*, p.303.
7   Biebrach, p 45.
8   Ibid., p.306.

Advance Guard – Colonel Wilkens
One troop, 2nd Squadron, 1st Mounted Regiment
I/2nd Infantry Regiment, preceded by 1st Schützen Company
Two guns of the 2nd Foot Battery, with one platoon, Hesse-Homburg Jäger

Support
Three troops, 2nd Squadron, 1st Mounted Regiment
II/2nd Infantry Regiment

Main Body – Colonel von Grolman
1st Infantry Regiment
Four guns of the 2nd Foot Battery, with Hesse-Homburg Jäger (minus one platoon)
4th Squadron, 1st Mounted Regiment.[9]

Encounters at Hain-Laufach

After a two-hour march, Colonel Wilkens reached the village of Weiberhof, some five kilometres west of Laufach. Here, he halted for two hours. Also approaching Laufach, but from the east, was Prussian Brigade of Wrangel, while that of Kummer was also marching on the town from the direction of Waldaschaff, some six kilometres south of Laufach.[10]

From Weiberhof, General Frey ordered the advanced guard, with the addition of two troops of the 2nd Squadron after a brief halt at the Weiberhöfe to the road towards Hain, and the II/ 2nd Infantry Regiment, Major Hauss, to advance with one troop of the 2nd Mounted Squadron into the Aschaff-Valley, towards Waldaschaff. Both detachments were ordered to feel out the enemy, make contact and maintain that contact. In case of retreat, Hauss was not to move to the road north of the Aschaff stream, but to remain south of the stream, at the railway, and to hold fast there.[11]

While these Hessian moves took place, the Prussian 13th Division had marched in two separate brigade columns from Lohr over Waldaschaff, and against Laufach. Goeben's force was, at this stage, about 15,000 strong. It had been the primary force in the struggle of Dermbach, and had also suffered heavy losses at Kissingen. Subsequently, the troops had marched over 50 kilometres in two days in the sultry heat, to Lohr. They had then broken camp at 04:00 that morning, and again marched a further 25 kilometres in hilly terrain. The exertions of these marches were very demanding thereby, just as it was for the Hessian troops, resulting in many cases of sunstroke, some of them fatal.

At about 14:00, the leading elements of Wrangel's Brigade, the Prussian 1/8th Hussars, Rittmeister Schmidt, accompanied by General Goeben himself, 'bumped' Colonel Wilkens' advance guard. Upon being fired upon by the Hessian skirmishers, the Prussians withdrew to the village of Hain, a little more than two kilometres to the east, where they sought the cover of a large railway embankment, where the valley was some 500 metres wide. The cavalry troop of Hessian Lieutenant Riedesel gave chase,

---

9   Ibid.
10   Zimmermann, p.308, is critical of this 'too long' a delay.
11   Ibid., p.307.

Hanoverian infantry, by Richard Knötel. (*Uniformenkunde*)

Hanoverian 3rd Jäger Battalion, by Richard Knötel. (*Uniformenkunde*)

Saxe-Coburg-Gotha Regiment at Langensalza, by Richard Knötel. (*Uniformenkunde*)

Lippe Detmold Füsilier Battalion, by Richard Knötel. The figure on the right shows a private in the campaign dress of 1866; an equivalent officer stands in the background, near the colours. (*Uniformenkunde*)

Oldenburg Infantry Regiment, by Richard Knötel. (*Uniformenkunde*)

Hamburg Infantry, by Richard Knötel. The campaign dress for other ranks in 1866 is on the far right. (*Uniformenkunde*)

Baden Infantry, by Richard Knötel. From left to right: Leib Grenadier Regiment grenadier, 3rd Infantry Regiment private, 5th Infantry Regiment officer, Leib Grenadier Regiment officer. (*Uniformenkunde*)

Hessen-Kassel Schützen and Jäger, by Richard Knötel. From left to right: Schützen private in campaign uniform, ditto in parade uniform, Jäger in campaign uniform, Jäger officer in parade uniform. (*Uniformenkunde*)

Bavarian schützen unterlieutenant from 9th Infantry Regiment, by Herbert Knötel. (*Deutsche Uniformen*)

Württemberg private from 2nd Infantry Regiment, by Herbert Knötel. (*Deutsche Uniformen*)

Soldier from the 1st Hesse-Darmstadt Infantry Regiment, by Herbert Knötel. (*Deutsche Uniformen*)

NCO of the Hesse-Cassel 1st (Leib) Hussar Regiment, by Herbert Knötel. (*Deutsche Uniformen*)

Bavarian prisoners move to the rear during the Prussian assault on the Nebelberg at Wiesenthal, July 4, by Ludwig Burger. (*Erinnerungs-Blätter aus dem Feldzüge der Main-Armee 1866*)

Vogel von Falckenstein at Hammelburg, July 10, by Ludwig Burger. (*Erinnerungs-Blätter aus dem Feldzüge der Main-Armee 1866*)

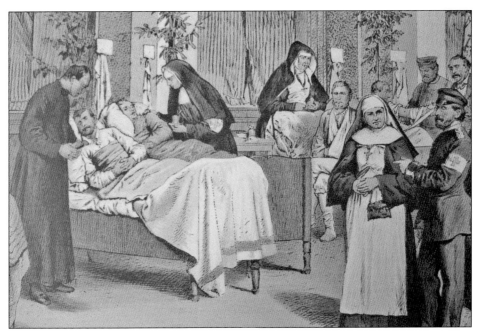

The wounded in hospital in Kissingen following the battle, by Ludwig Burger. (*Erinnerungs-Blätter aus dem Feldzüge der Main-Armee 1866*)

Austrian prisoners in the marketplace at Aschaffenburg following the battle, by Ludwig Burger. (*Erinnerungs-Blätter aus dem Feldzüge der Main-Armee 1866*)

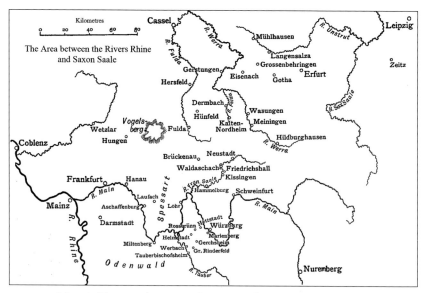

Map 1 The area between the rivers Rhine and Saxon Saale.

Map 2
The Langensalza
Campaign, June 17-23.

Map 3
The Langensalza
Campaign, June 23-27.

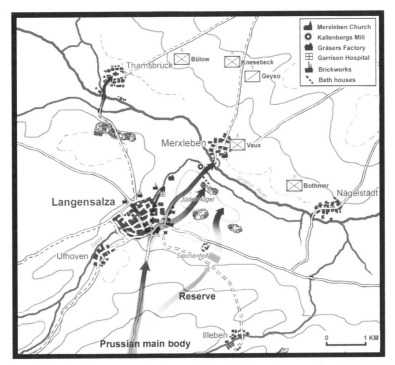

Map 4 Battle of Langensalza, June 27. Initial Prussian attacks, 1030-1300.

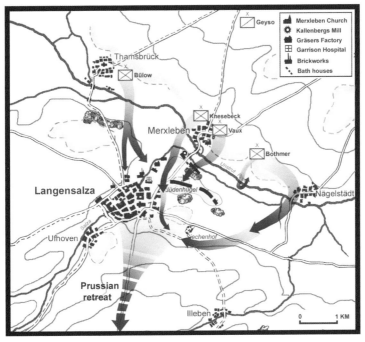

Map 5 Battle of Langensalza, June 27. Hanoverian counter-attack, 1330-1700.

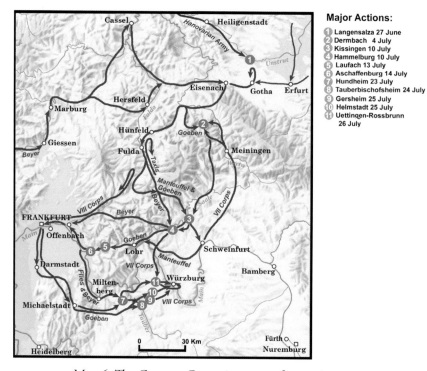

Map 6 The German Campaign, area of operations.

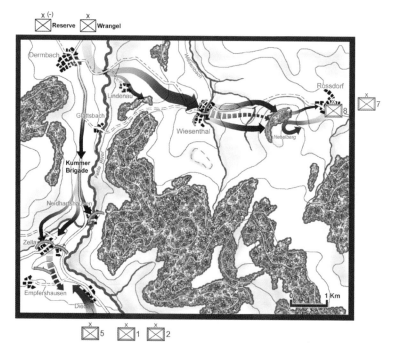

Map 7 Engagements near Dermbach, July 4.

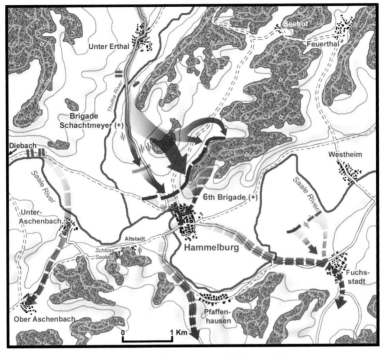

Map 8 Combat at Hammelburg, July 10.

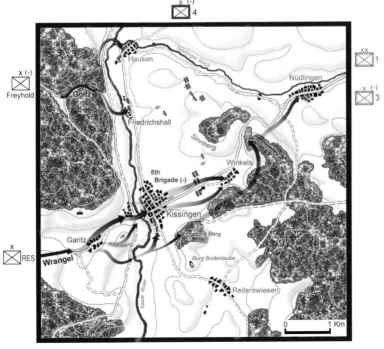

Map 9 Battle of Kissingen, July 10.

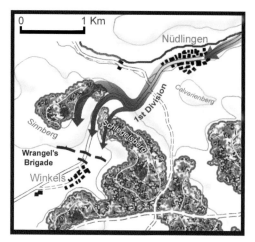

Map 10 Evening action at Winkels, July 10.

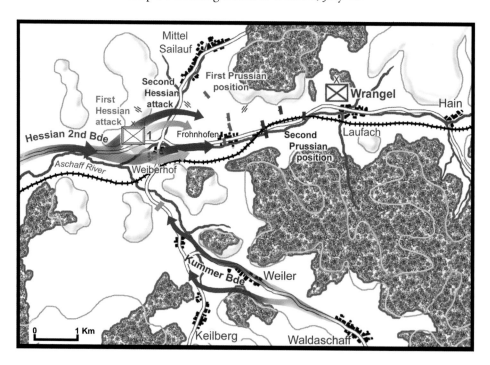

Map 11 Action at Laufach-Frohnhofen, July 13

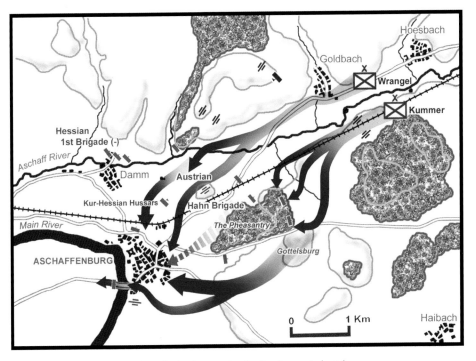

Map 12 Action at Aschaffenburg, July 14.

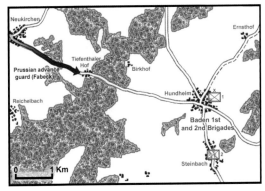

Map 13 Encounter at Hundheim, July 23.

Map 14 Engagement at Tauberbischofsheim, July 24.

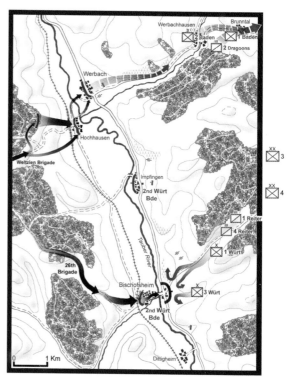

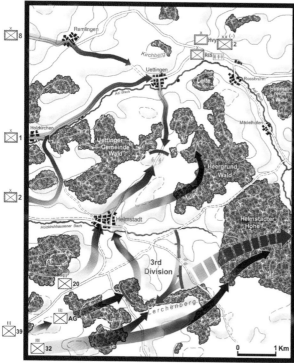

Map 15 Encounter at Helmstadt, July 25.

Map 16 Engagement at Gerchsheim, July 25.

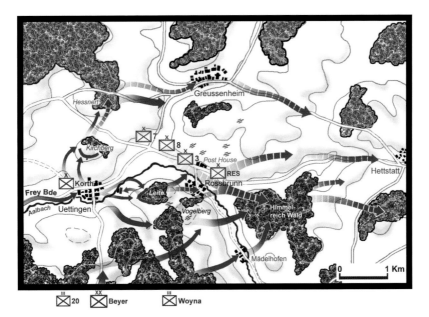

Map 17 Engagement at Rossbrunn, July 26.

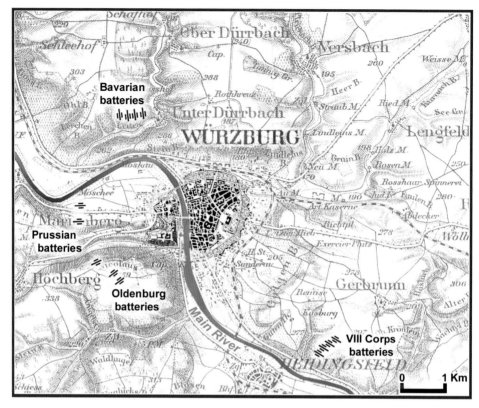

Map 18 Bombardment of Würzburg, July 27.

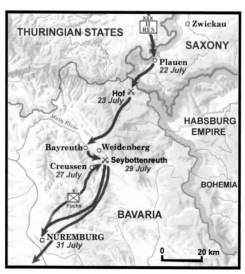

Map 19 Operations in north-eastern Bavaria, late July.

and there was an exchange of carbine fire, until the presence of Prussian infantry caused Riedesel to pull back.[12]

These leading Prussian infantry, F/IR55, Lieutenant-Colonel von Rex, had, at the sound of firing, almost reached the hamlet of Hain. They immediately halted, removed their packs, and hurried forward. Having then occupied Frohnhofen and Laufach, as well as its railway station, Wrangel resolved not to precipitate any further action, as his men were already exhausted from the day's exertions, having been up for some 12 hours. He was also, as noted, expecting the arrival of Kummer, who soon appeared. Kummer duly halted at Waldaschaff, around 15:00, and posted his own vedettes in the vicinity of of Weiler and Keilberg.

Encounters around Weiler and Hain

Major Hauss, as per his instructions, just after Noon, led his II/2nd Regiment along the road south-west, towards Weiler, accompanied by Lieutenant Roth's 2nd Mounted Squadron. This force clashed briefly with the outposts of Brigade Kummer near Weiler, subsequently pulling back, having lost one officer and two men killed, three men wounded, and a further eight men missing. One Prussian was killed, Gefreiter Ungerhausen, of IR13.[13]

As Hauss moved south-east, I//2nd Regiment, Major Gandenberger, at about 14:00, continued to advance towards Hain. The 'attack' was, however, slow and poorly coordinated. No real progress was made, and at around 16:30, Colonel Wilkens ordered a withdrawal.

After these halting and hesitant Hessian efforts, no further move was considered likely from them. Therefore, the Prussian troops then, as ordered, quickly prepared their bivouacs. Von Rex' F/IR55, remained as outposts at Laufach, and F/IR15, Baron Bönigt, did so in and around Frohnhofen. Without doubt, no one in the exhausted Prussian ranks expected any further emergency.

The Assault of 1st Hessian Regiment

After this, a lull ensued, as the Hessians considered their options. To begin with, during the earlier skirmishing, General Frey had held the two battalions of Colonel Grollman's 1st Infantry Regiment in reserve.

Of the main body then following the II/ 2nd Infantry Regiment at a considerable distance, the 1st Infantry Regiment and four guns of Captain Herget's 2nd Foot Battery, with its covering forces, had occupied the height of the Geisenberg in such a manner that on the left wing, the I/1st, Major Hoff, was deployed in line. To the right of these, the guns were deployed in a favourable position, on the right rear of this, facing south. II/1st, Major Lane, was deployed in line of company columns, with the 2nd Schützen Company deployed in front as skirmishers.

---

12 G.G.S., p.618 & Zimmermann, p.308. The latter times this episode at about 14:00.
13 Blume, p.177. For details of the reconnaissance, see Zimmermann, pp.314-318.

At about 17:30, Colonel von Grollmann received a brief order from General Frey, sent from the Geisenberg. It read simply, "The (1st) Regiment will advance". Accordingly, Grollman moved forward, with II/1st marching at the head, along the road to Laufach, accompanied by General Frey, followed by I/1st led by Grollman himself. The move was to be supported by the fire of the guns on the Geisenberg.[14]

After the earlier ineffectual Hessian probes, the Prussians had, as noted, assumed that operations had ended for the day. Indeed, General Goeben himself had given the order to make camp. As his very tired men began to bed down, however, word suddenly came of an enemy advance.

The attack of the Hessians came completely unexpectedly for the Prussians; at first only one complete company, Captain Fordenbeck's 10/IR 15, was able to take up a lively fire. All the other companies arrived piecemeal in their positions, to join the fire-fight. Soon, though, Kaweczynski's I/IR15 was moved forward to reinforce the right wing, and II/IR 15, Captain Hattorf, the left. With the companies arriving piecemeal, a unified command of the action was lacking at first, but, " ... once again the flexibility of the Prussian officers shone in a bright light".[15]

Meanwhile, Colonel Grollman's regiment advanced on the Prussians in three 'groups'. Along the main road marched Major Hoff's battalion, while Lane marched along the railway embankment, with three companies south of the road, and one to the north of it.[16]

Captain Krieg describes the Hessian approach:

> The enemy debouched with three heavy columns, and advanced with thick skir- misher screens from the railway embankment, which is about 2,000 paces from Frohnhofen, In the meanwhile, his battery took position to the north-east of the farm and threw grenades mainly at the woods south of the railway. Under the cover of this artillery fire, the enemy columns advanced in perfect order, with drums beating, on Frohnhofen.[17]

The advance was supported throughout by the artillery fire, which however failed to have any appreciable effect on the volume of the murderous Prussian small arms fire. The spirited assault continued to within some 150 paces of the Prussian positions, before faltering. Unable to push any further, the Hessians then fell back.

A second attack, chiefly launched by Major Lane's less II/1st, followed at around 18:45, once again being preceded by skirmishers. After a supreme effort, some elements actually entered Frohnhofen, before being swiftly driven out. Grollman's hard-used troops could do no more. The 2nd Hessian Brigade, however, was now nearing the field. The battle was certainly not over.[18]

---

14 Zimmermann, p.328.

15 Kunz, p.131. His quote above, at the end of the sentence, while appearing somewhat smug, does contain a kernel of accuracy here.

16 Schmidt, p.277, *Schlachtfelder*.

17 Krieg, p.66.

18 For 1st Hessian Regiment's attack, see Zimmermann, pp.328-336.

The approach and attack of 2nd Hessian Brigade

General Stockhausen's 2nd Brigade had been hurried towards Laufach, and upon arrival near Weiberhof went rapidly into action. First committed was the 3rd Infantry Regiment. Colonel von Ochtenstein, the 3rd Regiment's commander, ordered an immediate attack, emphasising to his officers the plight of their comrades of 1st Brigade. Their duty was made crystal clear. The two battalions commenced their advance a little before 19:00.[19]

After the Colonel's brief but definitive words of encouragement, the Regiment began its advance, led by its colonel and after a rapid march reached Weiberhöf shortly past 19:00, on the way marching past the divisional commander, who was riding back at Hösbach. In spite of the heat and the privations, the stance of the soldiers was good and they advanced with high confidence, when the gunfire and small arms fire became audible after leaving Hösbach. At Weiberhof, Colonel von Ochsenstein, following the example of the 1st Regiment, allowed the men to lay down their backpacks, and then continued the march along the road. About 100 paces west of the Kirchenhohle, when the enemy missiles were already hitting the forward companies of the regiment, the 1st Battalion deployed from the double file column, the 1st Company, at the head deployed into a dense skirmisher screen, with three platoons north and one south of the road, when Lieutenant Stammler was mortally wounded.[20]

Captain Scriba, the company commander of 3/3rd Hessian Regiment, described this attack in his subsequent report. His own company, which had until now been the head of the column, now still advanced directly along the road, but with 1 and 2/3rd to his left:

> The drummers, who were with the Leib (1st) and 2nd Companies, were beating the charge, and we all stormed valiantly forwards. During the charge the company came under the first enemy fire – 'rapid-fire'. The screams of pain and the moaning of the fallen wounded, as well as the jumping of the Battalion Adjutants horse, produced a hesitation for a moment. At the same moment the companies marching in the rear, wanted to advance through my company, so that the same would have been brought to disorder. Therefore, I commanded "Half left!", climbed the low edge of the road and attacked, with my company, in the direction of Frohnhofen. The first charge against the skittle alley and the fence was repulsed by murderous fire from the nearby houses. A second charge, during which Captain Stamm (who was to the right of me at the head of his company) was wounded, was also repulsed. Some individual soldiers, including Lieutenant Lauthard of the company, were yet still advancing within the fence of the skittle alley. After the second charge, I retreated to a hollow in the terrain, which is the southern continuation of the "Kirchenhohle". Here, I rallied my men. At this moment, Ensign Janson of the battalion appeared, and requested to join my company, and also bringing the following message: "Earlier, as I was with the 2nd Company, Major Kröll, who was at my side, grabbed my flag, shouted "Hurrah!", and desired to move forward with

---

19 Ö.K., p.96.

20 Ibid., p.337.

The Hessian infantry in action at the skittle alley, Fronhofen. (Cohn)

it. However I am not allowed to give (hand over) my flag, so I said: "Major, I may not give up my flag!" Whereupon, the Major left me and charged forward."[21]

The attack failed. The enemy was hardly visible and could not be dislodged, the high grain and the powder smoke denied a good oversight, the commands could not be heard due to the noise of battle, and with severe losses, the 1st and 2ndcompanies streamed back to the cover of the lower part of the Kirchenhohle. "Despite the attempts of Captains Schulz and von Hessert, order could not be restored, and the soldiers could not be made to renew the assault".[22]

Captain Krieg wrote later that,

> Under this concentric fire, the efforts of the enemy could not succeed. After three assault attempts, with enormous casualties that were delivered with great bravery, they began to fall back. Now, Colonel Baron von der Goltz undertook the offensive, with the 1st Battalion.[23]

Captain Scriba mentioned the Frohnhofen village skittle alley in his account. This structure, at the western edge of the settlement, was the scene of a bitter close-quarter

21   Zimmermann, p.402.
22   Ibid., p.338. These two officers were, respectively, the company commanders.
23   Krieg, p.67.

struggle. It was initially defended by the 4th Platoon of 10/IR15, Second-Lieutenant Hoffmann. The small Prussian force barely managed to hold the feature long enough for elements of Captain von Wülchnitz'11/IR55 to come their support, soon followed by others.[24]

4th Regiment's Assault

At about 18:00, the commanding officer of the 4th Hessian Infantry Regiment received the 'Alarm Signal', indicating imminent action. Colonel Schenck was then ordered forward, along the road embankment, with the 1st Schützen Company acting as advance guard. As with the other units previously, the troops then removed their packs before moving against the enemy.

General Stockhausen then directed Schenck to move north of the main road, in support of the 3rd Regiment. The attack was once again conducted in company columns, preceded by skirmish screens. There was no element of surprise here, and the Prussian defence was prepared. Fire was held until the Hessian columns were some three hundred paces. Then began the 'rapid fire' from a ready, and largely unseen enemy.[25]

The effect of this fire, supported by two artillery batteries, was devastating, not least to Hessian morale. Colonel Schenck was killed and General Stockhausen lightly wounded.[26] No progress could be made against the defensive fire. Soon after, the Prussians took the offensive, and rapidly swept the disordered Hessians from the field. Approaching darkness put an end to the combat at about 20:00.[27] The final assault had failed. There was now no alternative than to withdraw. A large number of the Hessian wounded also fell into Prussian hands, along with almost all of the baggage. The Prussian success was complete.

Once again, Prussian ammunition expenditure had been prodigious. The three battalions of IR 15, for example, alone fired the following.

> I/IR 15 – 550 rounds
> II/IR 15 – 522 rounds
> F/IR 15 – 10,022 rounds[28]

The amazing total fired by the Fusilier Battalion, in action from the start of the combat, is worthy of note. This unit alone expended almost ten times as much ammunition as had the other two battalions combined.

---

24 Kunz, p.132 & Krieg, p.66.
25 Kunz, p.133 & Schlachtfelder, p.277.
26 Lettow-Vorbeck, p.233. These units were Captain Cöster's four pounder battery, and the twelve pounder battery of Captain Eynatten II.
27 Sunset was officially 20:16, Kunz, p.133.
28 Hoffmann, p.68.

Hessian withdrawal and march to Aschaffenburg

By 21:00, all elements of the Hessian Division had withdrawn from the field, and were on the march to Aschaffenburg. With the exception of the 1st and 2nd Regiments, and their associated units, there was an understandable amount of confusion in places along the march route.[29]

The action at Laufach had been a model example of the use of the breech-loading small-arms in a defensive position. The gallant Hessians had been completely unable to close with their enemies. The primary error on the Prussian side was to completely misjudge their adversaries' intentions. They were most fortunate not to have paid a much higher price for it!

Nevertheless, both Generals Perglas and Stockhausen were subsequently sent before a court martial to explain their conduct in the battle. Stockhausen, particularly, taking this as a grossly unmerited affront to his honour, retorted by committing suicide on the day of the judgement.[30]

Casualties

Due to the nature of the conflict around Laufach, the losses incurred by the adversaries there were exceedingly one-sided. In essence, the Hessians attacked a difficult position head on. Their adversaries, many in cover, armed with breech-loading weapons, were presented with a series of ideal targets. The attackers themselves displayed admirable courage and discipline. Losses in this one-sided conflict were as follows:[31]

	Prussian		Hessian	
	Officers	**Men**	**Officers**	**Men**
Killed	–	5	12	163
Wounded	1	57	24	383
Missing/prisoners	–	3	1	123
Totals	1	65	37	669

The heaviest losses on the Prussian side were in the two fusilier battalions, F/IR 15 having 27 casualties, and F/IR 55, 13, respectively.[32]

Action of Aschaffenburg – July 14

Overnight, Federal troops converged on Aschaffenburg from both east and west. First to arrive were the retreating Hessians, who had commenced their retreat from the environs of Frohnhofen between 20:30 and 21:00. The Leib Regiment reached Aschaffenburg

---

29 Zimmermann, p.344.
30 Lecomte, p.229.
31 Lettow-Vorbeck, p.231. However, see Appendix XIV for further clarification.
32 Lettow-Vorbeck, p. 231 & Krieg p. 78.

around 23:00, and proceeded to bivouac in the streets of the town, as did the other units.[33]

The Austrian Brigade of Major-General von Hahn, which had left Frankfurt by train the previous afternoon, had arrived in Aschaffenburg by 05:00, on the 14th, under the personal command of the divisional commander, Count Neipperg.[34] Neipperg would sorely miss the presence of his Nassau Brigade in the coming battle. An additional factor for him to juggle was the need to consider the situation of the battered Hessians. A further issue would only become apparent during the action itself, though Hahn cannot have been unaware of it. The Hahn Brigade of seven battalions, two squadrons and two batteries, together with the rearguard of the

Kummer at Aschaffenburg. (Cohn)

Hessian Division, battalions and 1st Homburg Jäger Company plus three squadrons, and a six pounder rifled battery.

The position chosen was a cramped one, with no room to manoeuvre. More seriously, immediately the defenders had their backs to the river, crossed by the River Main bridge. Between the two, lay the town itself. Any withdrawal would be difficult. Hahn, however, had no choice.[35]

As the Federal forces made their defensive preparations, the Prussian advance resumed on the morning of the 14th. From 07:00, the seemingly tireless Goeben continued his march on Aschaffenburg. That day he again expected to engage the enemy. It was rumoured that Aschaffenburg was strongly held by the VIII Corps. In fact, as seen, only

33   Zimmermann, p.344 & Beck, pp.352-353.
34   Baur-Breitenfeld, pp.54-55. As previously seen, the division's other brigade, the Nassauers, had been temporarily recalled to the Duchy, to defend it from Prussian incursions from the west.
35   Sir Alexander Malet, no soldier, commented on this flaw, pp.281-282.

half the Neipperg Division had been rushed forward. on the evening of the 13th, by the Prince of Hesse, in order to relieve the defeated Hessians. Both the Badeners and Württembergers were not far distant.

For his attack on the town, Goeben formed his men in three attack columns. Kummer was on the left, by the railway and the high ground, with Wrangel in the centre, along the main road. On the right, Colonel von der Goltz led a detachment of IR/15 and a squadron of Hussars by a winding path through orchards. Treskow and the bulk of the artillery followed in reserve, behind Wrangel. In total, the division counted 16 battalions, 9 squadrons and 30 guns. One battalion and one squadron were detached to guard the 500 Bavarian prisoners who were destined to feature in the triumphal entry into Frankfurt.'

Lieutenant Tabouillot was advancing on the left that already warm morning, with Kummer's brigade:

> On the morning of the next day, it was July 14, the regiment advanced against Aschaffenburg; as it was again becoming rather humid, the march was not to be extended very far, Aschaffenburg was the objective, and there we were to take quarters. At about 9:30 AM, the advanced patrols reported that enemy cavalry was positioned in front of Aschaffenburg. The Four Pounder battery that was attached to us (Captain Weigelt) advanced at the gallop, unlimbered, and dislodged the enemy cavalry from their position with a few well-placed shots. At the double, they retreated into the cover of the town.
>
> In the meanwhile, the regiment had formed up for the assault.1st Battalion (v. Borries) advanced as an advanced guard along the railway line, followed by the 2nd Battalion (Captain Kerssenbrock) as the second echelon. The Fusilier Battalion was detached to the left, climbing across hill and valley, searching through the wooded sectors. Due to the rapid advance it was soon aligned with the 1st Battalion. In this formation the advance continued. At first, the very visible Fusilier Battalion (it was just climbing down another hill), and then the 2nd Battalion, both received a rapid and well-directed fire from a battery posted in front of Aschaffenburg. Fortunately, most of the shells landed where the battalion had just left, or hit to the rear of it. The damage was therefore minor; the order and cohesion was not affected, and the advance was accelerated instead of being slowed down as a result.[36]

The Prussian advance initially encountered Federal outposts near the villages of Hoesbach and Goldbach. Here, skirmishers of IR/13, supported by two batteries, engaged Austrian pickets of 35/FJB, Major Machalitzky, and a Hessian battery, Captain Herget's breech-loading six pounders.[37] The Imperial troops were slowly pressed back towards an ornamental wooded area known as The Pheasantry. After some 15 minutes of sustained fire, the Austrian Jäger occupied the buldings of the wood, continuing from there to exchange fire with the advancing I/IR13, Lieutenant-Colonel von Borries.

---

36 Tabouillot, pp.28-29.
37 Ö.K., p.102.

Wrangel's advance, meanwhile, had pushed the Federal outposts to the north beyond the village of Damm, but Herget's Hessian battery then forced a halt, and then a partial pull-back here. The two Prussian batteries attached to Wrangel, Captain Cöster's four pounders, and Captain Eynatten II's twelve pounders were brought forward, but were unable to dislodge Herget.[38] At this point, the general ordered forward three companies of IR 15, led by Colonel von der Goltz, followed by 10/IR55, Captain von Arnim, against the position. This move quickly caused the withdrawal of the guns.[39]

On the Prussian left, in and around the Pheasantry, the action had also grown in scale, as Lieutenant Tabouillot bore witness:

> Everyone was heading for the Pheasantry, its tight copses hid us from the sight and the bullets of the enemy; in it, a covered approach up to the town was possible. The 1st Battalion had to wheel to the left and leave the railway embankment to reach it. Near Aschaffenburg it suffered greatly from shellfire, as well as enemy rifle fire. Still the change of front succeeded in the best of order. 2nd Company (Oberlieutenant. Wuermeling) took with its rifle platoon (Lieutenant Klapheke) the edge of the Pheasantry which was only weakly held, and courageously, the few pursued the retreating enemy deeper into the woods. Here the assailants encountered two Austrian battalions that met them with heavy rifle fire. Our skirmishers staggered, and retired towards the main body so as to be better able to resist.
>
> Quickly, the rest of 2nd Company, as well as the 4th and 11th Companies (Captains Beckherrn and von Gillhausen I) advanced towards the edge with 11th Company, with their far advanced skirmishers forming a hook on our left wing. Rapidly, all were deployed and expecting the storm of the enemy, which was not long in coming. With rifles at the attack, and skirmishers swarming on either side, came both Italian battalions with drums beating.
>
> One salvo, then a terrible rapid fire smashed into their ranks. In rows, they sank to the ground; however again and again, they consolidated their thinned ranks. Nearer and nearer moved the overpowering enemy, silent but for the drums, when suddenly, the Imperial troops gave a resounding cheer, and, as if on parade, the ranks following the flag. The 2nd Battalion closed ranks, and threw itself at the enemy, closing with lowered rifles on their opponents. These hesitated, and before yet for its part a seeing, a new possible act, let loose a second salvo, followed by a second rapid fire ...[40]

The Imperial troops here, most particularly the two battalions of IR Wehrnhardt, were utterly demoralised by these encounters, and began to surrender wholesale. They had previously been made aware of the fact that a treaty had already been signed between Austria and Prussia's ally, Italy, whereby they were no longer to be Habsburg subjects. The effect of this can well be imagined. IR Wehrnardt largely fell apart, with many men shouting, 'Eviva Prussia' as the Prussians approached. This malaise soon, of course, encompassed

---

38   G.G.S., pp.624-625, insists that this was because the batteries had been unable to find a suitable position from which to do so.
39   Krieg, pp.72-73 & Zimmermann, pp.352-353.
40   Ibid., pp.31-32.

the 3rd Battalion, which was in reserve near the bridge

As his defence line east of the river came unhinged, General Hahn had little choice other than to order a withdrawal of his forces across the Aschaff Bridge. With no room to manoeuvre, and several units which would not fight, Hahn did his best to extricate what he could of his approximately 7,000 men.[41] The Imperial 35th Jäger stoutly defended the railway station, but a number were cut off there, and subsequently taken prisoner. Pulling back across the open ground between the Pheasantry and the town, the Imperial troops suffered from the heavy fire of the Prussian infantry, especially to the battalions of Hess and Nobili. Many prisoners were also being taken. General von Falckenstein, observing the action, allowed the

Austrian and Prussian infantry at Aschaffenburg, drawing by Hoffmann. (Regensberg/Mainfeldzug)

commander of his personal escort, Rittmeister Studnitz, to lead his squadron into the pursuit.[42]

Soon after the Austrian withdrawal to the west bank, General Goeben, invariably to the fore, crossed the bridge at around Noon. Confused fighting continued in the streets of Aschaffenburg continued for about another hour, but by around one o'clock, Tabouillot could say that, " … the last enemy barricade had been taken, and the bridge over the Main was in our hands."[43] With the vital bridge secured intact, the battle was over. The Federal forces were, by then, in full retreat, leaving many men still cut off in the town.[44]

---

41   Ö.K., Vol. V, p.101. This figure includes seven battalions, including the three of IR Wehrnhardt.
42   The squadron, 1/4th Cuirassiers, took 175 prisoners, Fontane, p.179 & Regensberg, p.105.
43   Tabouillot, p.33.
44   Ibid., p.33 & Lecomte, pp.231-232. G.G.S., pp.628-629 all emphasise that the troops of IR Wehrnhardt initially behaved well. This may, perhaps, involve a wish not too downplay the success too much.

A force from Wrangel's Brigade, commanded by Colonel von der Goltz consisting of his own regiment (IR15), two squadrons, and a battery, then pushed on along the east bank of the Aschaff, following the withdrawal route of the Hessians from Damm. A little over five kilometres further along, he was able to secure another intact bridge across the river, at Stockstadt.[45] Goeben's troops had achieved another resounding success.

Casualties[46]

	Prussian		Austrian		Hessian	
	Officers	Men	Officers	Men	Officers	Men
Killed	5	22	4	144	–	2
Wounded	12	132	16	321	2	17
Missing/prisoners	–	9	16	1,843	4	51
Total	17	163	36	2,308	6	70

Of the Prussian total loss, 11 officers and 103 men were from IR 13. Lieutenant Tabouillot, of the regiment, was also nursing a light injury.[47] Goeben's division, alone, had inflicted two stinging defeats on VIII Corps, on consecutive days, at comparatively minimal cost, not only completely confounding its opponents own plans, but also throwing them totally off balance.

By the evening of the 14th, the remainder of the Austrian Neipperg Division had set off for Babenhausen, along the road to Darmstadt. During the next morning they found the Headquarters of Prince Alexander and, soon after, also the bulk of the VIII Corps in full retreat, thus opening the road to Frankfurt for the Prussians.

These two engagements decided the fate of the German Federal Capital, and it had taken a little more than two weeks for the Prussians to achieve it. During the last two days the VII Corps had remained in the area of Schweinfurt. VIII Corps' Chief of Staff, the Württemberg Lieutenant-General Baur-Breitenfeld, was subsequently scathing about the handling of the operations in the Spessart at this time:

> On 13th and 14th of the month, all detachments of 3rd and 4th Divisions had fought with great courage and determination, and their losses in officers and men were considerable. However, in order to achieve a better result, on the 13th there was a lack of sharp determination of the task in hand and the reasonable employment of the forces, whereas on the 14th, it was a lack of joint action.

---

45 Zimmermann, pp.359-360.
46 The Federal losses here are primarily drawn from Ö.K., pp.109-110. There are, however, anomalies. IR Wernhardt losses are incomplete, being summarised as 1,125, for other ranks. The missing Hessians are not shown as such in Zimmermann, and the Kur-Hessian hussars are shown in Ö.K. as having lost one officer and 89 men taken prisoner, whereas G.G.S. states that these troops were actually not attacked due to the similarity of their uniforms to the Prussian, p.627.
47 Kunz, p.141.

Vogel von Falckenstein surrounded by men from IR 13 after Aschaffenburg. (Cohn)

Had all 17 available battalions been involved in the battle of Aschaffenburg, had the right wing of the deployment been given more attention right from the beginning, the fighting could have been strung out for another 1.5-2 hours, after which time reinforcements from the right and left bank of the River Main should have caused a favourable turnaround.[48]

General Goeben, upon considering the last few days, had wryly mused, "On the 10th Bavarians, on the 13th, the Hessians, and on the 14th, the Austrians; the joke is too good."[49]

The Prussian Occupation of Frankfurt and the Dismissal of Vogel von Falckenstein

In Frankfurt, events had, of course, been most carefully scrutinised since the developments along the Franconian Saale. On the 11th, indeed, the City Fathers had actually requested the Federal Parliament to evacuate the city. As the Prussian forces changed their direction westward, the matter rapidly became urgent for the concerned diplomats

---

48   Baur-Breitenfeld, p.59.
49   Bleibtreu, p.129.

and politicians. The Diet hastily accepted the proposal, and left the city for Augsburg on the 14th, that city now becoming its temporary capital.[50] Rather academically, Prince Alexander, having received the permission of the Federal Parliament to do so, also evacuated Frankfurt that same day. One military unit not on anyone's agenda, was the 'garrison', currently a Bavarian battalion, IV/2nd Infantry Regiment, Major Gradinger. With no Parliament to protect, Gradinger was at something of a loose end! Fortunately, the battalion was adopted by the Federal Nassau Brigade, with which it marched as far as the vicinity of Darmstadt, and subsequently followed VIII Corps' route east.[51]

The Federal VIII Corps now used the 15th to concentrate on the west bank of the Main, around Babenhausen, somewhat under 20 kilometres west of Aschaffenburg, in preparation to join the Bavarians to th east. The Prussians, meanwhile, stayed bivouacked in and around Aschaffenburg itself. Von Falckenstein also took his time to take stock, and plan his next move. There had, at this point, been no news from Beyer, and Manteuffel was still quite some distance behind. By that afternoon, though, information indicated that the Prince of Hesse, and most of the Federal Diet, had already evacuated Frankfurt.

The very tired Prussian troops camped in and around Aschaffenburg were, therefore, granted a well-deserved rest day on the 15th. The next day, however, von Falckenstein, in accordance with his instructions from Count Bismarck, moved north, marching on Frankfurt, following the railway via Hanau. His task force consisted of two cavalry regiments, six battalions, and four batteries, all from Goeben's Division. The remainder of this division, along with Manteuffel's, for now, remained in the area of Aschaffenburg. Beyer, in the meanwhile, had, by midday on the 16th, reached Gelnhausen, some 30 kilometres east of Hanau.[52] On the 16th, Falckenstein placed Wrangel's brigade in the van, sending it by train. At its head, he entered the Free City of Frankfurt at about 19:00. Flushed by his success, von Falckenhayn sent a telegram directly to the King, which read, "The Lands north of the Main lay at Your Majesty's feet".[53] The city would pay a heavy price for its defiance of Prussia, and particularly that of Minister-President Bismarck.

Frankfurt under Occupation

The Frankfurt Battalion, with fewer than 750 officers and men, was drawn up in the centre of the city, at a small fort, the 'Hauptwache', awaiting the arrival of the Prussians, ostensibly to greet them. The latter, understandably, were entering a potential enemy stronghold.The Frankfurt troops were largely ignored for some time, as von Falckenhayn's forces secured strategic locations around the city. Subsequently, the troops were disarmed, and marched to their barracks. The battalion was disbanded three days later.[54]

---

50 Sterne, pp.207-208. Muller, p.362, notes that the Federal Parliament had ensconsed itself in the Inn of 'The Three Moors', in Augsburg, an establishment particularly noted for its fine wines!
51 *Antheil*, footnote, p.153.
52 Winterfeld, p.260.
53 A number of sources place Prussian troops in the outskirts as early as 16:00. Quote in Regensberg, p.110.
54 Kanngiesser, pp.188-190.

The Prussians in Frankfurt.
(Cohn)

After announcing martial law throughout the entire city, von Falckenstein then ordered that his troops be given the best of quarters and, with a certain amount of vengeance toward that 'most liberal' of cities, he ordered the same. Not one to avoid comfort, he installed himself in a plush hotel, the Englischer Hof, along with his headquarters. In the name of his sovereign, he announced his governance of the entire area and to start with he hit the city with an order to requisition 300 of the best horses along with a levy of seven million florins.[55] Several days later,(the 20th) a second order arrived from Berlin announcing a further levy of 25 million florins, and a further 700 horses.

The city was also required to provide a pair of shoes for each many in the Prussian force. Along with the various forms of requisitioning, Prussian soldiers were billeted on the populace, not an unusual practice. In this instance, though, additional items were required to be supplied, specifically a bottle of wine, beer, and eight cigars per man, per day.

Another target for von Falckenstein's vengeance was, of course, the press. Perceived anti-Prussian journals were suppressed, and some editors detained. In one case, the editor of the *Postzeitung*, Dr. Fisher Goullet, had suffered a stroke, but was nevertheless taken under the arms by two soldiers, and dragged to headquarters. The paper was closed. Local Senators Bernus, Müller and Speltz were held hostage in the fortress of Cologne for a time, but later released.

Upon receiving the second demand for a second financial levy, on July 20, Mayor Fellner requested an audience with the Prussian commander, now Lieutenant-General Manteuffel, to to protest the imposition of the new penalty, demanded within 24 hours.

---

55 Malet, p.289. This represents approximately £600,000, at the time. Within this sum, was supposedly one year's of the Army of the Main.Ward, p.294, puts this a little under six million, as does Lecomte, p.234.

Manteuffel had no form of compromise to offer the Mayor. The levy was to be paid. Fully aware of the impossibility of compliance, Fellner returned home, and hanged himself.

The Mayor's action, of itself, solved little. Indeed, the local occupying force, now commanded by Major-General Röder, remained unyielding. More menacingly, on the 23rd, guns were emplaced on heights above the city. Röder, another martinet, merely continued the trend which had already been set.[56] All the civil authorities were declared disbanded and to be replaced by a 'Town Major' in the person of Röder along with a civil commissioner, Herr von Dienst.

Ultimately, part of the solution came from a completely unexpected direction. Details of affairs in Frankfurt came to the attention of Prussia's Queen Augusta. Upon her bringing the matter to his attention, the King subsequently remitted the second levy altogether.[57]

Although Frankfurt was saved from total bankruptcy, Bismarck still did not forget the Free City on the Main. The city itself was later subsumed in the in the new Prussian province of Hesse-Nassau.

Change of Command, and Reorganisation of the Army of the Main

As seen, Lieutenant-General Vogel von Falckenstein had, since the beginning of the campaign, taken a remarkably cavalier attitude to orders from the Army Chief of Staff, Count Moltke. Indeed, he almost appeared to deliberately goad him, while taking correspondence from Bismarck seriously. Such a situation at high level could not, of course, be allowed to continue. With a brief lull in operations after the capture of Frankfurt, the moment to resolve this issue had come.

On the evening of July 19, Vogel von Falckenstein was swiftly and unceremoniously superseded in command of the Army of the Main, by, the now Lieutenant-General Manteuffel. Having blatantly defied Moltke too often, he was then appointed Governor-General of Bohemia, an administrative post, and very quickly despatched to Prague.[58] Manteuffel's own division, perhaps surprisingly, was then placed under the command of Major-General von Flies.[59]

The changes in the command structure of the army were also reflected in a number of organisational alterations, including some not inconsiderable reinforcements. In addition, strategic needs had somewhat altered. No longer was there any threat to the western Prussian provinces from the Federal forces. The hostile territories north of the Main, including Nassau, were now firmly under Prussian control, with only the Federal fortress of Mainz being excepted.

Therefore, along with the change of command, the Prussian forces in the West underwent a number of organisational changes. Firstly, General Manteuffel formed an occupation force for Frankfurt itself. Commanded by Colonel Kortsfleisch, this primarily

---

56 It is difficult to consider this as a genuine prelude to a bombardment.

57 Malet, pp.298-299. The French Emperor also made representations.

58 Malet, p.292. Von Falckenstein's dismissal had actually been decided upon by a Royal Cabinet order of July 11, awaiting an opportune moment. He never again held a field command, although he was appointed as Governor-General of the German Coasts, a largely irrelevant post, during the later Franco-Prussian War.

59 Flies had clearly been either forgiven for Langensalza, or was never blamed.

consisted of the five 4th battalions, those of IR Nrs. 30, 32, 36, 39, and 70, and the three battalions of Landwehr Infantry Regiment Nr. 17, a total of eight battalions. Supporting these were one squadron of the 10th Landwehr Hussar Regiment, and four guns.[60]

Masking the Federal fortress of Mainz was a force commanded by Lieutenant-Colonel Fischer-Treuenfeld. This comprised:

Waldeck Fusilier Battalion
Schwarzburg-Rudolfstadt Fusilier Battalion
Two ersatz companies, IR Nr. 56
One combined Jäger company
One garrison squadron (from Coblenz)
One combined hussar squadron (Regiments 7 & 11)
Detachment, ersatz squadron, 8th Cuirassier Regiment
Artillery detachment – four rifled four pounder, and four smoothbore six pounder cannon
Approximate total: 5,000 men

In addition to the above, the three divisions of the Army of the Main also had the following troops attached:

Division Goeben
Regiment Oldenburg (three battalions)
Bremen Battalion
Three squadrons, Oldenburg Cavalry
One rifled six pounder battery
One smoothbore twelve pounder battery

Division Beyer
I/IR 30
II/IR 70
Two squadrons, Landwehr Hussar Regiment Nr. 10
One pioneer company
Two rifled six pounder batteries
One Bridging Train[61]

Division Flies
9th Jäger Battalion
Two Hamburg Infantry battalions
Battalion Lübeck
Two squadrons, Hamburg Cavalry[62]

---

60 Kunz, p.145. See below for details.
61 Knorr, Vol. 3, p 47.
62 See Appendix VII. Figures shown above are taken from Kunz, pp.145-146. Note that the Hamburg troops actually arrived with General Flies' Division just too late to take any active part in the campaign.

Failed Peace Talks – Prince Karl re-assembles VII Corps and links with VIII Corps

After the Bavarian army had withdrawn behind the Main at Gerolzhofen in mid-July, initially, little had been done once it was realised that there had been no serious Prussian pursuit. As in other circumstances, diplomacy took a hand. Talks as to the possibility of an armistice then took place.

Bavarian staff Colonel Bothmer later testified as to this matter in the 'Zander Trial',[63] stating that, "Here, the leadership was subject to the influence of political motives; in general, to us this concerned the conclusion of peace and an armistice; the days between the Battle of Kissingen and the move to Würzburg (10th-16th) were partly spent on these negotiations about a truce." In answer to another question by the accused's defence counsel, the colonel ended with a revealing question of his own, pondering as to, "… whether it would not have compromised these negotiations, if we had actively taken military action against Prussia".[64]

Colonel Booms concludes that all negotiations were probably finally broken off on the night of the 15th, after Manteuffel had discussions with a Bavarian delegation, at Lohr. If so, this appears tenuous, as the army's concentration, including the march of VIII Corps, was already well under way. Certainly, between the 14th and the 16th, Prince Karl had assembled his own forces between Würzburg, Dettelbach and Kitzingen, while also moving troops to the east bank of the Main, towards Markt Heidenfeld, on the 17th.[65]

After his rejection of possible armistice talks on July 13, though, Karl began to plan for a concentration of all of the Federal forces, south of the Main. He had, before this brief contact with the Prussians, already instructed Prince Alexander to march his force eastward through the Odenwald with a view to a rendezvous along the River Tauber. This plan was, therefore, to continue. In the meanwhile, though, Karl also, as seen, had his own army to move and re-assemble.[66]

By the 16th, the Bavarian army was once again concentrated, now around Würzburg.

A contemporary work supposed, "that doubtless explicit promises had been obtained from the Prussians that they would not be attacked, as long as a certain distance was kept", and that: "a condition for the armistice must have been that the Bavarians retreated across the Main". It presumes that, after the Bavarian withdrawal east of that river, it was no longer a threat to Prussian interests, which, from that point, were fixed upon a land-grab north of that river. Certainly, this occurred, but Bavaria did not then actually throw in the towel.[67]

---

63 Zander Trial, p.25.
64 Ibid., p.37.
65 *Antheil*, p.147 & G.G.S., p.435.
66 *Antheil*, pp.146-147, and also see Biebrach, p.44.
67 *Wirkungen und Ursachen*, pp.9-12.

VIII Corps' withdrawal through the Odenwald

After the stinging reverse at Aschaffenburg, Prince Alexander had also, as per his orders, resolved to finally achieve the goal of uniting VII and VIII Corps'. Beginning on the 16th, VIII Corps began a withdrawal south and east through the Odenwald towards the River Tauber. It was not an easy march, many units still being in varying states of confusion as a result of the previous several days. Fortunately, for reasons discussed, there was no Prussian pursuit, only a follow-up. The next day, the Bavarians threw a pontoon bridge across the Main, at Heidingsfeld, south of Würzburg, to allow the army to cross, and finally link with Prince Alexander.[68]

During the 18th, a small skirmish took place near near the town of Erlenbach, on the Main, some 12 kilometres north of Miltenberg. At around 04:00, the pickets of 2/2nd Baden Regiment, Captain Scharnberger, were suddenly attacked by Prussian hussars. In a swift melee, the Badeners had two men wounded, and lost seven more taken prisoner.[69]

VII and VIII Corps' Discuss Joint Plans

On that day, VIII Corps Headquarters was at Amorbach, along with the Württemberg Division. The Badeners lay in and around Miltenberg, with the Hessians at Michelstadt. The Austrian Brigade was at Hundheim. The Nassau Brigade lay to the east of the Baden Division. The march to the south and east continued.[70] A link of the two Federal corps' now actually appeared possible. Finally, also on July 19, the two corps commanders met at Tauberbishofsheim, to discuss joint plans, to be joined there by Prince Alexander's Chief of Staff, Lieutenant-General Baur-Breitenfeld, and his Bavarian counterpart, Baron von der Tann. The conference was certainly not a moment too soon. Was it, however, still in time?.[71]

As the combined Federal Staff pondered the situation, the three major columns of VIII Corps had made their way towards the River Tauber. By the 20th, the Corps was in place thus:

> Headquarters – Tauberbischofsheim
> 1st Division (Württemberg) – Groß Rinderfeld
> 2nd Division (Baden) – Hundheim
> 3rd Division (Hessian) – Hardheim
> 4th Division (Austrian/Nassau) – Gerlachsheim
> Reserve Cavalry and Artillery – Walldürn[72]

In Tauberbischofsheim, probably inevitably, disagreements as how to proceed immediately surfaced. However, on the 21st, designated a rest day, the two chiefs of staff spent the day planning a joint offensive, which was to be launched from the line of

---

68 *Antheil*, p.148.
69 Becker, p.103.
70 Alexander, *Feldzugs-Journal*, pp.16-17 & Wacker/Rosenwald, pp.121-123.
71 *Antheil*, p.150.
72 *Feldzugs-Journal*, p.17.

the Tauber. They were, of course, unaware that they were already one day behind their enemy. On the 22nd came reports of Prussian columns approaching along the Main. At this, Prince Alexander considered that measures need be taken to deal with the enemy forces appearing to their front. Karl, however, believed this premature, and also the Prussian force to be a small one, and no action, therefore, was taken.[73]

---

73   Ibid., p.18 & *Antheil*, pp.154-55.

9

The Return to the Main

The Prussian Advance to the River Tauber

As seen, General Manteuffel had assumed command of the army of the Main on July 20. Notwithstanding, his orders for the march to the Tauber were issued the same day. These specified that the army would commence its move the following morning.[1]

Leaving General von Röder to deal with matters to the west, including the masking of the Federal fortress of Mainz, Manteuffel then marched from Frankfurt on the 21st, with approximately 50,000 men and 286 guns. Reports had placed the Bavarians as being concentrated around Würzburg, and also VIII Corps in the vicinity of Miltenberg. He resolved to move against the latter. Once again, a bold and decisive course of action had been decided upon, while the Confederation High Command once again considered the situation.[2]

General Goeben's division proceeded in a loop via Darmstadt, while Beyer and Flies both initially marched along the Main itself. On the 22nd, Beyer pushed a reconnaissance in the direction of Heidenfeld. Commanded by Major Preuss, it comprised his own II/IR 70, and one squadron of the 9th Hussars.

Near daybreak on the 23rd, a cavalry patrol from Flies' division, led by Lieutenant Eisenhardt-Rothe, of the 5th Dragoons, clashed with Baden Jäger outposts, commanded by Lieutenant Froben, near Freudenberg. The Prussian officer was killed, and one NCO, and three of his men wounded. The Badeners lost one man wounded and another captured, before the Prussians pulled back. Several other minor exchanges also occurred during the morning.[3]

Goeben's division marched south, towards Darmstadt, while both Flies and Beyer proceeded south along the Main. Beyer despatched a column eastward, to reconnoitre towards Heidenfeld, north of Schweinfurt. This force, II/IR 70, Major Preuß, and a squadron, 1/9th Hussars, duly combed the area. Heavy concentrations of Bavarian troops were noted on the east bank of the Main, west of Würzburg, notably near Marktheildfeld.

By the evening of the 22nd, around 19:30, Manteuffel's major formations had reached the following points:

---

1   Knorr, Part 3, pp.45-46. Lettow-Vorbeck also gives this as the time that the Army of the Main universally adopted the white arm-band, on the left arm, Vol. 3, p.275.

2   G.G.S., pp.636-637 alludes to the general feeling of confidence in the Army of the Main at this time. Additionally, the Oldenburg-Hanseatic Brigade had, as noted, become operational with the Army.

3   Knorr, p.54-55 & G.G.S., p.638.

Manteuffel. (Cohn)

Goeben. (Cohn)

Division Goeben – Bad König (some 60 kilometres south-west of Frankfurt)
Division Flies – with his advance guard at Laudenbach (65 kilometres south of Frankfurt)
Division Beyer – Wallstadt (immediately to the west of Mannheim)[4]

Events on July 23

It was only on the 23rd, another designated rest day, that VIII Corps Headquarters actually learned of the current Prussian intent, as the Corps Chief of Staff later narrated: 'Early that morning came information, from the 2nd Division and private correspondence, that General Vogel von Falckenstein had been replaced by General Manteuffel, and that the whole Army of the Main was marching across the Odenwald'.[5] Prince Alexander's earlier fears of a Prussian offensive were proving accurate.

That morning, Major-General Flies received orders from the Army Commander to advance upon the town of Nassig. The advance that morning proceeded without incident until, just beyond the town, his advance pickets began exchanging fire with enemy patrols, which, however, made no attempt to stand their ground. The Division's main body subsequently ended up bivouacking near Neukirchen. One of Flies' subordinates, however, was to have an altogether different day.

To cover his right that day, Flies had detached a flank column, commanded by Colonel Fabeck, to move on the village of Hundheim, some 15 kilometres east of Miltenberg, south of Nassig. Fabeck, with his own Saxe-Coburg-Gotha Regiment (two battalions), a section of the 3rd Twelve Pounder Battery, and two half squadrons of the 6th Dragoon Regiment, duly moved off towards the objective.

The Encounter at Hundheim

Prince Wilhelm of Baden, naturally anxious to actually establish the nature of the Prussian advance, had already, as noted, pushed cavalry patrols westward, towards Freudenberg and Miltenberg, on the east bank of the Main, and then resolved to concentrate his division between Hundheim and Steinbach. Hundheim, roughly half way between Tauberbischofsheim and Miltenberg, was to be occupied by the 1st Infantry Brigade, and Steinbach by the 2nd Infantry Regiment, and the 2nd Fusilier Battalion. Two batteries supported each position. One battery remained in reserve, and the 2nd Dragoon Regiment was positioned behind Hundheim. A bridgehead across the Main and the Tauber, at Wertheim, was to be held by two companies of Lieutenant-Colonel von Peternell's Jäger, and a dragoon squadron.[6]

On the evening of July 22, Prince Wilhelm received a report that at Neukirchen, there had been a clash between Prussian and Hessian horse. Several other similar reports also appeared. At 02:30, on the 23rd, the Prince placed the Division on alert, and moved from Wertheim through Dedengefaess to Neukirchen. The first cavalry patrol sent

---

4   Knorr, pp.46-48 & Lettow-Vorbeck, Vol. 3, pp.275-276.
5   Baur-Breitenfeld, p.77.
6   *Zur Beurtheilung der Verhaltens der badischen Felddivision*, p.24.

The action at Hundheim. (Fontane)

earlier reported no sign of the enemy, though, and so, the Badeners then returned to their cantonments around Wertheim.[7]

As planned, on the morning of the 23rd, Baron La Roche's 1st Brigade duly took possession of Hundheim, and Steinbach, some two kilometres to the south, was also occupied by Colonel von Neubronn's brigade. Further south, the Baden Leib Dragoons covered the main road to Tauberbischofsheim, along with a battalion of the 3rd Infantry Regiment, and two guns.[8]

At around Noon, information arrived at Baden headquarters that a large enemy column was moving over Eichenbühl against Umpfenbach and Riedern. This was, in fact, the column of Colonel Fabeck.[9]

As Fabeck's own cavalry pickets moved towards the Tiefenthaler Hof, they encountered Baden infantry outposts of the Grenadier Regiment. The latter immediately pulled back. Fabeck, having deployed his I Battalion in company columns, then pushed it through the woods, with the 1st Company moving towards Birkhof, the 3rd through the woods to the left, with the 2nd Company linking the two. The 4th company followed, acting as the reserve. The Fusilier Battalion and the artillery remained assembled along the main road, along with a troop of the dragoons. The Baden Division, though no-one on either side knew it, was now engaged by the lone battalion of Colonel Fabeck, himself supported by only two guns.

---

7   Rüstow, p.322.

8   Baur-Breitenfeld, p.80.

9   Rüstow, p.323.

What followed was a series of 'partial encounters', with the Badeners, who were endeavouring to adhere to their orders to pull back, and being harried at every step by Fabeck. Now, Prince Wilhelm kept his troops to the south, and moved to a position on the heights before Hundheim and Steinbach, some 1,000 paces in front of the woods there. With a small advance guard of infantry and cavalry, and two rifled guns, the Prince personally moved along the main road from Hundheim to Neukirchen, when the first shot came from the detachment from Division Flies. The initial reports of a large enemy column were incorrect.

During the action, both troops of the Prussian 6th Dragoons individually recklessly attacked from their position south of Birkhof. In a 'swarm' attack, they approached to about 80 paces of the mass of Baden riflemen. Inexplicably, Lieutenant von Münchhausen, commanding the Prussian 6th Dragoon Regiment detachment present, then led his troop of about 30 men, and launched a bold attack on some Baden infantry, but was only very lucky to suffer a repulse without serious losses.[10] Fabeck's force now withdrew to its earlier positions in the woods. The Baden Division, in accordance with its previous orders, subsequently fell back towards Tauberbischofsheim.

The Prussian losses in these combats totalled 20. These were as follows:

> The Saxe-Coburg-Gotha Battalion suffered 16 casualties in total. These were:
> 1st Company – Two men wounded
> 3rd Company – Three men wounded
> 4th Company – Four men killed and seven wounded
> 6th Dragoon Regiment, detachment – One man killed and three wounded

Baden losses numbered three officers and twelve men killed, three officers and 53 men wounded, and one officer and 40 men taken prisoners or missing, a total of 105.[11]

Baden sources are quick to point out that comparatively few of their troops actually took part in the action, *Zur Beurtheilung des Verhaltens der badischen Felddivision*, commenting that only 11 companies, one battery, and a 'few' cavalry were actively involved. Nevertheless, the Baden Division had actually been faced down by a force of only two battalions, one squadron, and two guns. Equally, though, Fabeck had undoubtedly been very lucky.

At 23:00 on the 23rd General Orders were issued recalling the VIII Corps to the east bank of the Tauber. These instructions were particularly unwelcome to the Baden Division. The Badeners, however, obeying their orders, then pulled back, and on the 24th, moved back in the direction of Tauberbischofsheim, then being posted to the north, in Hochhausen and Wehrbach, with the Württembergers in and behind Bischofsheim itself.

---

10 Ibid., p.324 & Kunz, p.153.
11 Kehnert, p.51. Rüstow, though, gives the dragoons' loss as six men and 12 horses.

Cavalry skirmish of Waldürn

While these events occurred, the main body of Goeben's Division lay around Amorbach, south of Miltenberg. From here, a probe had been sent in the direction of Waldürn, along the main road to Tauberbischofsheim. As the advance elements of this column approached the town, they encountered Rittmeister Olewang's squadron of the Baden Leib Cavalry Regiment, just leaving it. Prussian Major Krug von Nidda, at the head of the 1 and 4/8th Hussars, immediately charged the Baden horsemen, rapidly putting them to flight.

Olewang's squadron was chased back through the town and back along the road to Bischofsheim, with a loss of two men killed, and one officer and 17 men taken prisoner, the officer being wounded. Two Prussian troopers were wounded. The rest of the fleeing Baden horsemen subsequently made their way to Tauberbischofsheim itself.[12]

---

12   G.G.S., p.641, Ö.K., Vol. V., p.129 & Baur-Breitenfeld, pp.79-82.

10

Across the Tauber

The Actions along the River Tauber – July 24

As Prince Alexander had now withdrawn his main forces to the east bank of the Tauber, General Manteuffel ordered a concentration of the Army of the Main for the 24th. Beyer and Goeben's very tired troops duly assembled that morning, and were encamped on the west bank, Beyer between Neukirchen and Hundheim, and Goeben at Hardheim and Wolferstetten. Flies, however, as seen, had in fact crossed the Tauber east of Hundheim, at Nassig, actually placing his division in a position between the Bavarians and Prince Alexander.[1] These moves would trigger several engagements along the Tauber during the day.

Alexander, himself, had established VIII Corps Headquarters at Gross-Rinderfeld, seven kilometres east of Werbach. He instructed that in the current position along the Tauber, the 1st (Württemberg) Division was designated as the advance guard, with the 2nd and 4th Divisions as the main body, and the 3rd acting as the Reserve.[2] 2nd (Baden) Division had bivouacked around Werbachhausen and Brunnthal, and deployed two companies in Hochhausen, on the west bank of the Tauber. On the east bank, in Werbach, stood two battalions and a battery. The bridge there had been barricaded.

Across the river, at 10:00, Manteuffel's morning march orders came into effect. Flies was on the heights of Nassig. Beyer's main force was at Neunkirchen, with his advance guard at Hundheim, while Goeben was on the road south of Külsheim, with a detachment moving along the Hardheim-Tauberbischofsheim road. This force was commanded by Colonel von der Goltz. Conversely, a Württemberg force, two squadrons of the 2nd Mounted Regiment, led by the regiment's commander, Colonel von Gudelen, moved west from Tauberbischofsheim, to reconnoitre in the vicinity of the same village.

The leading Prussian elements, a hussar squadron, closely followed by 2 and 3/IR 15, led by Premier-Lieutenant von der Busche soon contacted the on-coming Württemberg horsemen. These probes collided at about 14:00. Colonel von Gudelen's cavalry were roughly handled, and quickly withdrew to the Tauber, with a loss of one officer and 20 men, along with 12 horses.[3]

---

1   Manteuffel confirmed this position in his orders for the 24th, Kunz, p.155.
2   *Feldzugs-Journal*, p.20.
3   Baur-Breitenfeld, pp.84-85 & Kunz, p.157. The Württemberg account reports being repulsed by rifle salvoes.

Action of Tauberbischofsheim

The most serious action of the day took place in and around the picturesque town of Tauberbischofsheim itself, Goeben's primary objective. It would see a sharp struggle.

Brigade Wrangel, minus a detachment, moved on Tauberbischofsheim itself, directly from the west. Baron von der Goltz's detached force, consisted of two of his own battalions, I/IR 15, Captain Hattorf, and F/IR15, Lieutenant-Colonel Königl, three squadrons of the 8th Hussars, Major von Krug, and two guns. Goltz's task was to cover Wrangel's left flank. In all, Wrangel approached the town with five battalions, three squadrons, and two batteries, not including Goltz's troops.[4] The fiery General approached Tauberbischofsheim in full expectation of attacking it, seemingly regardless of the strength of the opposing force.[5]

Sir Alexander Malet gives an excellent contemporary description of this important crossing point on the Tauber:

> Bischofsheim is a town of 3,000 inhabitants, built in the narrow valley of the Tauber, and was formerly fortified, but the ancient walls and ditch have been converted into gardens and public walks. The railway from Heidelberg to Wurzburg (passes by the town on an embankment some 30 feet (9.1 metres) in height, and the Tauber, the bed of which has been artificially corrected and embanked, is crossed by a wooden bridge on piles of masonry about 75 yards (68.1 metres) long. The stream is barely 50 feet (15.24 metres) broad, and unless in time of flood, fordable everywhere, but on account of its high rough-stone-faced banks, is not easily traversed, even by infantry. The valley is about 400 yards (365 metres) in its mean breadth. The very steep hills on either side rise fully 300 feet (91 metres), being exceedingly abrupt on the left bank, but rather less so on the right, where they are covered with vineyards, and are cut in twain on that side by a brook called the Brehmback.
>
> The town therefore forms a defensible tête-de-pont, and the troops who hold it, protected by artillery, advantageously posted on the left bank of the Tauber, and being well covered by the railroad embankment, and by the position of the buildings and enclosures on that side of the stream, have a remarkably strong position.[6]

There was, however, an aspect to the position which Malet, the diplomat, had not noticed. It was not, though, to be overlooked by the advancing Prussians.

In anticipation of a likely Prussian against the line of the Tauber, the Württemberg Division began its deployment very early, on the 24th. Around 02:30, elements of Major-General von Fischer's 2nd Brigade were already on the march towards their designated positions along the Tauber.[7]

Von Fischer's brigade first moved to occupy positions in Tauberbischofsheim, and also the crossing at Impfingen, to the north. By around 10:00, the General stood in the town,

---

4   Kunz, p.159.
5   Note also that two Prussian companies, 6 & 7/IR 15, were detached along the west bank of the Tauber, as a link to the units further north.
6   Malet, pp.311-312.
7   Menzel, p.110.

Supplies of cartridges are carried across to IR 15 during the action at
Tauberbischofsheim. (Cohn)

with two battalions, two guns, and a squadron. The rest of the brigade, three battalions, one squadron, and four more guns of the artillery battery of Captain Roschmann, commanded by Colonel Baron von Hügel, had then also marched north to Impfingen, a river crossing roughly half-way between Tauberbischofsheim and Hochausen with his own 7th Infantry Regiment, the 2nd Jäger Battalion, one battery, and one squadron, and also occupied it.[8]

On the west bank of the Tauber, on the road south from Tauberbischofsheim to Dittigheim, stood two guns of the 6th Foot Battery, Captain Acker, along with a squadron of the 1st Mounted Regiment, Captain Mühlen, to work from here against any approach on the town from the south.

In Tauberbischofsheim itself, General von Fischer occupied the western heights of the town, the two battalions of Colonel Glaser's 2nd Infantry Regiment occupying positions largely along the three-metre high railway embankment, and the two cemeteries (The 'Old' and 'New'). Unfortunately, these positions were themselves dominated by the heights to the west of the town, the Imberg, from which direction any Prussian attack would come. Three companies of II/2nd were placed in reserve. 6/2nd, Captain von Baldinger, was deployed in open order along the river, and near the bridge. To Baldinger's left, stood Captain Weissenstein's 7/2nd, itself then linking to 8/2nd, Captain von Schröder.

---

8   Marx, p.66.

Further to the rear, the 3rd Württemberg Brigade, Major-General Hegelmaier, was posted east of the town, near the Lorenz Chapel, while the 1st, Major-General Baumbach, along with the rest of the cavalry, were stationed to the northeast, along the principal road to Gerchsheim and Würzburg. Two rifled six pounder batteries (16 guns), those of Captains von Faber (7th Battery) and Marchthaler (Horse Artillery), were positioned on the Hammberg, covering the north of the town. Again, however, this position was also dominated by the Imberg, across the river.[9]

Advanced Prussian elements were first reported on the heights west of the Tauber at around 11:30. Near mid-day, a strong enemy column coming from the direction of Impfingen was observed, which moved out of the Külsheim Woods. A part of this force was then reported to have advanced towards Hochhausen, and the rest against Bischofsheim.[10]

Around 14:00, the first cannon fire boomed over Bischofsheim, fired by the Prussian four pounder battery of Captain Coester (five guns), emplaced across the valley, on the Imberg. A little earlier, the sound of artillery fire had also been heard from the north. Coester's guns, though, were covering the advance of the infantry below.[11]

Following the bombardment, elements of 5/IR15, Premier-Lieutenant Bene, advanced in open order, into the western outskirts of the town, followed by the company columns of I/IR55, Lieutenant-Colonel Boecking, supported by the Lippe Battalion. Before this advance, the defenders gave ground, and the units of 2nd Regiment on the west bank then pulled back across the bridge, to the east bank of the Tauber, but leaving a number of men behind.[12] The main body of the regiment subsequently withdrew to the east, two companies initially remaining on the eastern edge of the town. By around 14:30, almost all of Tauberbischofsheim was already in Prussian hands.

The retreating troops of Colonel Glaser then had the misfortune to encounter a Württemberg supply column, of some 30 wagons, moving east, slowly ascending a particularly steep section of the road to Würzburg. This column attracted heavy Prussian fire, killing and wounding many horses, and understandably, causing the drivers to flee. This obstacle remained a difficult problem for the Württembergers for the duration of the action.[13]

In the meanwhile, Württemberg reinforcements from Major-General Baumbach's 1st Infantry Brigade hurried towards the town. First to arrive were II/5th Regiment, Major Schmalenberger. The Major ordered an immediate attack, with the battalion advancing with the first three companies in open order. The advance was brought to a halt by heavy rifle fire, on the heights of the Rector's Chapel (a height of 63 metres). The Württembergers' attack having stalled, they began to return fire.

---

9   Prussian sources make reference to 18 enemy guns at this point – as noted here, two of these were two kilometres south of town, near Dittigheim.

10 Baur-Breitenfeld, p.85.

11 At this point, only three of Coester's five guns were present with Wrangel's main body, along with three guns of Captain Eynatten II's twelve pounder battery (of six) – Lettow-Vorbeck, Vol. III, p.296. The remaining guns of both batteries subsequently appeared.

12 Lettow-Vorbeck, Vol. III, pp.299-300, G.G.S., p.645 & Krieg, pp.89-90.

13 Menzel, p.114, G.G.S., p.646 & Malet, p.313. Ö.K., Vol. V, (Westdeutschland) p.138, gives the number of vehicles as 40. The entire provisions train eventually fell into Prussian hands.

Württemberg artillery at Tauberbischofsheim. (*Illustrirte Kriegs-Chronik*)

Following Schmalenberger came I/5th, Lieutenant-Colonel Knölzer, moving on his subordinate's right. This advance also met heavy small arms fire, and was brought to a halt on the heights. Knölzer, too, then became involved in a firefight, at a range of some 400 paces, but could also make no progress, subsequently falling back.[14]

Although the Prussian infantry were confidently holding their ground, their artillery colleagues were having a difficult time. One of the two supporting batteries, that of Captain Eynatten II, was forced to withdraw from the action. Eynatten's twelve pounder smoothbores were simply targets at the ranges now involved. This left Coester's four pounder battery, which now had a gun dismounted, duelling with a much superior force.[15]

Across the river, General Hardegg also would not admit defeat. At about 15:00, a further assault was initiated by the Württembergers, against the bridge. Led by Major Starkloff, four companies of his 3rd Jäger Battalion launched a further assault, with four companies forward, and the fifth following on. The first half-platoons of the first line companies were deployed as skirmishers.[16] In a gallant effort, the Jäger approached to some 200 paces of the bridge, but the murderous defensive fire halted any further progress.

This effort, as with earlier assaults, attained the heights of the Rector's Chapel, but also broke down there, and becoming mixed with men from earlier moves. These attacks

---

14   Kunz, p.161.

15   This setback caused Coester, at roughly16:30, to pull back briefly, to re-organise before resuming fire, G.G.S., p.649.

16   The remaining company was temporarily detached.

were also unfortunate to have to also face the fresh, just committed III/IR55, led forward by the regiment's commander, Colonel Stoltz. The firefight on and around the heights continued. During these assaults, the commander of the Württemberg Third Brigade, Major-General Hegelmaier, had his horse shot from under him, and was also himself wounded.[17]

After these failures, some time around 16:00, the Württemberg I/8th Infantry, Captain Löffler, also launched an attack, with one company moving ahead of the other four as skirmishers for the main body. Though equally courageous, it was no more successful.

During the period that Captain Coester's Prussian four pounder battery had been out of action, the two Württemberg batteries had used the opportunity to close the range, and, for the first time, also to bombard the town itself.[18]

> For the fourth time, the Württemberg commander, General von Hardegg, had sent his attack columns of the 1st and 3rd Brigades of the Württemberg Division forward towards the Tauber, but again without success. Now he was giving up his assault on the bridge and town, but concentrated his entire artillery fire at the bridge as well as the buildings, behind which he was suspecting our columns, hardly had there been an open peaceful and friendly town that had been subject of such a rain of shells. Not even the white flags were spared, the sign for the field hospitals, where friend and foe were treated, everywhere balls and shells went screaming, spreading damage and fear and destroying the property of the frightened citizens.[19]

Reports of the fighting at Tauberbischofsheim from General Hardegg had first reached VIII Corps headquarters, at Gross-Rinderfeld at around 15:00, whereupon Prince Alexander himself immediately left headquarters, riding towards the Tauber.[20] Only now, he found that he was threatened not only at Tauberbischofsheim, but also at Wehrbach-Hochhausen, to the north, and between the two, at Impfingen, as well. He then began to bring forward his Reserve Artillery initially ordering two batteries forward, these subsequently being followed, less than hour later, by the main force.

Also, upon receipt of this information, a junior VIII Corps staff Hessian officer, Oberlieutenant Balser, was despatched to 2nd Division, then deployed to the north around Werbach. Balser was charged by the Corps Chief of Staff, Lieutenant-General Baur-Breitenfeld, to ascertain the situation with the Badeners, particularly in the holding of Werbach itself, and report back. Both Prince Alexander and the Chief of Staff were nervous as to the vulnerability of the right flank, and the consequent link with the Bavarians.[21]

---

17 Baur-Breitenfeld, p.88.

18 Lecomte, p.281-2, considers that this was the moment for an assault on the town, but as seen, no readily available formations were fit to do so. He also opines that the Württembergers feared a Prussian breakout.

19 Hoffmann, p.91.

20 *Feldzugs-Journal*, p 20 & Lettow-Vorbeck, p.301. G.G.S., p.649, though, times this an hour earlier!

21 Bleibtreu, p.141 & Lettow-Vorbeck, Vol. III, p.301.

Back in Tauberbischofsheim, gallantly try as they might to storm the bridge, all was to no avail. The Prussian 'rapid fire' rendered every effort a failure. II/1st, Major Gottschall, did no better in yet another supporting attack, just as was an attempt to storm the gardens on the east bank of the Tauber.[22] Nevertheless, the situation was uncertain. Determined Württemberg attacks had been repulsed, and the town securely occupied. On the other hand, the enemy was still present in force, and with growing artillery superiority.

Some two kilometres south of the town, there had also been Prussian moves. Here, on the road to Dittigheim, local initiatives took place. The approach of Prussian infantry along the river south of Tauberbischofsheim forced the withdrawal of the Württemberg artillery and cavalry posted in the area, and pushed back the infantry on hand:

> The infantry fire died down as the enemy had withdrawn his skirmishers from the heights opposite. Thus, a couple of companies had advanced on the far side of the river, crossing the bridge as well as wading through the (there) three-foot deep river upstream. Amongst these were the 1st and 2nd platoons of the 5th Company, under Premier-Lieutenant Bene, who took position on the road to Dittigheim, and from there exchanging a light fire with the enemy.[23]

Subsequently, by around 17:00, the Prussian troops south of town were able to push on, establishing a foot-hold in the Lorenz Chapel. The position was precariously held, however, as the ammunition supply at this point was largely dependent on men swimming or wading through the river to replenish it. This local situation existed, of course, within a general immediate shortage.[24]

Near 17:00, too, the Reserve Hessian Horse Artillery Battery, Captain von Lynker arrived, to be placed in support of the Württemberg infantry. Close behind von Lynker came the Baden battery of Captain Ehelius, for which there was currently no position available in the line, a situation also applying to the other batteries of the Artillery Reserve piling up behind them. At one point, up to 40 Federal guns were engaged here. During the cannonade, the four smoothbore six pounders of von Lyncker's battery were withdrawn from the line, by reason of their short range.[25]

Sometime near this point in time, Oberlieutenant Balser also returned from his ride to the 2nd Division, and reported that he had met Prince Wilhelm between Werbach and Werbachhausen, after a lengthy search, and also after the first-named place (Werbach) had already been evacuated by the Badeners, and the garrison had been on the march back. When Prince Wilhelm received Alexander's order, he replied that in order to execute it, Werbach would have to be retaken, which would only be possible with heavy losses, but that he would try it in any case. Balser had duly undertaken to report this.[26]

---

22 Kunz, p.162, Baur-Breitenfeld, p.88-89 & Lettow-Vorbeck, Vol. III, p.300. Also mentioned in Krieg, p.92. Kunz also offers the view that I/3rd Regiment was less aggressive than other Württemberg units here.

23 Hoffmann, p.92 & Knorr, Vol. III, p.99.

24 G.G.S., p.649.

25 Lettow-Vorbeck, p.320. Kunz, p.164 & G.G.S., p.650.

26 Ibid, pp.302-303. No attempt to retake Werbach was, in fact, actually made.

Subsequently, at about 18:00, Prince Alexander having by now received definitive word that the Baden Division had, indeed, abandoned Werbach, he ordered that the Württembergers be withdrawn, to be replaced by the 4th (Austrian-Nassau) Division, prior to a pull-back.[27] This process then took place, though not without confusion, some elements of both divisions becoming entangled with one another, but with the early stages still being covered by the powerful Federal artillery. By 19:00, most units were on their way to the east, towards Gross-Rinderfeld, on the main road to Würzburg.[28]

The initial phase of the withdrawal was in places far from orderly, with many retreating groups containing men from different units, causing varying degrees of confusion and understandable lack of apparent purpose or control. Certainly, it was fortunate that there was no pursuit. Equally, though, just prior to the Federal retreat from Tauberbischofsheim, General Wrangel had committed his own last reserve, the Lippe Battalion. It is most unlikely that any advance was on his mind!

In fact, it had never been Goeben's intention to advance beyond the Tauber, on the 24th. Rather he set out to secure crossing points over the Tauber for the army. This, he had certainly achieved. At the same time, the Württembergers had also received a bloody nose.

Casualties[29]

	Prussian		Württemberg		Other	
	Officers	Men	Officers	Men	Officers	Men
Killed	–	16	6	55	–	1
Wounded	10	97	20	433	–	2
Missing/prisoners	–	3	2	176	–	1
Totals	10	116	28	664	–	4

Encounter at Impfingen

As noted, at Impfingen, north of Tauberbischofsheim, by 10:00 that morning, stood Württemberg General Fischer, with three battalions, one squadron, and the artillery battery of Captain Roschmann (six guns). As a result of the morning's general orders, the Württemberg Colonel, Baron von Hügel, had then marched to Impfingen, a river crossing roughly half-way between Tauberbischofsheim and Hochausen, with his own 7th Infantry Regiment, the 2nd Jäger Battalion, one battery, and one squadron, and occupied it. Accordingly, the Colonel deployed his men thus: I/7th Regiment, in and around the village itself, and II/7th mainly to the north-west, with 8th and 10th

---

27 Kunz, p.167 & Biebrach, p.67.
28 Ö.K., p.140. Some formations detoured via Impfingen.
29 These figures from Baur-Breitenfeld, p.94. The four 'other' losses are from 4th Division. The total shown here includes losses for Impfingen; for details, see 'Casualties', in 'Action of Hochhausen & Werbach', below.

Companies held in reserve, in the centre of Impfingen The Jäger battalion was assembled east of the village.[30]

Around 13:00, shots were exchanged with troops of Wrangel's flank guard (Half-Battalion Hattorf, 6 & 7 IR15) and hussar patrols, moving along the river, causing a number of casualties on both sides.[31] Around half an hour later, the leading elements of the Hanseatic Brigade, of General Weltzien, appeared on the heights above the Tauber, west of Hochhausen. This column was swiftly engaged by the rifled battery of Captain Roschmann, posted north-east of Impfingen.

Equally rapidly, Weltzien deployed his own artillery, the Oldenburg rifled six pounder battery, Captain Nieber. From his superior position on the heights, Nieber was able, after a short time, to dominate the exchange, and by 14:00, had forced Roschmann to withdraw. Around this time, too, Weltzien's second battery, the Oldenburg twelve pounder smoothbore battery, Captain Baumbach, was able to come up on Nieber's left.[32] Both batteries would presently be engaged against a brigade of the Baden Division of VIII Corps.

The immediate area around Impfingen now fell quiet, as the centre of action switched to the north.

Action of Hochhausen and Werbach

North of Impfingen, at Werbach and Hochhausen, two additional river crossings were to be defended by troops of the Baden Division. Prince Wilhelm had, at about Noon, on the 24th, arrived along the Tauber from Külsheim. Upon reaching the river here, he occupied the area around the crossing, as ordered, though in a somewhat haphazard manner, especially considering he was covering the corps' right flank.

In the lead was Colonel Neubronn's Second Brigade. The village of Hochhausen, on the west bank of the Tauber, was occupied by two companies of 2nd Infantry Regiment. 7/3rd Company Captain Enderlin, was posted in the west of the village, and 8/3rd, Captain von Gemmingen to the south, between the railway and the village. Across the river stood the other six companies of Colonel von Billiez' 3rd Infantry Regiment, the six rifled six pounders of Battery Hoffmann, and one squadron. The remainder of 2nd Brigade was posted, as noted, across the river in Werbach, with 1st Brigade remaining in Brunnthal.[33]

The bridge across the deep railway cutting there was pulled down, and replaced by a smaller one, suitable only for foot-soldiers. Colonel Billiez's 3rd Infantry Regiment was posted in Werbach. The remaining two companies of 2nd Regiment, along with the main body of Second Brigade (10 companies, one battery, and eight squadrons) stood in reserve in Werbachhausen. First Brigade, Major-General Laroche, and one battery were, at this point, still encamped at Brunnthal, some four and a half kilometres to the east.[34]

---

30 Marx, pp.66 & 67.
31 Knorr, pp.117-8 & Krieg, p.93.
32 Knorr, p.122 & G.G.S., p.653. Marx, p.67 says that this was achieved after about 15 rounds.
33 Becker, p.113.
34 Lettow-Vorbeck, pp.305-6 & G.G.S., p.653. 1st Baden Brigade was not engaged on the 24th, *Zu Beurtheilung*, p.32.

After the silencing of the Württemberg guns near Impfingen, as discussed, the commander of the Hanseatic Brigade, General von Weltzien, opened the action here with the fire of both of his batteries, placed on the west bank of the Tauber. Captain Nieber's rifled four pounder battery stood south of Hochhausen, with the smoothbore twelve pounder battery, Captain Baumbach, to the north. Both batteries presently directed their fire against Baden columns, which were advancing along the road from Werbachhausen, though with little discernible effect.

Two Baden batteries were then pushed forward to counter Weltzien's artillery, the rifled six pounder batteries of Captains Dienger and Hoffmann (six guns each). These were positioned near Werbach Cemetery, and opened fire. A short engagement then occurred, during which one Baden gun was dismounted, and one man killed, along with four horses. This precipitated a rapid withdrawal of the Baden guns.[35]

During this artillery exchange, General Weltzien took advantage of the cover offered by the extensive woods to deploy his infantry on the heights. II/ Oldenburg Battalion, Lieutenant-Colonel Lamping, was placed in the centre, opposite Werbach. On the left, stood the Bremen Fusilier Battalion, Lieutenant-Colonel Niebour, and on the right, I/Oldenburg Battalion, Colonel Beaulieu-Marconnay, stood directly opposite Hochhausen. III/Oldenburg Battalion, Lieutenant-Colonel Kellner, was held in reserve.

The Hanseatic infantry, having formed up in company columns, at about 15:00, the three assault battalions advanced to the attack. The advance was somewhat hindered both by the steep descent and the railway cutting. They were also, though, peripherally supported by a company of the FR/70, detached from Beyer's division.

The Badeners were quick to evacuate Hochhausen, but the struggle was more intense around Werbach, where the barricaded bridge over the Tauber downstream from Werbach was attacked by the Bremen Battalion. It was this crossing which decided the outcome of the engagement. Attacked from three sides, the town was soon in 'Prussian' hands.

The Baden troops which had defended the two villages then withdrew along the Welsbach Valley towards Welsbachhausen, still under fire from the Oldenburg artillery, which by then had been brought up to the east bank of the Tauber.[36] The Baden Division subsequently retreated to Unter-Alteraltheim, north of Gross-Rinderfeld.[37]

In an odd postscript to these actions, at about the time that firing died down around Werbach, the Württemberg battery of Captain Roschmann, near Impfingen, reopened fire on Hochhausen from a fresh position, causing a fire. Two fresh Prussian batteries, Six Pounder Battery Wasserfuhr, and Four Pounder Battery Schmidts (both units of Division Beyer) then silenced Roschmann once more. The Württemberg units still in this area also subsequently withdrew to the east, from around 19:00 onwards.

---

35 *Zur Beurtheilung*, p.29 & Knorr 126. The former says five horses.
36 Rüstow, pp.328-329.
37 Kunz, p.171. Two Baden ambulances were also abandoned.

Casualties

	Prussian		Baden	
	Officers	Men	Officers	Men
Killed	2	10	1	6
Wounded	5	54	1	59
Missing/prisoners	–	–	–	16
Totals	7	64	2	81

As noted, the losses of the Württemberg troops around Impfingen are generally given as three killed and 18 wounded, and added to the general total for Tauberbischofsheim, as here.[38] Marx gives the loss of 7th Württemberg Regiment here as six killed or died of wounds, and eight wounded, leaving a further seven from other units, including Roschmann's battery.[39]

That evening, Division Goeben occupied the immediate vicinity of Tauberbischofsheim, while Beyer's troops halted in and around Hochhausen, Werbach, and Impfingen. Flies' division was assembled in the area about Wertheim. The Army of the Main had once again forced a defended river line. Far from running out of steam, however, the Prussian offensive was set to continue, with the city of Würzburg, on the east bank of the River Main, as its next objective.

Tauberbischofsheim – Postscript: Lieutenant Balser's Ride to the Baden Division

If any event encapsulates the perhaps unavoidable confused state of VIII Corps' communications on July 24, it is the episode of the Hessian Staff Officer, Oberlieutenant Balser.

The conversation of Lieutenant Balser, in his report of 21/01/1867, to Prince Alexander, that his message was actually delivered at 16:30, is incorrect, since the 'Prussian' attack on Werbach itself only came at 16:00. The meeting with the Baden divisional commander, Prince Wilhelm can, therefore, only have taken place at 16.45, at the very earliest.

The ride itself, via Brunnthal and Gross Rinderfeld (11 kilometres) must have taken longer than one hour, because as far as Brunnthal, Balser was forced to pass the retreating columns of (Baden) troops at a walk. On the outward run he must have fared similarly, because from Brunnthal to Werbachhausen he must have met the advancing troops of 2nd Baden Brigade, and he actually met Prince Wilhelm on the side of the road, only after he had already come close to Werbach and then turned about. He can hardly have received his task from General Baur-Breitenfeld before 15:15.[40] In any case, the mission achieved nothing.

---

38   G.G.S., p.652.
39   Marx, pp.68-69.
40   Lettow-Vorbeck, p.302.

Manteuffel marches on Würzburg

Despite many platitudes, there had still been precious little real cooperation between the two Federal Corps', as the actions along the Tauber had again shown. Decisive action by the Army of the Main, however, had once more brought its own rewards. With the main force of both sides now in close proximity, it remained to see whether or not this situation would alter. On the morning of July 25, the dispositions of the opposing were:

Prussian movements

As seen, Division Flies had crossed the Tauber the previous afternoon and evening, and now had its pickets pushed well forward, reaching Werbachhausen, some 15 kilometres north of Tauberbischofsheim.On the morning of the 25th, Goeben's Division remained in and around Tauberbiscofsheim, with Beyer at Urphar, eight kilometres east of Helmstadt.[41]

At around 09:30 on the 25th, Prussian Army Orders for the day were issued by General Manteuffel. These specified that Division Beyer was to break camp at 10:00, and then march via Hochhausen, Werbach, and Böttigheim, to Neubrunn. A detachment was also to proceed through Wehrbachhausen in the direction of Welzbach-Thale.At 12:30, Division Goeben was to move along the main road through Gross-Rinderfeld to Gerchsheim. Division Flies was initially to proceed only to Dertingen, east of Helmstadt.

Federal movements

VII Corps

Early on the morning of the 25th, Prince Karl received the news of the previous day's actions along the Tauber, and the consequent withdrawal of VIII Corps. This determined him to continue the concentration of his own forces. Prince Luitpold's 3rd Division was moved further west, with instructions to scout the area between Neubrunn and Kembach, to the south-west of Helmstadt. In the meanwhile, the Reserve Infantry Brigade, and part of the Reserve Cavalry were to join the 2nd Division (Feder) at Rossbrunn. 1st Division (Stephan) was to move to Unter-Alterheim, probing to the west, and 4th Division (Hartmann), for the moment, to remain near Würzburg.

VIII Corps

On the morning of the 24th, Prince Karl had informed his counterpart that he was moving his own headquarters further west to Remlingen, a village some eight kilometres north of Helmstadt, and that he would be concentrating his forces in the area between there and Rossbrunn. From Remlingham, the next morning, he had sent instructions to VIII Corps that both Corps should make a joint advance against the Tauber. The orders for this probably already unrealistic plan were then badly delayed. Major Massenbach,

---

41 Manteuffel had originally intended to turn VIII Corps' flank to the north. He did not expect a fight over Tauberbischofsheim.

of Prince Karl's staff, was unable to find Alexander until about Noon. By this time, his force was already withdrawing towards Gerchsheim, about 15 kilometres north-east of Tauberbischofsheim, where it would re-group.[42]

Early on the 25th, Beyer's division was given the order "…to, as early as possible, hold itself ready to repel a counterattack against the positions which it had gained." At this point, the main body, the reserve artillery, and the cavalry of the division were in a state of readiness on the high plateau on this side of Hochhausen, and above Impfingen. The advance guard and infantry reserve held the Tauber villages of Werbach, Hochhausen, and Impfingen, and their advance posts had reported the enemy's forward positions in front of Groß Rinderfeld and Wenkheim (at distances of from some 4 to 5.5 kilometres). As an enemy attack seemed unlikely, the troops were allowed to brew coffee.[43]

At 10:00, orders came from General Manteuffel, still in Bischofsheim, that the division was to advance towards Neubrunn and, from there, if the report of the enemy occupation of Steinbach and Alterheim in the Welz Valley was true, to attack these positions in the flank. Should this not be the case, it was to advance to Helmstadt. A detachment was also to be sent ahead into the Welz Valley, as a right flank guard.[44]

Consequently, Beyer ordered the following movements of the division:

A.   The main body, Major-General von Glümer, IR/20, Major Baron von Hertzberg (acting), IR/32, Lieutenant-Colonel von der Lundt, 2/9th Hussars, Captain von Rommel, Twelve Pounder Battery Richter, & Six Pounder Battery Wasserfur (six battalions, one squadron, & two batteries) was to proceed via Werbach and Niclashausen, towards Neubrunn.

B.   The Advance Guard, Colonel von Woyna I, II/IR30, Major von Mützschefal, F/IR70, Major de L'Espinol, 5/9th Hussars, Captain von Böttiger, and Four Pounder Battery Schmidts (two battalions, one squadron, one battery) proceeded from Werbach via Böttingheim also against Neubrunn.

C.   F/IR 30, Major von Frankenberg-Ludwigsdorff, along with 4/9th Hussars, went as the right flank guard through the Welz Valley up to Ober-Alterheim and then, when no enemy was found, from there to Helmstadt.

D.   I/IR 30 (Major von Griesheim) were to occupy Hochhausen and Werbach as the support for the detachment v. Frankenberg

E.   The 3rd and 4th squadrons of the 10th Landwehr Hussars (Major von Kuylenstjerna) proceeded as the connection between the main column (A) and the right flank guard (C) from Werbach directly over the heights against Neubrunn.

---

42   *Feldzugs-Journal*, pp.23-26, *Antheil*, p.160 & G.G.S., pp.658-660, Malet, p.333. Two very similar orders to VIII Corps appear to have been sent.

43   Scherff, p.93.

44   Ibid., pp.93-94.

Action of Helmstadt-Uettingen, July 25

As the Division was under march, at 11:00, in the directions ordered – General von Beyer led the column towards Böttingheim. No enemy interference was expected, since the Bavarians were thought to be further north, as indicated by Flies' presence. As the marching columns passed through Werbach, a high-ranking Baden officer was encountered, who had been sent as an emissary. The officer was doubtless directed to the appropriate authority.

The area around Helmstadt at that time is well described in a Bavarian regimental history:

> The terrain around Helmstadt, and forward up to Neubrunn and Holzkirchhausen, is hilly with slopes that are gentle towards the west, and steep towards the east, which are sometimes cultvated with wine but mostly with grain. These heights are covered by deciduous and spruce forest, afford a good view, and are well suited for defensive positions – towards Waldbrunn the terrain is gently rising up to the so called Helmstadter Hill.
>
> Helmstadt, an open place of 215 lightly built houses with 1,170 inhabitants, is situated in a flat depression stretching from west to east, and is dominated by the surrounding heights, and therefore not suited for defence.
>
> From there extend:
> to the north a good road towards Uettingen
> to the east a trail to Waldbrunn
> to the south a road to Ober- and Unteralterheim
> to the southwest across the heights an excellent district road to Neubrunn,
> and to the west a road to Holzkirchhausen
>
> The bottom of the valley is watered by the Holzkirchhausen stream which, from the military point of view, is completely unimportant.
>
> Holzkirchhausen is close to 45 minutes and Neubrunn, and one hour distant from Helmstadt …[45]

As Captain Boetticher's Prussian hussars approached the village of Böttigheim, they encountered Bavarian chevauleger pickets. The latter quickly pulled back, but not before two of their number were taken prisoner.[46] Beyer's two primary columns approached Neubrunn at almost the same time, about 13:30. The Bavarian commander here, Colonel Fink, presumably considering the position indefensible in the circumstances, withdrew three of the four companies present, leaving one, 1/15th Regiment, to slow the advance as far as possible. The company found

---

45 *Geschichte des Königlich bayerischen 15. Infanterie-Regiments*, p.45.
46 Biebrach, p.82. Other sources make no mention of captives.

itself split by the attack, the two segments joining the units on either side.[47] The position was also subjected to a brief bombardment from the two Prussian batteries, causing a withdrawal to two small hills to the north-east, the Amiesenberg on the (Prussian) left and the more wooded Forstgrund, on the right.

Due to the volume of fire coming from a height known as the Sesselberg, about a kilometre south-west of Helmstadt, General Glümer then sent Baron von Hertzberg's IR 20 to take the feature. This was duly accomplished, but the action also caused a Bavarian battery, placed on a hill east of Helmstadt, to open fire. In reply to this, Prussian Battery Wasserfuhr, near Neubrunn, also became engaged.[48]

The other Bavarian troops in the immediate vicinity of the attack, drawn from First and Second Brigades, were deployed thus:

> Holzkirchhausen (two kilometres east of Helmstadt) – Lieutenant-Colonel Höggenstaller, with II/Leib Regiment, Major Dörmühl, II and III/8th Regiment, Captain Count Tattenbach and Major Ritter von Reichert, respectively.

> Wüstenzell (a little over two kilometres south-west of Holzkirchen) – Colonel Dietl, with II & III/2nd Regiment, Majors Duntze and Murmann. From there, the Colonel proceeded to extend his left to remain in contact with Höggenstaller.

Also on the march from Helmstadt to Holzkirchhausen, under Major-General von Welsch, were 4th Jäger Battalion, Major Hebberling, a half squadron, and four guns.[49]

Welsch's column reached Holzkirchhausen, three and a half kilometres south-west of Uettingen, at around 13:00, the General then taking command from Höggenstaller. He immediately posted the Jäger Battalion in a wood south of the village. As he moved to consolidate his position, however, he received a delayed, relayed message from the Divisional Commander, Major-General Stephan, who ordered an immediate withdrawal to Helmstadt. Welsch quickly moved to comply.[50]

Stephan, then in Uettingen, and at this point himself also in the midst of conflicting instructions, had decided that he would concentrate his Division between Holzkirchausen and Helmstadt. By 14:00, his column was nearing Helmstadt, skirmishing on the left flank along the way, only to find it to be already occupied by Prussians. The whole Division was forced to detour to the north, via Holzkirchen.

Assault on the Lerchenberg

While one of General Glümer's regiments had been engaged on the Sesselberg, the other, Lieutenant-Colonel von der Lundt's IR 32, had remained in reserve. For a short time, firing had largely ceased, with some on both sides wondering whether the action had actually petered out. With the resumption of Bavarian artillery fire, though, the battle

---

47   *Geschichte des Königlich bayerischen 15. Infanterie-Regiments*, p.48.
48   Lettow-Vorbeck, p.329.
49   This latter move was made at the behest of Prince Luitpold, *Antheil*, p.162.
50   *Antheil*, p.164.

resumed in earnest. Units of Prince Luitpold's 3rd Division were to be the next Prussian targets.

Near 14:00, von der Lundt's regiment was sent forward, deployed in company columns. I/IR 32, Lieutenant-Colonel von Donat, and II/IR32, Captain Redies, formed the first line, and F/IR 32, Lieutenant-Colonel Wülcknitz, the second. The Regiment was to advance against the Lerchenberg (Lark Hill), on the Bavarian left, supported by the fire of the twelve pounder smoothbore battery of Captain Richter.

On the Bavarian side, the rifled battery of 1st Division withdrew towards Uettingen as it had no covering infantry, and so the artillery of the 3rd Division had to make do with their own forces. Arriving partly from the Sesselberg, north-east of Neubrunn, came I/8th Regiment, Major Lachemair, and half battalions of I/15 and II/15 from 1st Division, which took position on the right wing of 3rd Division.

The first push of the Prussians was not long delayed. It struck the 6th Brigade of Colonel Schweizer forcefully, rapidly scattering the two battalions of 6th Regiment; these, in turn disordered and scattered Major Göriz's 1st Jäger Battalion, rendering all three units 'hors de combat' in the heavily forested terrain. Prince Luitpold now called forward two fresh battalions II/14th Regiment, Major Dichtel, and III/15th, Major Pöllath.

Prussian infantry advance during the actions at Helmstadt-Uettingen. (Cohn)

This attempt fared little better, with these units soon also losing all cohesion and control. Yet another battalion, III/11th, Major Wernhard, pulled from the right wing, was committed to the combat, making a most gallant assault, though perhaps predictably in the circumstances, again without altering the situation. As the units fell further into confusion, the troops would no longer advance. Prince Luitpold, himself set a noble example, but to no avail. His son was also severely wounded in the upper leg. The claustrophobic struggle here lasted some two hours. The action, however, was very far from an easy for either side. Kunz writes:

> Despite of all this success, the combat of the 32nd Regiment made slow progress. The Prussians had to break tenacious and tough resistance, because the forward Bavarian skirmishers defended themselves bravely.[51]

Prince Luitpold, now with only four and a half effective battalions, supported by two batteries and four squadrons, was in a very difficult position. Efforts to rally the rest of the division were under way, but certainly, no more could be expected that day. I/14th Regiment, Ritter von Täuffenbach, had, and continued to behave in exemplary fashion in covering the retreat, notably on the Zotterain, the highest point of the Lerchenberg.

Having enabled the pull-back of the two artillery batteries, the battalion, near a feature known as the Ziegelhütte, east of Helmstadt, was now forced to form squares at the sudden appearance of Prussian cavalry. In an encounter witnessed by Lieutenant-General Manteuffel, a cavalry action took place. Two distinct clashes took place, the first involving the General's escort, 3/9th Hussars, Rittmeister Klaatsch, after which the sides briefly separated. The second melee saw the intervention of a further Prussian squadron, led by the commander of the Prussian regiment, Major von Cosel. The net result was a repulse for the Bavarian horse, the commander of the 2nd Chevauleger Regiment, Lieutenant-Colonel Horadam, being captured, as were two captains, one being Prince Taxis, and the latter severely wounded.

Major von Täuffenbach was finally able to withdraw his battalion to Waldbrunn, to the north-east, along with two squadrons of the 2nd Chevaulegers. Losses for the Bavarians in this equine affair were five officers and 28 men. The Prussian casualties numbered two officers and 26 men.[52]

At about 17:30, Manteuffel ordered the relief of IR32 by FR39, Colonel von Woyna II, the advance of the former having slowed somewhat.[53] First to move up was III/FR 39, Major Kurth, deployed in company columns, followed by, in the second line, I/FR 39, Major von Cederstolpe, in half-battalions. II/FR 39, Major Kruse, brought up the rear. Richter's twelve pounder battery of the main column had earlier shelled the edge of the Hausacker Woods (north of the Lerchenberg). The four companies of Major Kurth's battalion, joined by elements of all three battalions of IR 32, then threw themselves,

---

51 Kunz, pp.183-184 & *Antheil*, pp.168-169. The latter describes these woods as 'without trails'. Six battalions had temporarily largely disintegrated.
52 *Antheil*, p.169. Casualties taken from Kunz, p.186. He also lists 12 of the Prussians as being lightly wounded.
53 Note that, as a Fusilier Regiment, the 39th had no musketeer battalions.

with a cheer, at the edge of this wood and quickly crowded considerable numbers of their adversaries back, deep into the forest.

From here, I and II/39 were subsequently ordered towards Helmstadt, as were all three battalions of Regiment Nr. 32, once all of these units had re-grouped.

In the meanwhile, Captain Wasserfuhr's rifled six pounder battery of Beyer's 'Main Body' had found itself in a most challenging situation. Positioned on the north-eastern slope of the Mausberg, some two kilometres south-east of Helmstadt, the battery came under a crossfire from 16 Bavarian guns, firing from positions near Uettingen. Subsequently, the rifled Four Pounder Battery Schmidts arrived in support, and then both batteries moved to a more favourable location on the Katzenbuckel, just south of Helmstadt. Somewhat later, these were also joined here by the twelve pounder smooth-bore Battery Hoffbauer, from the Reserve, finally making a total number of 18 Prussian guns here.[54]

Struggle around the Frohnberg

General Stephan, in the face of the Prussian attacks, had by 16:00 concluded that he must pull back to Walldbrunn, along the Würzburg Road, about eight kilometres to the east. The main road was the only route suitable in the circumstances, particularly for wagons and artillery. Before the withdrawal began, though, a fresh battery of the Reserve Artillery, the twelve pounder battery of Captain Otto Schropp, reported directly to Stephan. The General took this as a message that Prince Karl wished that the height of Frohnberg, the only feature of consequence between Uettingen and Helmstadt, to be held.[55]

Earlier, upon learning of the occupation of Helmstadt by the enemy, he had detached the 2nd Jäger Battalion, Major Baron von Treuberg, as a flank guard in that direction. At this time, Stephan also directed that III/Leib Regiment, Major Reuss, a squadron, and two guns, to keep open the route to Dertingen, to the west.

By around 18:00, Stephan had reached and occupied the Frohnberg. Placing Schropp's battery near the road, he positioned II/2nd Regiment (three companies), Major Duntze, to the right, and III/2nd Major Murmann, to the left. The two other battalions present, II/1st, Captain Jouvin, and III/1st, Captain Ritter von Stubenrauch, were placed in a second line.

Shortly after this deployment had been finalised, troops were observed, approaching from the south, through the extensive crops towards the position. These were Prussian troops of IR 30 and IR70, hurriedly diverted by General Beyer to meet this 'new' threat. F/IR 70, Major d'Espinol, and two companies of I/IR70 made their way across from the area near the Ziegelhütte, while, to their left, II/IR 30, Major von Schnehen, with the other two companies of Major Mützschefahl's I/IR70, also moved up in support.

---

54 Kunz, p.185. It will be recalled that Bavarian batteries comprised eight guns.
55 *Antheil*, pp.171-172. This appears to have been Stefan's interpretation.

Further on the Prussian left, IR20, Baron von Hertzberg also moved on the Frohnberg, but from east of Helmstadt, with Major Brüggemann's Fusilier Battalion in the lead. The Major's initial push thrown back, largely due to II and III/7th Regiment, Majors Gambs and Bohe, but the weight of all of these continued assaults was too much, forcing General Stephan to withdraw.[56]

As the combat flared for the Frohnberg, the two detached Bavarian battalions of Treuberg and Reuss had found themselves out on a limb. Encountering one another north of Helmstadt, the joint column then stumbled into the action flaring near Uettingen.

The Leib Regiment history describes the confusion of the situation:

Prussian infantry at Uettingen, drawing by Hoffmann. (Regensberg/*Mainfeldzug*)

The trail led upwards, through dense forest. The forest trail became increasingly narrow. One was forced to march in column of twos. All of a sudden a hailstorm of bullets hit the troops. The Jäger fall back on Uettingen. A loud 'Hurrah' echoes through the woods. Already the Jäger think that they are taken in the rear. The excitement is growing. But then the Leib Regiment appears. From them came the battle cry. There was no hesitation amongst the 'Life Guards'. Immediately after the first shots, our leader ordered "Fix bayonets!", and with a "hurrah" the Leib Regiment came to the rescue of their comrades. Lieutenant-Colonel Höggenstaller is shot through the leg. He is carried from the field by Private Zwenger from the 9th Company. With closed ranks, the companies broke through the superior enemy. At some points small groups are being pushed aside, but they find their way through. Up to Uettingen the Prussians followed, but the battalion was saved from encirclement.[57]

---

56   Ibid., pp.174-175.
57   Illing, pp.55-56.

Stephan withdrew from Uettingen at about 18:00, pulling back just over a kilometre to the east, to a good position with secure flanks. Intermittent skirmishing took place for some time, but firing finally died away by 19:30. Rüstow, somewhat unkindly, comments that, "Both sides fired at and kicked one another for five hours, finally ending up in exactly the same positions that they had occupied at the beginning."[58] At 21:00, the main body of Flies' Division, six battalions, two squadrons, and a battery, commanded by Major-General von Korth, reached the area west of Uettingen and bivouacked there. A detachment occupied the Ober-Mühle to the east of Uettingen. This force had been diverted here directly by General Manteuffel, upon his learning about the fighting around Helmstadt.[59]

That night, the entire Bavarian Army lay tightly bivouacked in the area of Waldhüttelbrunn (1st and 3rd Divisions), the 2nd Division about Mädelhofen, and the 4th, at Rossbrunn. Both the Infantry and Cavalry Reserve were encamped close to Hettstadt, along with the Army Staff. The whole array occupied only some four square kilometres![60]

Just to the south, that same day, the Federal VIII Corps had also been involved in an encounter with the Prussians, in this case, with Division Goeben. The nature of the conflict there, however, was very different.

Casualties

	Prussian		Bavarian	
	Officers	Men	Officers	Men
Killed	1	30	6	37
Wounded	12	273	24	384
Missing/prisoners	–	37	6	273
Totals	13	340	36	694

Engagement of Gerchsheim, July 25

At dawn on the 25th, VIII Corps commenced its planned withdrawal towards Gerchsheim, some 15 kilometres fromTauberbischofsheim, along the Würzburg Road to the north-east. First to move was the Austrian-Nassau (4th) Division, which initially moved as far as Grossrinderfeld, and then on to Gerchsheim. By the afternoon, the Hessian (3rd) Division, and the 2nd Brigade of the Württemberg (1st) Division had joined 4th Division there.[61] The Baden (2nd) Division was posted to the north, at

---

58 Rüstow, p.332.
59 Biebrach, p.82.
60 Klingenstein, p.20.
61 The First and Third Württemberg Brigades were held in reserve, on account of their part in the previous day's action.

Steinbach. The Artillery and Cavalry Reserve were already stationed respectively in Gerchsheim and Kist.

As previously noted, at around 10:00 that morning, a courier from Prince Alexander, Major Massenbach, reached Prince Karl, with details of the previous day's events, and the news that VIII Corps was now making for Gerchsheim. Karl then reiterated his wish that the line of the Tauber was to be held. The Prince of Hesse personally rode to Gerchsheim and here, at Noon, received the order from Prince Karl, which began," The 8th Army Corps will move, with its entire force, to the line of the Tauber …"[62] While on the march, probably around 11:00, Prince Alexander, while with the command of the Baden Division, instructed that that two Baden battalions, one battery, and one squadron, were to be sent to Neubrunn, as a link with the Bavarians.[63] The troops of the Hessian Division were also noted as being tired.

Goeben's Prussian division, also assembled, but in and around Tauberbischofsheim that morning, then commenced its eastward advance, the majority of it also along the main road to Würzburg, at about 13:00. Brigade Kummer composed the advance guard, with Brigade Weltzien the main body, and the reserve, Brigade Treskow. On the right, the detached brigade of General Wrangel would subsequently march via Schönfeld.

Near 16:00, some half an hour's march from Gerchsheim, large numbers of hostile infantry were observed on the heights around that town, supported by powerful artillery. Without hesitation, Goeben then ordered Kummer's brigade to form for action to the left of the road there, in the wooded area midway between Gross-Rinderfeld and Gerchsheim. At the same time, word was despatched to Major-General Wrangel to hurry the pace of his own march, and to proceed to turn the enemy left.

What Goeben had encountered was, in fact, the 4th Division of VIII Corps, with the Austrian Brigade of Hahn on the (Federal) left, with General Roth's Nassauers to their right. These were, as on the previous day, strongly supported by artillery. In addition, further to the rear, and unknown to Goeben, was all of the rest of Prince Alexander's force. Alexander had now resolved to make a stand here, midway between Tauberbischofsheim and Würzburg, a little over 11 kilometres from each, thus allowing him to maintain contact with the Bavarians on his right. At long last, immediate close cooperation between the two Corps' appeared a realistic possibility.

Goeben's original instructions, in fact, were to act in concert with Beyer, but the latter, as seen, had already become entangled with the Bavarians, further north. This minor point, however, would in no way inhibit his perception of his own freedom of action.

At around 16:00, perceiving the possible strength of the hostile force, Goeben instructed Major-General Kummer to deploy his brigade for action in the Hachtel Wood, to the (Prussian) left of the Würzburg Road, while Major-General Wrangel, several hours behind was to be pushed his to the right, via a secondary road through the villages of Ilmspan and Schönfeld. Wrangel's march would be difficult and slow, but vital.

VIII Corps' Chief of Staff, General Baur-Breitenfeld, observed the initial advance of the Prussian left:

---

62   Kunz, p.196. Malet, p.326, places this as about 11 am, while withdrawal already under way. The second document is likely a copy. It is clear that Alexander had no intention of obeying the order.

63   Ö.K., Vol. V, p.144.

At first skirmishers appeared in the Hachtel Woods facing (across to) Schönfeld, and soon a battery deployed and there was also artillery fire at the road. At once, the fire of the batteries of 4th Division commenced. The enemy did not advance, but the intensity of the artillery bombardment still increased. After this, when enemy columns tried to advance on Schönfeld, the Reserve Cavalry as well as the two attached rifled horse batteries von Wagner as well as the rifled Baden foot battery Ehelius of the reserve rained shells upon them so that the fighting here came to a standstill here as well. An ammunition caisson of an Austrian battery blew up and several Prussian guns were put out of action.

This moment was used by the Nassau Brigade to advance on the enemy position, but the closer they came to the woods the more intense became the rapid fire of the enemy, and finally, the battalions were forced to withdraw towards their former position.[64]

To support Kummer's infantry, two Prussian batteries, the six four pounders of Captain Weigelt, and the six six pounders of Captain Eynatten I, were deployed at the edge of Hachtel Wood, to the left of the road. This move had provoked an immediate response from Federal Batteries in front of Gerchsheim. Two Austrian batteries, Four Pounder Battery Klopetz – eight guns, and Eight Pounder Battery Burger – eight guns, initially engaged the Prussians, to then be joined by the two Nassau half-batteries, a total of 24 guns.

As General Baur-Breitenfeld mentioned, units of the Nassau Brigade had advanced, though not to attack, but in an attempt to avoid the galling Prussian fire. This move was later misinterpreted by the Prussian Official History, as Kunz explains:

> If the work of the Prussian General Staff is speaking about an attack of the Nassau Brigade, this is an error. This brigade had intended to get out of the intensive fire of the Prussian cannon firing shrapnel. For this reason, the 1st Nassau Regiment sought cover further forward, while pushing forward their two skirmish companies. The remaining three Nassau battalions sought to find a cover in a position to the rear, in which they succeeded at Gerchsheim.
>
> There can be no discussion about an attack on the woods by the Nassauers, nor of a repulse of any such attack.[65]

In the meanwhile, Kummer's supporting artillery had been targeted by the VIII Corps batteries near Gerchsheim, at ranges mainly between 1,500 and 2,000 metres. This counter-battery fire was not only heavy, but also accurate. After a combat of around 45 minutes, both Prussian batteries were forced to withdraw behind the cover of the woods.

Prince Alexander, who was now only some 15 kilometres fromWürzburg, had moved his headquarters the previous day, and had before Gerchsheim the entire Reserve Artillery available for use against the advancing Prussians. The VIII Corps had some 50

64 Baur-Breitenfeld, p.102.
65 Kunz, p.197-198. See G.G.S., pp.670-671.

guns, against which Kummer's brigade could only bring 12 to begin with. Subsequently, the Oldenburg-Hanseatic brigade (Weltzien) reinforced it with another 12 pieces, to which, finally, were then added a further 12 from Wrangel's brigade which had advanced towards Schönfeld against the left flank of the Confederation forces.

The last-mentioned of these forces, was, by 19:00, finally approaching Schönfeld, from where Wrangel could indeed now threaten that flank. He proceeded to deploy the four pounder battery of Captain Coester in a position on the left of the Federal artillery, swiftly causing these to pull back. This also allowed Kummer's two batteries to re-engage near the Hachtel Wood, joined there by the newly committed Oldenburg Battery. Under the cover of this counter-bombardment, both brigades were able to advance against an increasingly off-balance enemy. In addition, upon the appearance of enemy infantry on his left flank, Prince Alexander had resolved to break off the action. Reports as to the situation of the situation of the Bavarians, to the north, were sketchy.

The operational situation within VIII Corps itself was, however, far from clear. Orders were then issued for a general retreat to Kist, a little under ten kilometres to the north-east, along the Würzburg Road. As Rüstow commented, since the previous day, "An immense, deplorable confusion reigned in the headquarters of Prince Alexander."[66]

The final encounter of the day took place on the Prussian right, in the oncoming darkness in the woods around the Forester's lodge at Irtenberg, along the Würzburg Road, to the northeast of Gerchsheim. As Prussian Colonel von der Goltz led his II and F/IR 15 along the road, his force was suddenly counter-attacked by elements of I/2nd Württemberg Regiment, Major von Hügel, and pushed back along the same road. Darkness, sometime around 21:00, finally halted the fighting here.[67]

Captain Schleussner, commanding the (Hessian) Homburg Jäger Company, described his day in his subsequent report:

> After a very difficult march, in great heat, and without having any food, the company, along with the regiment, arrived in the woods behind Gerchsheim. In a state of exhaustion they deployed on the left wing of the regiment at the edge of the woods. Here they received ineffective enemy artillery fire for some time. Later, as dusk was setting in, the company came under lively small-arms fire on its left flank. Oberlieutenant Schleussner, seeing himself completely flanked, led the company back, covered by a platoon deployed as skirmishers under Lieutenant Rauenfels. Without taking any losses, the company joined II Battalion / 3. Infantry Regiment on the wine road leading through the woods. Unified with this battalion, a further retreat towards Kist was begun.[68]

Division Goeben camped for the night in and around Gerchsheim. There had been no battle there, only a delayed retreat. Kunz commented:

66 Rüstow, p.331.
67 Baur-Breitenfeld, p.306 & Menzel, pp.116-117.
68 Hessian *Antheil*, pp.415-416.

The combat of Gerchsheim demonstrated quite clearly how it suffices in no way to meet an important numerical superiority on the battlefield, in order to obtain the victory, but rather the victory depends only upon the correct use of the troops.

On the morning of July 25, the entire 8th Bundes-Army Corps stood united against Division Goeben, which, on its part, had no support at all. Taking into account the losses suffered by Division Goeben at Tauberbischofsheim and Werbach-Hochhausen, and detachments to cover the baggage trains etc, on July 25, it numbered 14,300 bayonets, 1,450 sabres, and 43 guns, of which 25 were rifled. The VIII Corps, on the morning of July 25, numbered roughly 31,500 bayonets, 3,800 sabres, and 133 guns, 93 of them rifled.[69]

Casualties[70]

	Prussian		Federal	
	Officers	Men	Officers	Men
Killed	–	8	1	12
Wounded	3	48	2	87
Missing/prisoners	–	1	5	146
Totals	3	57	8	245

Federal Disarray

Given that any retreat across the valley of the Main in the face of the enemy could end in complete disaster, but also that now, at last, VII and VIII Corps were finally in close proximity, Prince Karl, to his great credit, once again considered that a joint offensive was the required move. Unaware of the details of events around Gerschsheim, he quickly made plans for an attack to be carried out at first light on the 26th. Prince Alexander, once again, was intended to advance to the south-west, along the Tauberbischofsheim Road against Goeben, who was, as seen, at Gerchsheim. The Bavarians, meanwhile, would move on Helmstadt and Uettingen, thus splitting the Prussian forces.

Karl's hopes of a concerted attack were soon dashed once again by the news that Prince Alexander was adamant that his troops were in no condition to fight a battle, and that, in fact, an immediate withdrawal across the Main must actually be undertaken instead.[71] That morning, Major Suckow, attached to Bavarian headquarters, chanced upon Prince Alexander and his Chief of Staff, in the Hotel de Russie. In answer to a loaded question from the Prince as to the effort that the Bavarians were making, the gallant Suckow replied, "Yes, Your Highness, the Bavarian army is fighting for its sheer survival up there."[72]

---

69 Kunz, p.200.
70 Ö.K., Vol. V, p.159. The highest number of missing, four officers and 86 men, were from the Hessian Division.
71 *Antheil*, pp.178-179.
72 *Rückschau*, p.107.

Prussian Intent

In the main Prussian headquarters, it was known that they faced the entire enemy army, and General von Manteuffel was determined to retain the initiative by attacking this force on the 26th. Having already sent Flies' main body ahead, he further instructed that, "The division v. Flies should advance towards Uettingen in the morning with all forces. Until their arrival, the division v. Beyer and the division v. Goeben should remain in their positions. Further orders will be sent." Flies certainly required no prodding. His own two remaining columns were both on the march at 03:00.

Major-General von Korth, with main body of the division von Flies – six batallions, two squadrons, and one battery – reached the area west of Uettingen at 21:00, and bivouacked there. A detachment occupied the Ober-Mühle to the east of Uettingen. No further security measures could be undertaken because of the darkness.[73]

Action of Rossbrunn, July 26

Bavarian dispositions on the morning of the 26th were as follows:

> 2nd Division (Feder) lay in the positions which they had occupied at the end of the previous day's combat. Hartmann's 4th Division lay astride the road between Uettingen and Greussenheim, the 8th Brigade not having arrived until 20:00, the previous evening, and the 7th, not until 22:00. The Reserve Infantry Brigade was camped north-east of the Post House, while the Reserve Artillery was partly located at Hettstadt, and partly around Rossbrunn. Stephan's 1st Division had made camp on the heights west of Rossbrunn. 3rd Division (Prince Luitpold) eventually ended up bivouacking east of Waldebüttebrunn, with the majority of the Reserve Cavalry to the west of the same village.

Fight for the Kirchberg

Unsurprisingly, given the close proximity of many of the protagonists, preparations began early that day. Around 04:00, what was to prove the final major field action of the Bavarian Army during the campaign spluttered into being. General Flies, riding well in advance of his other two marching columns, immediately grasped the importance of the Kirchberg. Seeking out General Korth in Uettingen, he had two battalions, II/GR 11, Major von Bonin, and II/IR 59, Major des Barres, despatched to secure it.[74]

Sometime earlier, around 03:15, three Bavarian companies of I/5th Infantry Regiment, led by Captain Kress, ascended the hill, the captain then reporting back that it was too large to be held by his existing force. The decision was made to deploy the remainder of the battalion there, with Major Schwalb leading the rest of the men up. As he did so, the Prussians were also making their ascent at about 04:15. As Biebrach wrote: 'The first

---

73   G.G.S. pp.674-75.

74   Note that GR11 was a Grenadier Regiment. Knorr, p.230, has pickets of IR59 reporting the presence of " … the entire enemy army …" as early as 02:30.

shots that fell here were the signal for battle along the entire line from the Kirchberg to the Geisberg" (a height just west of Mädelhofen)'.[75]

As von Bonin's grenadiers climbed through the vineyards of the south face of the Kirchberg, they came under heavy fire from Schwalb's skirmish lines. Within about 15 minutes, the firing became general. The Bavarian rifled six pounder battery of Captain Girl, of the Reserve Artillery on the Vogelberg, also opened fire.

Bavarian Colonel Bijot, commanding 7th Brigade, now ordered I and II/13th Regiment (Majors Faber and von Kramer) from reserve over to the right for a counter-attack. The 8th Jäger Battalion, Major Rudolf, and II/5th, Major Högele, constituted the second line. The attack went forward, only to be hit in the right flank by heavy small-arms fire. The advance failed, Major Rudolf's battalion being particularly hard hit, losing over 120 officers and men.[76]

For additional reinforcement of the Bavarian troops on the Kirchberg, II/9th Regiment, Major Schrott, received orders to immediately advance. However, as the battalion's 5th and 6th companies were still absent, guarding the trains, while 7th and 8th were already in a position north of the main road, guarding artillery, only the 3rd and 4th Schützen companies were actually sent there. The former (Captain Baur) occupied the far edge of the woods deployed as skirmishers; the latter company (Captain von Tein) was placed in support, along with the colours. These troops now comprised the Bavarian right wing on the hill.[77]

As these two companies deployed, General Korth also pushed a further battalion forward, I/GR11, Lieutenant-Colonel des Barres. On the Bavarian right wing, as the Prussians were increasing their pressure, the decision was taken to gain breathing space by launching a counterattack. Baur's Bavarian skirmishers then "…threw themselves at the enemy with a hurrah", causing them to fall back hastily. Hardly were the assaulting troops half way down the slope on the western side, though, than they received a murderous rapid fire, again in their own right flank: Prussian infantry had moved unde-tected along the road from Remlingen.

The two companies were precipitately driven back, Major Schrott being wounded in the process, and Oberlieutenant Weber killed. The mixed Bavarian units here were thrown back with considerable losses, and pushed back behind the road leading into the Hessnert Woods. All other remaining detachments had to withdraw. The Kirchberg was, and remained, lost.[78] The majority of Bavarian troops from here were then directed to the area around the Post House.

Korth's troops then pushed on against the wooded heights of the Hessnert, coming under fire from the Bavarian rifled six pounder battery of Captain Königer, which had moved to a position some 800 paces north of the main road, from where it engaged Prussian guns near Uettingen, as well as Prussian infantry. Around 06:15, though, with Prussian skirmishers approaching, the captain was forced to pull back about 800 paces closer to Greussenheim, and again deploy. Having cleared the Hessnert, Brigade Korth

---

75   *Antheil*, p.180 & Biebrach, p.83.
76   *Antheil*, Appendix III, pp.12-13.
77   Käuffer, p.77.
78   Ibid.

itself then halted to reorganise. Near this time, too, the last elements of Division Flies reached the field.

Around half an hour before this, von Flies had sent the following urgent message directly to General Manteuffel:

> Division Flies is in action from Uettingen, over Rossbrunn. I am interfereing on his (the enemy) right wing. The reconnaissance under Colonel von Krug (von Nidda) is cancelled.[79]

Facing him now, another Bavarian battery, the eight smoothbore twelve pounders of CaptainWill, had been positioned on the heights above Greussenheim, near the 'Post House', where they were joined by two more twelve pounders of Battery Hang, for now effectively halting Prussian progress here. Käuffer describes the defences:

> After the unfavourable result of the earlier combat made itself felt, a fall back position at the Post House was taken up. Therefore, the 1st Battalion of our (9th) regiment took position on a height north of the building, whereas the 3rd Battalion at first did the same, and the VI Schützen Company covered the guns. The 10th Company took position to cover the right wing, and the 11th company occupied and defended Rossbrunn.[80]

Assault on the Leite/Vogelberg[81]

To the south, Beyer's Prussian troops became aware of the nature of the encounter a little less than an hour after its beginning: "Then suddenly, at about 5 o'clock, far behind the left wing, which was facing east, renewed lively cannon fire could be heard from the direction of Uettingen."[82] Upon his own arrival on the field, also around 05:00, General Freyhold received instructions to attack the hills east of Uettingen, particularly the Leite and the Vogelberg.

Defended by troops of Major-General Hanser's 4th Bavarian Brigade, the dispositions of the defenders of those features on the morning of the 26th were unchanged from those of the previous evening. The Leite was occupied by I/7th Regiment, Major Narciss, and the Vogelberg by III/7th, Major Böhe, with II/7th, Major Gambs, in between them. Now, however, there was artillery support. Captain Redenbacher's rifled six pounder battery was positioned on the Leite, and Captain Girl's, on the Vogelberg.[83]

Tied by the urgency and detail of his instructions, Freyhold swiftly made his dispositions for his attack. The objectives were difficult, and flexibility out of the question. First

---

79 Von Werner, *Manteuffels Operationen in Bayern von der Tauber bis zum Beginn der Waffenruhe 1866*, p.17.

80 Lieutenant Haag undertook this on his own initiative – *Antheil*, p.183.

81 The height was known as the Leite or the Ossnert. Some sources also make reference to the 'Brunnschlag'. For all practical purposes, this is a part of the same feature as the Vogelberg.

82 *Division Beyer*, p.104.

83 *Antheil*, pp.183-184.

to advance were II/FR36 Major Baron von Kayserlinck and four pounder battery von Blottnitz.

The battery unlimbered directly south of Uettingen, on a hill called the Taubenheerd, to be joined there, some 15 minutes later, by rifled six pounder battery von der Goltz. Both batteries were tasked with bombarding the enemy troops on the Leite, rather than Bavarian batteries around the Post House. Kayserlinck's troops now attacked a little south of the Vogelberg.

On Kayserlinck's left, III/FR36, Major Liebeskind advanced against the south of the Vogelberg, with 10th and 11th companies in skirmish lines, and followed by 9th and 12th, both formed in company columns. Bavarian Battery Redenbacher bombarded both these guns as well as the approaching infantry. The heavy Bavarian fire pushed these Prussian formations south, to their own right, leaving numbers of skirmishers and stragglers behind.

Meanwhile, accompanied by General Freyhold, I/FR36, led by Colonel von Thile, assembled in half-battalions, with skirmishers to the front, advanced directly on the Leite itself. This height was completely free of foliage for the first 800 metres of the climb to the tree-line. The attackers were, consequently, subjected to intense fire.

Between the two heights, Bavarian Major Gambs' II/7th Regiment, under pressure from both sides, was being pushed back, while the two supporting batteries were withdrawn. Redenbacher was running out of ammunition, and Captain Girl's battery had no position in which it could deploy. The latter was moved to the Post House. From there, after exhausting its ammunition, the battery withdrew. Ammunition for several other batteries was also now running low.

After heavy fighting, by 07:00, these important positions were in Prussian hands, with the Bavarians withdrawing, in their turn, under heavy small-arms fire.[84] It had, however, been far from easy, with FR36 alone suffering over 400 casualties. Lettow-Vorbeck was scathing as regards to the operation, stating that:

> Since at this time the enemy had already been dislodged from the Kirchberg, the flanking support of the Division Beyer, which had been requested, should have been waited for.[85]

About 07:00, additional Prussian troops had also been committed against the heights. Three more battalions went sent forward, I/IR59, Major Haak, F/IR59, Lieutenant-Colonel von Köppen, and F/GR11, Major von Busse, it being felt necessary now to strongly support the hard hit IR36. The latter was, most deservedly, pulled out of the line about an hour later. After the Prussian capture of the Leite/Vogelberg, the troops there were reorganised before any further move. This done, the advance could be continued.

Since 07:00, Ritter Hartmann's 4th Bavarian Division had been slowly pulling back, still exchanging fire with the enemy. Now, the Post House, too, was finally ordered to be abandoned:

---

84 Scheibert, p.212.
85 Lettow-Vorbeck, p.362. *Antheil*, p.186, places the beginning of IR36's attack as 07:30, surely much too late.

When this position also had to be abandoned due to the progress of the enemy, the entire 3rd Battalion (9th Regiment, Major Dietrich), together with one battalion of the 12th Regiment occupied the Post House building, and the garden wall in front of it, as well as the road ditch in front of that. In the meanwhile, the enemy had occupied the Vogelberg and advanced through the Thalgrund (Valley floor), when a lively and effective fire was opened up from the occupied positions, by which the retreat of the division was covered, and an enemy attack was prevented. In this the artillery supported us in a splendid way.[86]

Having been driven from the Leite/Vogelberg position, General Hanser's 4th Brigade retreated to the Himmelreichwald (woods), there linking with Major-General Schumacher, with three of his own battalions. At 09:00, orders arrived to retreat to Hettstadt.[87] Prussian Four Pounder Battery Schmidts now took position on the Leite, while Six Pounder Battery Wasserfuhr was deployed near the village of Platten.

At about the same time, General Beyer also committed his own infantry against the high ground further south, around Mädelhofen.[88] Here, Colonel Woyna's IR20 moved through the village of Platten, against Mädelhofen itself, and the Himmelreichwald beyond. Beyer followed this up with both the Main Body and Advance Guard of the Division. The Prussian momentum, though, was slowing, especially under artillery fire. Of Bavarian guns, there were five batteries deployed between Greussenheim and the Himmelreichwald at this time.[89]

Bavarian withdrawal to Hettstadt

For the Prussians, the situation had already become a matter of consolidation. There seemed no further additional advantage in prolonging the already costly hard-fought action. Indeed, Biebrach commented that subsequently, "…the last Bavarian troops withdrew towards Hettstadt and Waldbüttelbrunn, where the entire Bavarian army, with the artillery to the fore, had marched. A further Prussian advance was not possible, because of the numerous enemy artillery".[90] The firing therefore fell silent around 10:30 almost completely." *Antheil* closely mirrors this:

> By 10:30, small arms fire was abating. Half an hour later, fighting had effectively ceased, with only the occasional cannon shot being heard.[91]

Further to counsel caution, General Manteuffel himself, had no news at all of the whereabouts of VIII Corps, and Goeben's tired division, still assembled around Gerchsheim,

86 Käuffer, p.77.
87 The three other battalions of 3rd Brigade, II/3rd, III/3rd, and 7th Jäger, due to conflicting orders, did not come into action at all; *Antheil*, footnote, p.190.
88 G.G.S., p.681.
89 *Antheil*, p.195 & Kunz, p.213 – a total of 40 guns, 32 rifled six pounders, and eight smoothbore twelve pounders.
90 Biebrach, p.83.
91 *Antheil*, p.193.

Beyer's infantry near the Mädelhofen, Rossbrunn, July 26. (Cohn)

was also short of ammunition. There would be no immediate further continuation of the Prussian advance. There would, however, be a sting in the tail!

The Cavalry Clash on the Hettstädter Heights

Although the fighting around Rossbrunn had largely lapsed with the Prussian seizure of the Leite (Ossnert), some time after 11:00, a Prussian cavalry force moved against the Bavarian right wing. Colonel Krug von Nidda, with a Combined Cavalry Brigade (three squadrons, 6th Dragoons, two squadrons of 10th Landwehr Hussars, 4/9th Hussars, Captain von Lücken, and Captain König's horse artillery battery), now advanced from Greußenheim, west of the Heßnert, against the Hettstadt Heights, north-west of the village of that name, allegedly on instructions from General Flies.[92] The force proceeded to take position in a dale, where it was joined by two more squadrons, of the 5th Dragoons, under Major von Westfal.

The Colonel's push soon attracted Bavarian attention, and the Reserve Cavalry was moved forward along the north of the main road towards the enemy, in two lines, the

---

92   Manteuffel/Flies. One troop of the hussars was withdrawn at the last moment. It will be recalled that earlier that morning, a planned probe by the Colonel had been cancelled.

The cavalry clash at the Hettstädter Heights, Rossbrunn. (Fontane)

First and Second Cuirassiers comprising the first line, and the Third Cuirassiers and the Third Uhlans, the second.

Lieutenant-General von der Tann himself rode forward to observe, with Captain Girl's rifled six pounder battery, which engaged the Prussian guns.[93]

Major Baumüller, commanding the Bavarian 6th Chevauleger Regiment, pushed a squadron forward to probe, but this force was charged and driven back by two squadrons, 2/6th Dragoons, and 3/10th Landwehr Hussars. Baumüller then committed his remaining two squadrons, with equal bad luck. Now, however, the Bavarian 1st and 2nd Cuirassiers both entered the action (695 officers and men)[94]

There followed a rolling melee which drifted in the direction of the Prussian battery, Captain König managing to discharge some grape-shot against the Bavarian horse. The swirling mass then moved within range of Captain Girl's guns, the fire of which, in turn, drove off the Prussians. The second echelon of Bavarian horse then proceeded to push the Prussians, until Colonel Krug von Nidda withdrew, covered by the artillery.

The Prussian loss probably numbered 84 officers and men, there being seven dead, 42 wounded, and 35 missing. Of this total, over a third of the casualties belonged to the Magdeburg Dragoon Regiment, with this corps losing six men killed, 22 wounded, and eight missing. In contrast, the Bavarian horse suffered less than half the Prussian number, with three killed, 25 wounded, and three men missing.[95] They also, without

---

93 This was a total of 19 squadrons, with one squadron of the 3rd Cuirassiers being absent on escort duties.

94 Kunz, p.215. *Antheil*, pp.197-198, states that, in their excitement, some elements of the cuirassiers attacked before they had deployed. One chevauleger squadron screened the Bavarian battery.

95 Knorr, Vol. I, p.266. *Antheil*, appendix XIV, however, gives the Prussian total loss as 85, as does the regiment's history, Schulenberg-Hehlen & Briesen, p.43. Kunz, however, p.216, gives the

doubt, considered the clash as "Revenge for Hünfeld", almost a month earlier. Certainly, on this occasion, the outnumbered Prussian cavalry had been chased from the field.[96]

Coincidentally, shortly after the end of this combat, Prince Karl was forced to ordere a general withdrawal across the Main.[97] Hardly had the last Bavarian troops arrived on the plateau of Hettstadt and Waldbütteln, when he received a report from the VIII Corps, that it had evacuated the position on the Nicolausberg and was assembling on the east bank of the Main. There was no longer any choice to be made. The Bavarian Army must conform to Prince Alexander's retreat, and also cross to the east bank of the Main, at Würzburg.Consequently, orders for this were now prepared.[98] Subsequently, Bavarian formations began to appear near the city from 14:00.[99]

Casualties[100]

	Prussian		Bavarian	
	Officers	Men	Officers	Men
Killed	4	97	9	82
Wounded	35	680	32	575
Missing/prisoners	–	40	2	187
Totals	39	817	43	844

Despite the other relevant factors, Colonel Kunz was certain that the Prussians had missed an important chance. He wrote:

> Without doubt, around noon on July 26 there was an excellent opportunity to inflict a catastrophe on the Bavarians. General Manteuffel, however, did not yet know about the retreat of the 8th Federal Corps behind the River Main, and also the troops were highly exhausted and the ammunition rather depleted. Therefore, a good military opportunity was not taken advantage of.[101]

VIII Corps on July 26

After its own withdrawal from Gerchsheim, on the evening of July 25, VIII Corps had bivouacked in the area of Kist, in a state of some confusion, in some places intermingled with Bavarian troops. At 20:00, Lieutenant-Colonel Werra, of Prince Karl's staff, encountered Prince Alexander there. It was now abundantly clear that a joint offensive

---

Prussian loss as seven officers and 80 men.
96 Von Bredow, p.124.
97 Ö.K., Vol. V., p.170 & Koch, p.58.
98 Biebrach, p.83.
99 *Feldzugs-Journal*, p.30.
100 22 officers and 436 other ranks were from FR36. As already noted, Kunz adds three further Prussian officers as wounded during the cavalry action.
101 Kunz, p.214.

was not now feasible. This being the case, the Bavarian army would now have to gain time for VIII Corps. It was urgent for Alexander to hold the Nicolausberg, a height on the west bank of the Main, opposite Würzburg, at the very latest by midday. At the same time, two pontoon bridges was to be used to facilitate the withdrawal. These moves were to be screened that day, as seen, by the stand of the Bavarians.

Consequently, Prince Karl ordered that the 1st and 3rd Divisions, along with the Reserve Cavalry should hold the Waldbütteln Plateau. Additionally, the troops around Rossdorf were to move there as well, in case of a major enemy attack. VIII Corps, meanwhile, was to hold the village of Höchberg and the Nicolausberg. These directives were sent near daybreak on the 26th, as cannon fire echoed from Rossbrunn.

Hardly had the last Bavarian troops arrived on the plateau of Hettstadt and Waldbütteln, at around 13:00, than Prince Karl received a report from the VIII Corps, that it had already evacuated the position on the Nicolausberg, and was establishing itself on the right (east) bank of the Main. The Prussians, fortunately, were also completely unaware of this.[102]

At around 04:00, that morning, the Nicolausberg had, as instructed, actually been occupied by troops of the Württemberg, Baden, and Hessian divisions. At the same time, the 4th (Austrian-Nassau) Division was sent south, towards Heidingsfeld to secure the railway and the pontoon bridge there. The Reserve Cavalry and Artillery had already been sent back across the Main. VIII Corps remained in these positions – with 34½ batallions, 16 squadrons, and 48 guns – without any attack.

VIII Corps had reported to Prince Karl on the night of the 25th that it had withdrawn across the Main, on account of the exhaustion of the troops. As for the firm order to hold the position on the Nicolausberg on the 26th in order to pin Goeben, this instruction was followed until 11:00. Then, however, a withdrawal took place, since the aforementioned 'exhaustion' would not allow the force to take up a renewed fight. Without doubt, some in the higher ranks of VIII Corps required a period of stability and a firm hand. Time, however, had run out. Biebrach commented that:

> The invisible power, called the influence of morale, which prevails in war, called forth by the results of unlucky battles, by withdrawals, by strains, and by the lack of sleep, had gained the upper hand.[103]

---

102 G.G.S., p.685.
103 Biebrach discusses this at length, pp.84-86.

11

The Federal Army east of the Main and the end of the campaign

The morning of July 27 found the bulk of the Federal forces safely on the east bank of the Main. Much of the Bavarian force was now deployed around Rottendorf, with Lieutenant-General Feder's division (2nd) covering the river crossings near the fortress city of Würzburg.[1] The principal dispositions were:

VII Corps:

Rottendorf – 10 kilometres east of Würzburg – Headquarters, 3rd Division, & Artillery Reserve
Gerbrunn – six kilometres east of Würzburg – 1st Division
Veitshöchheim – eight kilometres north-west of Würzburg – 2nd Division
Versbach – six kilometres north-east of Würzburg – 4th Division
Dürrbach – immediate north-west of Würzburg – Infantry Reserve
South of Schweinfurt – Reserve Cavalry

VIII Corps:

Biebelried – 15 kilometres east of Würzburg – Headquarters and Artillery Reserve
Ochsenfurt – six kilometres east of Würzburg – 2nd (Baden) Division
Wöllried – three kilometres east of Würzburg – 3rd (Hessian) Division
Versbach – Between Würzburg, Heidingsfeld – 1st (Württemberg) Division
Heidingsfeld – eight kilometres south of Würzburg – 4th (Austrian-Nassau) Division – Westheim

The Bombardment of Würzburg, July 27

On the morning of the 27th, a number of probes were made by detachments of both Brigade Kummer and Brigade Wrangel against Bavarian positions around the Marienberg Fortress, on the west bank of the river. It was noted that, besides the works

---

1   *Antheil*, p.200.

The bombardment of Würzburg. (*Illustrirte Kriegs-Chronik*)

of the Marienberg itself, artillery positions were being prepared on the east bank of the Main.

As discussed, the Army of the Main possessed no siege train, the heaviest weapons available being its twelve pounders. It is, however, curious that General von Goeben appears to have actually considered that his field artillery might have a major effect against the fortress. In any case, the decision having been made, there was no alternative under the circumstances, for the Prussian batteries chosen for the operation, but to try it and hope for the best, however unrealistic that prospect may be.

Deployed for the effort were 3rd Six Pounder Battery, and the 4th Four Pounder Battery, placed so as to engage the fortress, whilst the 3rd Four Pounder Battery and the Oldenburg Battery were to bombard the Hexenberg and the Nicolausberg respectively. The first lies directly across the river from the Marienberg fortress, while the second lies immediately south of it.

At around 12:00, Goeben ordered the batteries to open fire. The prime target was the citadel, known as the Marienberg, on the west bank of the river, with the ranges varying from one and a half to over two kilometres. This fire was answered not only from the citadel, but also from above the city by Bavarian guns, and also by the two Austrian and the Nassau Battery, of VIII Corps, on to the heights south of the city. The latter were later also joined by two Württemberg batteries, the Six Pounder Battery of Captain Roschmann, and the 1st Horse Artillery Battery, making a total of 38 rifled cannon engaged in this area. All of these guns east of the river were engaged at a considerable distance, some over three kilometres. At length, a fire was started in the citadel, by the Prussian shelling, and approximately 1,000 rifles in the arsenal there were destroyed.[2] The defending fire nevertheless continued unabated, both from the Marienberg, and also the Federal batteries on the east bank of the Main, both north and south of the city.

---

2   Lecomte, p.301.

At 14:30, with no result in sight, a most annoyed General Manteuffel finally accepted defeat, and ordered that the exposed batteries be withdrawn. Thus, the firing soon ceased.[3] The Prussian troops returned to their bivouacs in Hettstadt, Waldbüttelbrünn, and Höchberg, with General Manteuffel's own headquarters remaining at Eisingen. Casualties in this inconclusive bombardment totalled one officer, Rittmeister von Legat, and five men killed (two IR 15), and three officers and 17 men wounded (two men, IR 15) on the Prussian side, with one officer and eight men wounded on the Bavarian.[4] The blaze in the Marienberg was subsequently extinguished.

A later Bavarian reconnaissance by one and a half platoons of the 9th Regiment, from the fortress resulted in an encounter with Prussian pickets, men from two platoons of 10/IR 53, Lieutenant Müller, on the Nicolausberg. Five of the latter were taken prisoner.[5]

The attempt to pound Würzburg into surrender, with only the means at hand, had unquestionably failed. Indeed, given the open nature of the ground, the Prussians were very fortunate not to have suffered more losses. The habit of victory, for once, had not overcome presumption, albeit academically. The next morning, although various overtures and rumours of a possible armistice came and went, the troops on both sides were held in readiness. Indeed, the Prussians continued preparing new earthworks.

The immediate military situation here was now a temporary stalemate, with the Prussians presently unable to force the Main at this point. The political situation, though, was a very different matter.[6] In addition, a new threat to the Federal Army had appeared, this one from the east.

Formation and Advance of Prussian II Reserve Corps into North-East Bavaria

While these events occurred, further 'Prussian' troops were being allocated to the German theatre. The newly created, and still incomplete II Reserve Corps, commanded by General of Infantry Friedrich Franz, Grand Duke of Mecklenburg-Schwerin was committed to the campaign in mid-July.[7] It was to operate along the Upper Main and in north-east Bavaria.

The corps was composed of two divisions, the Prussian Combined Division of Lieutenant-General von Horn, and the Mecklenburg-Schwerin Division of Major-General von Bilger. Totalling 24 battalions, 14 squadrons, and 10½ batteries, the force numbered a little over 26,000 men. For the first time, though still outnumbered by their enemies, the odds against the Prussians would no longer be some 2-1. Even so, these additional troops were presently still to the north.

---

3   Baur-Breitenfeld, pp.115-116. Malet gives the time as 14:00, p.362.
4   Knorr, pp.288-290. Ö.K., Vol. V., p.173, does not mention a Prussian officer, possibly because he died subsequently. Lettow-Vorbeck, p.377, gives Prussian losses as two officers and 22 men. The VIII Corps batteries on the east bank of the Main appear to have suffered no losses.
5   *Antheil*, pp.202-203 & Käuffer, p.79.
6   It should be noted that, for a number of operational reasons, Prussian telegraphic communication between Supreme Headquarters, and the Main Army at this time was somewhat erratic, G.G.S., pp.694-695.
7   Formed by a Royal Order, dated July 3. See Appendix VII.

The Grand Duke commenced his advance south from Leipzig on July 20, along the roads through Zwickau and Werdau. The Corps Advance Guard was sent ahead by train to the Saxon town of Plauen, on the 22nd, from where the force then made an overnight march on the Bavarian town of Hof, a little over 20 kilometres to the south-west. This force consisted of Fusilier/4th Guard Regiment, one company of the Mecklenburg Jäger Battalion, one squadron of the Mecklenburg Dragoon Regiment, and two guns of the Mecklenburg Artillery, the whole under the command of the Fusiliers' Major von Loos.

The pitifully weak Bavarian presence in this area comprised a mere five companies of IV/13th Infantry Regiment, Major Wirthmann, who also had a small number of chevaulegers at his disposal, for use as couriers. Wirthmann had stationed two companies in Hof itself, and placed one company each in the adjoining villages of Schwarzenbach, Münchberg, and Culmbach. His nearest support was in Bamberg, over 30 kilometres to the south-west. Even this, however, was composed only of two infantry battalions, I/4th and II/10th, with a chevauleger squadron, all commanded by Major Höfler. To complete the tale of woe for the defenders, a garbled message of a five-day truce had also been mistakenly received by them.

The next morning, von Loos' troops, having no knowledge of any such truce, swept the Bavarians from Hof, cutting off a detachment, and the dragoons taking three NCOs and 62 men prisoner.[8] The Mecklenburg artillery also briefly fired upon a train loaded with Bavarian troops and stores, just as it was leaving Hof station, but caused it no damage. Major Wirthmann was able to withdraw the bulk of his command to Münchberg, where the meagre Bavarian force was now concentrated.

On the 24th, Wirthmann, with little choice, continued to withdraw before the advancing Prussians, as further scattered detachments joined him. By the 26th, the Bavarian position had coalesced along the line of Windisch-Eschenbach-Kemnacht. The following day, Major-General Fuchs arrived to take command; a surely dubious honour for Fuchs! That same day, the main body of The Grand Duke's II Reserve Corps reached Hof.[9] No effective defence was possible against this force. There were no measures that General Fuchs could undertake without considerable reinforcements, and there was no prospect of this.

Fuchs' command, now somewhat grandly titled the 'East Corps', consisted of seven battalions, positioned south-east of Bayreuth, between the towns of Creussen and Weidenberg. His intention was to occupy Bayreuth on the 28th, and he also sent an emissary to his counterpart, insisting upon the existence of an armistice, whilst also attempting to occupy as much territory as possible for possible future negotiations. That morning, IV/Leib Regiment, Major Count Joner, like all 4th battalions, full of recruits, was to be despatched to occupy Bayreuth, along with the only artillery available, these being four rifled breech-loading six pounders of the 4th Artillery Regiment. In the meanwhile, a Prussian infantry company in wagons and a dragoon squadron, under Major von Loos were also pushed ahead towards the city. Confusion as to the use of the railway by the Bavarians in this move badly slowed operations, and a single company, 8th Schützen, Captain von Parseval, reached the outskirts of the city at around

---

8   175 Knorr, Vol. III, p.349.
9   Ö.K., Vol. V, pp.182-183, Fontane, pp.266-269, Winterfeld, p.263, *Antheil*, pp.212-214 & Appendix XVII. Fontane and Winterfeld both give the number of prisoners as 60.

15:00, closely followed by Joner's advance guard, only to find that Prussian dragoons had already taken control of the station, just ahead of him.

Bluffing, Parseval informed the Prussian commander that his orders were to occupy Bayreuth pending the outcome of negotiations. This 'news' elicited a curt reply from the Prussian commander, Major von Loos, that no information of any ceasefire had reached him, but that the report of it would be despatched to the Grand Duke's Headquarters.[10]

While this lull occurred, Parseval telegraphed the information of Bayreuth's occupation by the enemy, and then proceeded back along the road to Creussen, encountering the main body of his battalion at Ober-Connersreuth. In the meanwhile, word having arrived from Corps Headquarters that no armistice existed, the Prussian force in Bayreuth, F/4th Foot Guards, two dragoon squadrons and 1/Mecklenburg Jäger Company, along with two guns, commenced its advance against Joner's command, with further troops available.

Encounters around Weidenberg and Creussen, July 29

After this rebuff at Bayreuth, at around 20:00, Major Joner himself moved, in accordance with the previous instructions from General Fuchs, to occupy positions around the villages of Weidenberg and Creussen, to the east of Bayreuth. Although initially uncertain of the situation regarding the cease-fire, and by now marching in the failing light, he led two companies towards Weidenberg, and sent one towards Creussen. He also sent an officer to ensure that his other three companies, as yet unaware of these moves, would conform to them.

Despite understandable confusion in the pitch-darkness, most units were indeed, remarkably, despite occasional exchanges of fire with the now advancing Prussians, able to conform to their instructions. The unfortunate exception was Oberlieutenant Aretin's 13th Company. 13/Leib Regiment was now split in half, with one platoon making its way to join the rest of the battalion at Weidenberg. The other, with the company commander, completely lost, halted for the night in the village of Emtmannsberg. From here, at daybreak, Aretin continued his march.

Overnight, a Bavarian staff officer, Captain Schanzenbach, was sent to Joner, instructing him that he was now to move his battalion to Seybottenreuth, from where he was to entrain. Near this village, the unlucky Aretin was attacked by 1 and 3/ Mecklenburg Dragoon Regiment, and forced to surrender, having lost 18 killed or wounded, Baron Aretin, himself being among the wounded. The remaining 68 unwounded were also taken prisoner.

While this took place, Captain Parseval's 8th Schützen Company, having exchanged fire with Prussian pickets in the darkness, was able, in the early hours of the 29th, able to make its way to Weidenburg. The remainder of Major Joner's battalion was not so fortunate.

Joner, with the remaining four companies of his battalion, having been given several contradictory orders, at about 07:30, was once again directed towards Seybottenreuth,

---

10   *Antheil* & G.G.S., p.696. The information of a cease-fire was indeed incorrect, and this fact was confirmed later that evening.

by General Fuchs. Completely unaware, the Major was now attempting towards Creussen, heading straight towards the main Prussian force. Engaged by two Prussian guns, Joner's force was pushed into a cutting along the railway, and there attacked by the 10 and 11/4th Foot Guards, along with the Mecklenburg Dragoons. In attempting to withdraw from this position, Joner's command stumbled into Captain von Zulow's 1/ Mecklenburg Jäger Company. Exhausted, completely surrounded, and without any chance of assistance, the Bavarian force surrendered.

Bavarian losses in this confused series of encounters numbered five men killed, four officers and 59 men wounded, and seven officers and 186 men taken prisoners or missing. Prussian losses, all suffered by the Mecklenburg Dragoons, totalled one officer, 11 NCOs, and 28 men wounded. In hindsight, it is abundantly clear that any Bavarian attempt to hold territory here, pending oft-discussed negotiations, was a pointless exercise.[11]

The end of the campaign

Encounter at Gotsmannsdorf

While matters appertaining to a possible armistice took their tortuous course, both armies remained in the field, their prime immediate concern being food for both men and animals. On the morning of July 29, a number of Prussian foraging parties from Division Goeben moved east, from Kist, to fulfil a number of requisition requirements. This force consisted of IR 19, one and a half squadrons of Hussar Regiment Nr. 8, and two and a half squadrons of Oldenburg Cavalry.

The Oldenburg horsemen left their bivouac in Höchhberg at 06:00, that morning, with instructions to requisition supplies in the villages of Darstedt and Gossmansdorf. The 2nd Squadron was despatched to the latter settlement. As the lead troop, under Lieutenant von Büsching, approached the village, a Baden infantry patrol, already there, opened fire upon them. In a short exchange, the Oldenburgers suffered casualties of one NCO, and four men badly wounded, two of whom were taken prisoner, then beating a hasty retreat. The Badeners had no loss, and no follow-up occurred.[12]

Events Relating to the Fortress of Mainz – June-July 1866

It will be recalled that the Federal fortress at Mainz, at the confluence of the Rhine and Main Rivers, was already garrisoned by Federal troops prior to the outbreak of hostilities (See Appendix XI), the Governor being the Bavarian Major-General Ludwig Count von Rechberg und Rothenlöwen.

With the Prussian invasion of Hesse-Cassel and Hanover, in mid-June, the crisis became a conflict, the establishment therefore moving on to a war-footing. On the night of June 26, Forts Hardenberg and Hartmühl were both armed (with field guns) and provisioned, by order of Colonel von Hofmann. Having been inspected by Prince Alexander of Hesse on June 29, the Hesse-Cassel Division of General von Loßberg was

---

11   G.G.S., pp.696-698, Illing, pp.56-59, Ö.K., Vol. V, p.184, *Schlachtfelder*, pp.298-308.
12   Knorr, Vol. 3, p.320 & Anon., *Zur Beeurtheilung des Verhaltens der badischen Felddivision im Feldzuge des Jahres 1866*, p.40.

considered unfit for field service, and sent to join the fortress garrison, with the exception of two squadrons. The situation at Mainz, though, then remained quiet until after the Prussian 'raid' on Nassau, in mid-July.

From July 20, the Prussians formed a 'Corps of Observation' covering both Wiesbaden and Mainz, commanded by Major-General Roeder. Wiesbaden was the responsibility of Colonel von Kortzfleisch, with eight battalions, one squadron, four guns, and a light bridging train, in all, some 6,000 men. Around Mainz, Lieutenant-Colonel von Fischer-Treuenfeld had six and a half battalions (two companies of which were from an ersatz battalion), one company, two squadrons, four rifled four pounders, four smoothbore twelve pounders. With a pioneer detachment, this numbered some 5,000.[13]

Around this time, Prussian vedettes first began to appear. A patrol of the Kur-Hessian Garde du Corps clashed with a detachment of Prussian Landwehr Hussars on the 18th, bringing in one officer and 17 men as prisoners.[14] A Federal river steamer was also fired upon. News also arrived of the Prussian occupation of Frankfurt. These events caused the Governor, Count von Rechberg, to declare a State of Siege, and to close the Rhine to traffic.[15]

The next day, two Kur-Hessian battalions undertook a reconnaissance to the west, around Finthen and and Budenheim. One wounded Prussian was brought back. On the 20th, the four Prussian four pounders bombarded the Castle. Intermittent probing and shelling continued until the 26th, when Count Rechberg agreed a cease-fire with General Roeder. This was ratified on August 4, and the fortress handed over on the 26th.

Armistice

As chance would have it, firm news regarding the agreement of an armistice reached the opposing armies facing one another at Würzburg on July 28 with Prince Karl being informed of an immediate suspension of military operations until August 2. Fortunately, they would not subsequently resume.

Most significantly, the armistice was not all-embracing. Whereas suspensions in hostilities were granted to the southern states, this was not the case with Hanover, Hesse-Cassel, and Nassau, and others ripe for annexation. In the case of Württemberg, General Manteuffel was authorised to allow a cease-fire, while also engaging in a more modest land grab. Dramatic change was in the wind.[16]

Aftermath

That the Prussian Army of the Main had triumphed against a far more numerous foe cannot be disputed. The following figures show the rough comparative figures at three points during July 1866:

---

13   Ö.K., Vol. V, p.126.
14   Bockenheimer, p.73.
15   *Antheil*, p.225.
16   Malet, p.367.

Army of the Main Combined Federal VII & VIII Corps[17]
July 4	51,000	92,440
July 25	53,542	94,354
July 27	54,900	91,236

These, admittedly Prussian, figures make it clear that, by the end of hostilities, General Manteuffel's forces were still outnumbered by more than 35,000 men. Even this 'cushion', however, was about to be offset by the appearance of the Grand Duke of Mecklenburg's Prussian II Reserve Corps, thus rendering the Federal troops' situation completely untenable, let alone without any additional assistance from the huge Prussian armies further east. It is unsurprising, therefore, that the Prussian General Staff History accords the Army of the Main the following accolade, comparatively modest though it is: "It was thus possible, with 47,000 men against 100,000, to take the offensive, and in 47 days, advance from the Elbe to the Iaxt" (A distance of just over 885 kilometres, the Iaxt being a district of Württemberg).Though smug, this was, in the circumstances, quite reasonable.

---

17 *Militär-Wochenblatt*, Vol. 52 1867, p.471. Note that this does not include II Reserve Corps.

12

Epilogue

An Alternative?

What issues, then, led to this apparently easy victory, and what, if anything, could have altered the situation? Perhaps the most tantalizing 'what if' is assuredly that surrounding the attempt on the Prussian Chancellor's life in early May 1866.

Once the die had been cast, though, Prussia possessed some definitive advantages in Germany. Firstly, the loss of the Hanoverian Army, in its entirety, right at the beginning of hostilities was certainly a considerable blow to the Federal forces, although it does not appear to have been perceived at the time as such, by their allies to the south. In reality, not only some 16,000 troops of the mobilised army were lost, but also were several thousand more recruits, and additional numbers of men who had been unable to reach their units during the unavoidably rapid mobilisation. On the other hand, however, logistical issues might have severely hampered the Hanoverians had they managed to join the VII and VIII Corps. The hesitancy and lack of urgency by the latter forces, though, were also to blame for the early demise of their allies, as were the uncertainty and gullibility of King George himself, and some of his commanders. These same factors were to plague the other Federal forces throughout the rest of the campaign.

Command and Control

Bavarian

The timidity and lack of purpose of many of the Bavarian Army's operations during the campaign had most certainly not gone un-noticed at home. The firebrand editor of the popular Catholic journal, the *Münchener Volksbote*, Ernst Zander, had, as discussed, been scathing in his criticism of much of the conduct of the campaign. This criticism, directed at the General Staff, and more specifically of Baron von der Tann, was bitterly resented by them, and resulted in that body rather foolishly bringing a court case of slander against Herr Zander.

The case was heard in open court, in Munich, and tried before a jury. Only one witness was presented by the General Staff, the most unfortunate Colonel Bothmer. The unanimous judgement went in Zander's favour, and he was acquitted, much to the discomfiture of General Staff. The ruling can only be described as an accurate critical assessment of a great deal of the lackadaisical, indecisive, and often directionless conduct of operations.

This said, the Wittelsbach forces were the heart of the coalition. This was particularly so in the latter part of the campaign. Had these early performances mirrored some of the spirit and determination shown subsequently, matters might have appeared somewhat differently.

Hanoverian

The army of King George V of Hanover went to war for less than two weeks, in the summer of 1866. It took to the field while still under organisation, led by its blind King. No novelist would presume to invent the tale.

Prussian

The senior commanders of Prussian Army of the Main, in general lacked neither energy nor enterprise. Only at the very top was there serious friction, as Vogel von Falckenstein often casually treated orders from the Army Chief of Staff almost as options. As a consequence, he was relieved of his command and transferred to an administrative position in occupied Bohemia. His replacement, by Edwin Manteuffel, who was held in high esteem by the King, was hardly a surprise, but the change did not cause any operational difficulties.

Equally, the next tier of command down the chain exhibited no major problems. The brigade commanders normally carried out their instructions competently, and could be relied upon to act on their own initiative. It is notable, though, that Major-General Flies, who, on his own initiative started the Battle of Langensalza, and lost it, was given command of General Manteuffel's after the latter became Army Commander, following the dismissal of von Falckenstein. Such are the machinations of power.

VIII Federal Corps

Of all the major forces to take the field in Germany in 1866, the VIII Army Corps was by far the most disparate. As seen, its troops were provided by myriad of different sovereign states', all serving their own rulers. In such circumstances, perhaps was inevitable.

Far too often, orders were used as a basis for further discussion; and that discussion could be prolonged. The stubborn wilfulness of Prince Wilhelm of Baden on several occasions comes to mind. Such behaviour also applied at the top. VIII Corps' commander blatantly ignored instructions from Field Marshal Prince Karl more than once, though fortunately without immediate disastrous consequences.

So much for conjecture. As in Bohemia, the forces opposed to Prussia in Germany had been definitively defeated. By default, Prussia's ally, Italy, had also prevailed, though defeated on the battlefield. The face of Germany was about to change, and with it, that of Europe. For the forces opposed to the Prussians within the territories of the German Confederation during the campaign there, it had indeed been too many cases of, 'Too Little, Too Late'

Appendix I

Order of Battle of the Prussian Army of the West, June 16 1866[1]

Commander   General of Infantry Vogel von Falckenstein
Chief of Staff   Colonel von Kraatz-Koschlau
Artillery Commander   Colonel von Decker
First Engineer Officer   Colonel Schulz I

13th Infantry Division
Commander   Lieutenant-General von Goeben
Chief of Staff   Captain von Jena

25th Infantry Brigade
Commander   Major-General von Kummer
Infantry Regiment Nr. 13, Colonel von Gellhorn (3 battalions)
Infantry Regiment Nr. 53, Colonel von Treskow (3 battalions)

26th Infantry Brigade
Commander   Major-General Baron von Wrangel
Infantry Regiment Nr. 15, Colonel Baron von der Goltz (3 battalions)
Infantry Regiment Nr. 55, Colonel Stolz (3 battalions)

Pioneer Battalion Nr. 7 (1st & 3rd companies)

13th Cavalry Brigade
Commander   Colonel von Treskow
Cuirassier Regiment Nr. 8, Colonel von Schmidt (4 squadrons)
Hussar Regiment Nr. 8, Colonel von Rantzau (5 squadrons)

3rd Foot Detachment, Field Artillery Regiment Nr. 7 (4 batteries, 24 guns)
3rd and 4th Horse Artillery Batteries, Field Artillery Regiment Nr. 7
    (2 batteries, 12 guns)

---

1   Divisional totals taken from Kunz, pp.2, 3 & 5.

Provisional Rifled Six Pounder Battery (from captured Hanoverian materiel) (6 guns)[2]
Three munitions columns, Field Artillery Regiment Nr. 7
Division Total: 11,100 infantry, 1,260 cavalry, 24 guns

Combined Division Manteuffel

Commander   Major|-General Baron von Manteuffel
Chief of Staff   Colonel von Strantz

Combined Infantry Brigade
Commander   Major-General von Freyhold
Infantry Regiment Nr. 25, Colonel Baron von Hanstein (3 battalions)
Fusilier Regiment Nr. 36, Colonel von Thile (3 battalions)

Combined Infantry Brigade
Commander   Major-General von Korth
Grenadier Regiment Nr. 11, Colonel von Zglinski (3 battalions)
Infantry Regiment Nr. 59, Colonel von Kessler (3 battalions)

Combined Cavalry Brigade
Commander   Major-General von Flies
Rhineland Dragoon Regiment Nr. 5 (4 squadrons)
Magdeburg Dragoon Regiment Nr. 6 (4 squadrons)
Division Total   11,100 infantry, 1,120 cavalry, 24 guns

Combined Division Beyer

Commander   Major-General Beyer
Chief of Staff   Major von Zeuner

32nd Infantry Brigade
Commander   Major-General von Schachtmeyer
Infantry Regiment Nr. 30, Lieutenant-Colonel von Koblinski (3 battalions)
Infantry Regiment Nr. 70, Colonel von Woyna I (3 battalions)

Combined Infantry Brigade
Commander   Major-General von Glümer
Infantry Regiment Nr. 19, Lieutenant-Colonel von Henning (3 battalions)
Infantry Regiment Nr. 20, Colonel von der Wense (3 battalions)
Rhineland Hussar Regiment Nr. 9, Major von Kosel
Division Total: 16,650 infantry, 700 cavalry, 18 guns

---

2   Note that these guns were captured in the Hanoverian fortress of Stade, on 17th June. See Lettow-Vorbeck, Vol I, pp.147-148.

Appendix II

Reinforcements despatched to reinforce the Prussian Army of the West up to June 26 1866[1]

4th Foot Guards (2 battalions)	2,058 men	
Coburg-Gotha Regiment (2 battalions)	1,300 men	
2 battalions, 3rd Brandenburg Landwehr Infantry Regiment Nr. 20	900 men	
1 battalion, 2nd Magdeburg Landwehr Infantry Regiment Nr. 27	450 men	
2 battalions, 2nd Thuringian Landwehr Infantry Regiment, Nr. 32	900 men	
Combined Battalion, Thuringian Infantry Regiment Nr. 71	250 men	
Garrison Squadron, Landwehr Hussar Regiment Nr. 12	80 men	
Garrison Squadron, Westphalian Dragoon Regiment Nr. 7	80 men	
Combined Squadron, Magdeburg Hussar Regiment Nr. 7	80 men	
Two Provisional six pounder batteries	270 men	12 guns[2]
Half 'Sally' Battery, Fortress Artillery Regiment Nr. 4	86 men	4 guns
Approximate total:	6,500 men	16 guns

---

1   Ö.K., Volume I, Appendix II. Kunz, p.15 gives the total as 6,400 men.
2   These formations were organised using captured weapons and materiel found in Hanover.

Appendix III

Order of Battle of the Royal Hanoverian Army, June 20 1866[1]

Royal Headquarters
His Majesty, King George V
His Royal Highness, Crown Prince Ernst August

General Adjutant	Colonel Dammers
Flying Adjutants	Lieutenant-Colonel Kohlrausch Rittmeister Second Class Count Wedel
Adjutant to the Crown Prince	Major von Clenk (Garde du Corps)
Attached to the Royal Staff	General of Infantry Baron von Brandis Minister of War
Army Commander	Lieutenant-General von Arentsschildt
Chief of Staff	Colonel Cordemann
Chief of Adjutants Staff	Colonel Dammers
Cavalry Commander	Major-General von Wrede
Artillery Commander	Colonel von Stolzenberg
Engineers Commander	Lieutenant-Colonel Oppermann
Director, Remount Commission	Lieutenant-Colonel Lüderitz
Intendant-General	Counsellor Flügge
Chief of Medical Services	General Staff Dr. Strohmeyer
Military Justice Bureau	General-Staff Auditor Dr. Lueder & Senior Staff Auditor Ekherdt
General Adjutants	Lieutenant-Colonel Bremer
	Major Koch
	Captain Gündell
	Captain Krause
	Captain Schaumann
	Lieutenant von Klenk
General Staff	Lieutenant-Colonel Rudorf
	Major von Jacobi

---

1 Sichart, pp. 28-36, Reitzenstein, pp. 41-44 & *Österreichs Kämpfe*, Vol. I, Appendix I. The latter shows Battery Röttiger as being attached to the Reserve Cavalry.

1st Brigade   Major-General von der Knesebeck
Guard Regiment (2 battalions)
1st (Leib) Regiment (2 battalions)
Guard Jäger Battalion
Queen's Hussar Regiment (4 squadrons)
5th Foot Artillery Battery (6 guns)
Total: 5 battalions, 4 squadrons, 1 battery – 6 guns

2nd Brigade   Colonel de Baur
2nd Infantry Regiment (2 battalions)
3rd Infantry Regiment (2 battalions)
1st Jäger Battalion
Duke of Cambridge Dragoon Regiment (4 squadrons)
9th Rifled Six Pounder Battery (6 guns)
Total: 5 battalions, 4 squadrons, 1 battery – 6 guns

3rd Brigade   Colonel Bülow-Stolle
4th Infantry Regiment (2 battalions)
5th Infantry Regiment (2 battalions)
2nd Jäger Battalion
Crown Prince Dragoon Regiment (4 squadrons)
4th Rifled Six Pounder Battery (6 guns)
Total: 5 battalions, 4 squadrons, 1 battery – 6 guns

4th Brigade   Major-General Bothmer
6th Infantry Regiment (2 battalions)
7th Infantry Regiment (2 battalions)
3rd Jäger Battalion
Guard Hussar Regiment (4 squadrons)
1st Horse Artillery Battery, short smoothbore twelve pounders (4 guns)
6th Rifled Six Pounder Battery (4 guns)
Total: 5 battalions, 4 squadrons, 2 batteries – 8 guns

Reserve Cavalry Brigade   Colonel von Genso
Garde du Corps (4 squadrons)
Guard Cuirassier Regiment (4 squadrons)
Total: 8 squadrons

Artillery Reserve   Major Hartmann
2nd Horse Artillery Battery, short smoothbore twelve pounders (4 guns)
2nd twenty-four pounder Howitzer Battery (4 guns)
3rd Rifled Six Pounder Battery, breech loaders (4 guns)
Artillery Park (10 guns)
Army Strength: 20 battalions, 24 squadrons, and 42 guns (excluding Artillery Park)

The total number of men listed as present and available on June 20 with the main body of the army was given as 20,569, of whom 4,392 were recruits, engineer, medical, or ancillary personnel. This left the following troops on hand for immediate operations:

Infantry	13,390
Cavalry	1,730
Artillery	1,056
Total	16,177[2]

---

2   Schwerdt, p. 20, states some 18,000 men in all, and 52 guns.

Appendix IV

Order of Battle of Prussian 'Detachment' von Flies at the Battle of Langensalza, 27 June 1866[1]

Commander   Major-General Eduard von Flies

Advance Guard   Colonel von Fabeck
Coburg-Gotha Infantry Regiment, Lieutenant-Colonel von Westernhagen
2 battalions   1,200 men
Magdeburg Landwehr Hussar Regiment, Nr. 12
1 combined squadron, Merseburg 70 men
3rd Four Pounder Battery, Silesian Field Artillery Regiment, Nr. 7
1 battery   6 guns
Detachment, Erfurt provisional battery, Magdeburg Fortress Artillery Regiment, Nr. 4
1 section   2 guns

Main Body   Colonel Baron von Hanstein
1st Rhineland Infantry Regiment, Nr. 25, Baron von Hanstein
2 battalions   1,800 men
Second Silesian Grenadier Regiment, Nr. 11, Colonel von Zglinski
3 battalions   2,700 men
Garrison Battalion, 2nd Thuringian Landwehr Regiment, Nr. 32 (Torgau)
1 battalion   400 men
Combined Squadron, Magdeburg Hussar Regiment, Nr. 10
1 squadron   80 men
3rd Horse Artillery Battery, Westphalian Artillery Regiment, Nr. 7
1 battery   6 guns

---

1   These numbers are taken from Kunz, p. 29. Only approximate figures can be offered. *Die Hannoveraner in Thüringen und die Schlacht bei Langensalza 1866*, pp. 61-62, however, gives different figures for most units, though the total figures for both sources are close.

'Reserve'	Major-General von Seckendorff
First Echelon	Colonel von Helmuth

3rd Battalion (Naumburg), Landwehr Regiment Nr. 32

1 battalion	400 men

3rd Battalion (Aschersleben), Landwehr Regiment Nr. 27

1 battalion	400 men

Second Echelon	Major Baron von Wintzingerode

Battalion (Potsdam), Landwehr Regiment Nr. 20

1 battalion	425 men

Battalion (Treuenbrietzen), Landwehr Regiment Nr. 20

1 battalion	425 men

Provisional Battalion, Thuringian Infantry Regiment, Nr. 71, Baron Wintzingerode

3 companies	350 men

Garrison Squadron, Westphalian Dragoon Regiment Nr. 7,

3 troops	70 men

Third Horse Artillery Battery, 7th Field Artillery Regiment, Captain Metting

	6 guns

Detachment, 4th Artillery Brigade, Lieutenant Hupfeld

Sally Battery 'Erfurt'	2 guns
Misc. 2 7-pounder howitzers	2 guns

Approximate Total:	8,100 infantry, 340 cavalry, c. 200 artillery with 22 guns

Appendix V

Order of Battle of the Royal Hanoverian Army at the Battle of Langensalza, June 27 1866[1]

Royal Headquarters

His Majesty, King George V
His Royal Highness, Crown Prince Ernst August

General Adjutant	Colonel Dammers
Flying Adjutants	Lieutenant-Colonel Kohlrausch Rittmeister
	Second Class Count Wedel
Adjutant to the Crown Prince	Major von Clenk (Garde du Corps)
Attached to the Royal Staff	General of Infantry Baron von Brandis[2]
	Minister of War
Army Commander	Lieutenant-General von Arentsschildt
Chief of Staff	Colonel Cordemann
General Staff	Lieutenant-Colonel Rudorf
	Major von Jacobi

1st Brigade   Major-General von der Knesebeck

Guard Infantry Regiment
1st Battalion   525 officers and men
2nd Battalion   773 officers and men
1st (Leib) Regiment
1st Battalion   771 officers and men
2nd Battalion   742 officers and men
Guard Jäger Battalion   738 officers and men
Queen's Hussar Regiment
4 squadrons   290 officers and men
5th Foot Artillery Battery (Meyer) 167 officers and men – 6 guns
Total: 5 battalions, 4 squadrons, 1 battery – 6 guns

---

1   1.Present on the field, from Wyatt, pp. 68-72.
2   Lieutenant-General.

2nd Brigade   Colonel de Baur
2nd Regiment
1st Battalion
2nd Battalion   1,473 officers and men
3rd Infantry Regiment
1st Battalion
2nd Battalion   1,763 officers and men
1st Jäger Battalion   906 officers and men
1st (Duke of Cambridge's) Dragoon Regiment
3¼ squadrons   276 officers and men
6th Foot Artillery Battery (Laves)   138 officers and men 6 guns
9th Rifled Six Pounder Battery
Total: 5 battalions, 3¼ squadrons, 1 battery – 6 guns

3rd Brigade   Colonel Bülow-Stolle
4th Infantry Regiment
1st Battalion
2nd Battalion   1,043 officers and men
5th Infantry Regiment
1st Battalion
2nd Battalion   1,122 officers and men
2nd Jäger Battalion   699 officers and men
Crown Prince Dragoon Regiment
4 squadrons   276 officers and men
6th Foot Artillery Battery (Eggers)   138 officers and men 6 guns
Total: 5 battalions, 4 squadrons, 1 battery – 6 guns

4th Brigade   Major-General von Bothmer
6th Infantry Regiment
1st Battalion
2nd Battalion   1,134 officers and men
7th Infantry Regiment
1st Battalion
2nd Battalion   991 officers and men
3rd Jäger Battalion   810 officers and men
Guard Hussar Regiment
2 2/3 squadrons   222 officers and men
Rifled Six Pounder Battery (Müller)   149 officers and men 4 guns
Total: 5 battalions, 2 2/3 squadrons, 1 battery – 6 guns

Reserve Cavalry   Lieutenant-Colonel von Geyso
Garde du Corps
3 squadrons   245 officers and men
Guard Cuirassier Regiment
4 squadrons   370 officers and men
Horse Artillery Battery Böttiger   100 officers and men 4 guns[3]
Total: 8 squadrons, 1 battery – 4 guns

Artillery Reserve   Major Hartmann
2nd twenty-four pounder Howitzer
    Battery (Hartmann)   134 officers and men 4 guns
3rd Rifled Six Pounder Battery (Blumenbach)   153 officers and men 4 guns
Total: 2 batteries
Artillery Park (10 guns)
Army Strength on the field: 20 battalions, 21 squadrons, and 42 guns
    (excluding Artillery Park)
Total on the Field: 13,930 infantry, 1,731 cavalry and 1,056 artillery.[4]

---

3   Attached, from the Artillery Reserve.
4   Wyatt, p. 70. Schwerdt, however, p. 20, states some 18,000 men in all, and 52 guns. Kunz, p.28,
     gives the Hanoverian infantry present as 13,742 officers and men.

Appendix VI

Order of Battle of the Royal Bavarian Army (VII Corps, Federal German Confederation), June 21 1866[1]

Commander	His Royal Highness, Field-Marshal and Inspector General, Prince Karl Theodor of Bavaria
Chief of Staff & General Adjutant	Lieutenant-General Baron von der Tann
Deputy Chief of Staff	Major General von Schintling
Artillery Director	Lieutenant-General Ritter von Brodesser
Engineer Director	Lieutenant-Colonel Limbach
Attached to Headquarters	FML Count Huyn (Austria)
Major Suckow (Württemberg – Liaison officer from VIII Corps)	

1st Infantry Division

Commander	Major-General Stephan
Chief of Staff	Major Diehl

1st Infantry Brigade   Major General von Steinle

Leib Regiment – 2nd and 3rd Battalions
1st Infantry Regiment – 2nd and 3rd Battalions
2nd Infantry Regiment – 1st Battalion
2nd Jäger Battalion
Total: 6 battalions: 5,398 men

2nd Infantry Brigade   Major-General Ritter von Welsch
2nd Infantry Regiment – 2nd and 3rd Battalions
8th Infantry Regiment – 1st, 2nd and 3rd Battalions
4th Jäger Battalion
Total: 6 battalions: 5,398 men

---

1   Figures based on ration strength of 21 June.

Divisional troops
3rd Chevauleger Regiment (4 squadrons)   507 men
Divisional Artillery – from 1st Artillery Regiment
Battery Hutten (8 rifled six pounders)
Battery Mussinan (8 smoothbore twelve pounders)
Total: 2 batteries   412 men 16 guns
Munitions Reserve   537 men
Engineer Detachment   45 men
4th Medical Company   174 men

2nd Infantry Division

Commander   Lieutenant-General von Feder
Chief of Staff   Lieutenant-Colonel Baron von der Tann

3rd Infantry Brigade   Major-General Schumacher
3rd Infantry Regiment – 1st, 2nd and 3rd Battalions
12th Infantry Regiment – 1st and 2nd Battalions
7th Jäger Battalion
Total: 6 battalions: 5,398 men

4th Infantry Brigade   Major-General von Hanser
7th Infantry Regiment – 1st, 2nd, and 3rd Battalions
10th Infantry Regiment – 1st and 3rd Battalions
7th Jäger Battalion
Total: 6 battalions: 5,398 men

Divisional troops
4th Chevauleger Regiment (four squadrons) 507 men
Divisional Artillery – from 1st Artillery Regiment
Battery Zoller (8 rifled six pounders)
Battery Kirchhoffer (8 smoothbore twelve pounders)
Total: 2 batteries   412 men 16 guns
Munitions Reserve   537 men
Engineer Detachment   45 men
3rd Medical Company   174 men

3rd Infantry Division

Commander   Lieutenant-General Baron von Zoller
Chief of Staff   Major von Heckel

5th Infantry Brigade   Major-General von Ribaupierre
11th Infantry Regiment – 1st, 2nd and 3rd Battalions
15th Infantry Regiment – 1st, 2nd, and 3rd Battalions
5th Jäger Battalion
Total: 7 battalions: 6,298 men

6th Infantry Brigade   Major-General Walther
6th Infantry Regiment – 1st and 3rd Battalions
14th Infantry Regiment – 1st and 2nd Battalions
1st Jäger Battalion
Total: 5 battalions: 4,498 men

Divisional troops
2nd Chevauleger Regiment (four squadrons) 507 men
Divisional Artillery – from 1st Artillery Regiment
Battery Lottersberg (8 rifled six pounders)
Battery Schuster (8 smoothbore twelve pounders)
Total: 2 batteries   412 men 16 guns
Munitions Reserve   537 men
Engineer Detachment   45 men
3rd Medical Company   174 men

4th Infantry Division

Commander   Lieutenant-General Ritter von Hartmann
Chief of Staff   Colonel Dietl

7th Infantry Brigade   Major-General Faust
5th Infantry Regiment – 1st, 2nd and 3rd Battalions
13th Infantry Regiment – 1st, and 2nd Battalions
8th Jäger Battalion
Total: 6 battalions: 5,398 men

8th Infantry Brigade   Major-General Cella
4th Infantry Regiment – 2nd and 3rd Battalions
9th Infantry Regiments – 1st, 2nd, and 3rd Battalions
6th Jäger Battalion
Total: 6 battalions   5,398 men

Divisional troops
6th Chevauleger Regiment (four squadrons) 507 men
Divisional Artillery – from 1st Artillery Regiment
Battery Königer (8 rifled six pounders)
Battery Hang (8 smoothbore twelve pounders)
Total: 2 batteries   412 men 16 guns
Munitions Reserve   537 men
Engineer Detachment   45 men
2nd Medical Company   174 men

Reserve Infantry Brigade

Commander   Colonel Bijot
4th Infantry Regiment – 1st Battalion
6th Infantry Regiment – 2nd Battalion

10th Infantry Regiment – 2nd Battalion
12th Infantry Regiment – 3rd Battalion
13th Infantry Regiment – 3rd Battalion
14th Infantry Regiment – 3rd Battalion

Total: 6 battalions	5,610 men

1st Chevauleger Regiment – 2nd and 3rd Squadrons

Total: 2 squadrons	240 men

Battery Kriebel (8 rifled six pounders)

Total: 1 battery	206 men eight guns
Munitions Reserve	268 men
Medical Detachment	86 men

Reserve Cavalry

Commander	General of Cavalry Prince Karl Theodor von Thurn and Taxis
Chief of Staff	Lieutenant-Colonel Weiß

1st Light Cavalry Brigade   Major-General Duke Ludwig of Bavaria
1st Uhlan Regiment (four squadrons)
2nd Uhlan Regiment (four squadrons)

Total: 8 squadrons	1,026 men

2nd Light Cavalry Brigade   Major-General Count zu Pappenheim
5th Chevauleger Regiment (four squadrons)
3rd Uhlan Regiment (four squadrons)

Total: 8 squadrons	1,026 men

Heavy Cavalry Brigade   Major-General Baron von Rummel
1st Cuirassier Regiment (4 squadrons)
2nd Cuirassier Regiment (4 squadrons)
3rd Cuirassier Regiment (4 squadrons)

Total: 12 squadrons	1,533 men

3rd Horse Artillery Battery (Massenbach)	172 men	8 guns
4th Horse Artillery Battery (La Roche)	72 men	8 guns[2]
Munitions Reserve	332 men	

Reserve Cavalry Total: 28 Squadrons, two batteries

---

2   Smoothbore twelve pounders.

Reserve Artillery

Commander   Major-General Count Bothmer

1st Division (from 3rd Artillery Regiment)
1st Horse Artillery Battery (Lepel)   177 men   6 guns
2nd Horse Artillery Battery (Hellingrath)   177 men   6 guns[3]

2nd Division (from 4th Artillery Regiment)
Rifled Six Pounder Battery Redenbacher   211 men   8 guns
Rifled Six Pounder Battery Girl   210 men   8 guns

3rd Division (from 1st Artillery Regiment)
Twelve pounder Smoothbore Battery Gramich[4]   211 men   8 guns
Twelve pounder Smoothbore Battery Cöster   210 men   8 guns

4th Division (from 2nd Artillery Regiment)
Twelve pounder Smoothbore Battery Minges   211 men   8 guns
Twelve pounder Smoothbore Battery Mehler   210 men   8 guns

---

3   Smoothbore twelve pounders.
4   Subsequently, transferred to Reserve Infantry Brigade.

Appendix VII

Order of Battle of the Prussian Army of the Main, July 1866[1]

Commander	General of Infantry Vogel von Falckenstein[2]
Chief of Staff	Colonel von Kraatz-Koschlau
Artillery Commander	Colonel von Decker
Engineer Commander	Colonel Schulz I

13th Infantry Division

Commander	Lieutenant-General von Goeben
Chief of Staff	Captain von Jena

25th Infantry Brigade

Commander   Major-General von Kummer
1st Westphalian Infantry Regiment, Nr.13, Colonel von Gellhorn
3 battalions
5th Westphalian Infantry Regiment, Nr. 53, Colonel von Treskow
3 battalions
Total: 6,172 men

26th Infantry Brigade

Commander   Major-General Baron von Wrangel
2nd Westphalian Infantry Regiment, Nr. 15, Colonel Baron von der Goltz
3 battalions
6th Westphalian Infantry Regiment, Nr. 55, Colonel Stoltz
3 battalions
Total   6,172 men

---

1   Note that unit strengths shown here represent full strength. For approximate numbers of effectives, see below.

2   Replaced by Baron Manteuffel on July 19.

13th Cavalry Brigade
Commander   Colonel von Treskow
1st Westphalian Hussar Regiment, Nr, 8, Colonel von Rantzau
5 squadrons
Westphalian Cuirassier Regiment, Nr. 4, Colonel von Schmidt
4 squadrons
Total: 1,042 men

Artillery
Commander   Major Petzel
3rd Foot Division, 7th Artillery Regiment
4 batteries   580 men, 25 guns
3rd Horse Division, 7th Artillery Regiment
1 battery   270 men, six guns
3rd Munitions Column, 7th Artillery Regiment   270 men
Two companies (1st & 3rd), 7th Pioneer Battalion   308 men
Total: 13 battalions, 2 companies, 9 squadrons, 5 batteries
13,368 infantry, 1,405 cavalry, 1,428 artillery etc., 31 guns

Oldenburg-Hanseatic Brigade[3]
Commander   Major-General von Weltzien
Oldenburg Infantry Regiment
3 battalions   3,072 men
Bremen Fusilier Battalion
1 battalion   1,024 men
Lübeck Fusilier Battalion
1 battalion   1,024 men

Combined Division Manteuffel
Commander   Major-General Baron von Manteuffel[4]
Chief of Staff   Captain von Gottberg

1st Combined Infantry Brigade
Commander   Major-General von Freyhold
1st Rhineland Infantry Regiment, Nr. 25, Colonel Baron von Hanstein
3 battalions
Magdeburg Fusilier Regiment, Nr.36, Colonel von Thile
3 battalions
Total: 6,172 men

---

3   The units of this brigade were attached to the division 20-27 July.
4   From July 19, Major-General von Flies.

2nd Combined Infantry Brigade
Commander   Major-General Korth
4th Posen Infantry Regiment, Nr. 59, Colonel von Kessler
3 battalions
2nd Silesian Grenadier Regiment, Nr. 11, Colonel Zglintski
3 battalions
Total: 6,172 men

Combined Cavalry Brigade
Commander   Major-General von Flies[5]
Rhineland Dragoon Regiment Nr. 5, Lieutenant-Colonel von Wedell
4 squadrons
Magdeburg Dragoon Regiment Nr. 6, Colonel Krug von Nidda
4 squadrons
Total: 1,024 men

Artillery
Commander   Lieutenant-Colonel von Seel
8th Six Pounder Battery, 6th Artillery Regiment
8th Twelve Pounder Battery, 6th Artillery Regiment
3rd Four Pounder Battery, 6th Artillery Regiment
4th Four Pounder Battery, 6th Artillery Regiment
Total: 4 batteries   580 men 24 guns
3rd Light Field Hospital

Combined Division Beyer
Commander   Major-General von Beyer
Chief of Staff   Major von Zenner

32nd Infantry Brigade
Commander   Major-General von Schachtmeyer
4th Rhineland Infantry Regiment, Nr. 30, Colonel von Selchow
3 battalions
8th Rhineland Infantry Regiment, Nr. 70, Colonel von Woyna I
3 battalions
Total: 6,172 men

---

5   From July 19, Major-General von Below.

Combined Infantry Brigade Glümer

Commander   Major-General von Glümer

2nd Posen Infantry Regiment, Nr. 19, Lieutenant-Colonel von Henning

3 battalions

3rd Brandenburg Infantry Regiment, Nr. 20, Colonel von der Mense

3 battalions

Total: 6,172 men

Attached

2nd Thuringian Infantry Regiment, Nr. 32, Colonel von Schwerin

3 battalions

Lower Rhineland Fusilier Regiment, Nr. 39, Colonel von Woyna II

3 battalions

Total: 6,172 men

Cavalry

2nd Rhineland Hussar Regiment, Nr. 9, Major von Kosel

5 squadrons

10th Landwehr Hussar Regiment

2 squadrons

Total: 1,093 men

Artillery

Commander   Major Stumpff von Rhein

1st Four Pounder Battery, 8th Artillery Regiment

1st Twelve Pounder Battery, 8th Artillery Regiment

12th Twelve Pounder Reserve Battery

Total: 3 batteries   435 men 18 guns

3rd Light Field Hospital

Total effectives: Approximately 45,000, on June 2[6]

---

6   Scheibert, p. 192.

Appendix VIII

Order of Battle of the Federal VIII Corps[1]

Commander	Grand Duke, General of Infantry, Prince Alexander of Hesse
Chief of Staff	Lieutenant-General von Baur (Württemberg)
Deputy Chief of Staff	Major Krauss (Baden)
Artillery Director	Lieutenant-General von Faber (Baden)
Engineer Director	Major von Orelli (Austrian)

1st Division (Württemberg)

Commander	Lieutenant-General von Hardegg
Chief of Staff	Major-General von Kallée

1st Infantry Brigade　　　Major-General Baumbach
1st Infantry Regiment (2 battalions), Colonel von Starkloff
5th Infantry Regiment (2 battalions), Colonel Hermann von Hügel
3rd Jäger Battalion, Major von Starkloff
Total – 5 battalions:　　　　4,474 men

2nd Infantry Brigade　　　Major-General von Fischer
2nd Infantry Regiment (2 battalions), Colonel von Majer
7th Infantry Regiment (2 battalions), Colonel Albert von Hügel
2nd Jäger Battalion, Lieutenant-Colonel von Hayn
Total – 5 battalions:　　　　4,474 men

3rd Infantry Brigade　　　Major-General Hegelmaier
3rd Infantry Regiment (2 battalions), Colonel von Lipp
8th Infantry Regiment (2 battalions), Colonel von Reitzenstein
1st Jäger Battalion, Major von Berger
Total – 5 battalions　　　　4,474 men

1　Baur-Breitenfeld, Appendices 1-8, also quoted in Ö.K, Vol. V, Appendix II. Note that strengths shown represent establishments, rather than actual.

Cavalry Brigade   Major-General Count Scheler
1st Mounted Regiment (four squadrons), Colonel von Harling
4th Mounted Regiment (four squadrons), Colonel von Sukelen
2nd Squadron, 2nd Mounted Regiment
Total – 9 squadrons   1,260 men

Divisional Artillery   Colonel von Leube
1st Horse Artillery Battery (eight rifled six pounders), Captain von Marchtaler
6th Foot Artillery Battery (eight rifled six pounders), Captain Roschmann
7th Foot Artillery Battery (eight rifled six pounders), Captain Faber du Faur
Total – 3 batteries   714 men   24 guns
Divisional Pioneers, Captain Schmoller   55 men
Medical Company, Captain Flaischlen   222 men

2nd Division (Baden)

Commander-in-Chief   Lieutenant-General Prince Wilhelm of
                                            Baden
Chief of Staff   Colonel Keller
Divisional Commander   Lieutenant-General Waag

1st Infantry Brigade   Major-General Baron von La Roche
1st Leib Grenadier Regiment (2 battalions), Colonel Baron von Degenfeld
5th Infantry Regiment (2 battalions), Colonel Keller
Jäger Battalion, Lieutenant-Colonel von Peternell
Total – 5 battalions   4,266 men

2nd Infantry Brigade   Colonel von Neubronn
2nd Infantry Regiment (2 battalions), Colonel Hoffmann
3rd Infantry Regiment (2 battalions), Colonel von Billiez
Fusilier Battalion, Lieutenant-Colonel Bauer
Total – 5 battalions   4,266 men
2nd Dragoon Regiment (four squadrons),
Colonel von Laroche   487 men

Divisional Artillery   Colonel Count Sponeck
1st Artillery Battery (six rifled six pounders)
2nd Artillery Battery (six rifled six pounders)
5th Artillery Battery (six rifled six pounders)
Total – 3 batteries   498 men   18 guns
Divisional Pioneers   61 men
Medical Company   149 men

3rd Division (Grand Duchy of Hesse)

Commander   Lieutenant-General Baron Perglas
Chief of Staff   Colonel Becker

1st Infantry Brigade   Major-General Frey
1st Leibgarde Infantry Regiment (2 battalions), Colonel von Grolman
2nd Infantry Regiment, Grand Duke (2 battalions), Colonel Wilkens
1st Homburg Jäger Company, Captain Wernigt
Total – 4 battalions & 1 company   3,735 men

2nd Infantry Brigade   Major-General von Stockhausen, Senior
3rd Leib Infantry Regiment (2 battalions), Colonel von Ochsenstein
4th Infantry Regiment, Prince Carl (2 battalions), Colonel Schenck
2nd Homburg Jäger Company, Captain von Buseck
Total – 4 battalions & 1 company   3,735 men
Sharpshooter Corps, Lieutenant-Colonel von Grolman
Total – 1 battalion   880 men

Cavalry Brigade   Major-General Ludwig of Hesse
1st Mounted Regiment (four squadrons)
Total – 4 squadrons   581 men

Divisional Artillery   Major Scholl
2nd Artillery Battery (six rifled six pounders)
3rd Artillery Battery (six rifled six pounders)
Total – 2 batteries   387 men   12 guns
Divisional Pioneers   60 men
Medical Detachment   91 men

4th Division (Austria-Nassau)

Commander   FML Count Neipperg
Chief of Staff   Captain von Ratschiller

Austrian Brigade   Major-General Hahn
IR Nr. 16 (3 battalions)
IR Nr. 21 (1 battalion)
IR Nr. 49 (1 battalion)
IR Nr. 74 (1 battalion)
Feld-Jäger Battalion Nr. 35
Total – 7 battalions   7,053 men

Nassau Brigade   Major-General Roth
1st Infantry Regiment (2 battalions)
2nd Infantry Regiment (2 battalions)
Jäger Battalion
Total – 5 battalions   4,503 men

Divisional Cavalry
Kur-Hessen Hussars (two squadrons)   331 men

Divisional Artillery
Nassau
1 battery (rifled six pounders)
Austrian
Foot Battery Nr. 1 (rifled four pounders)
Foot Battery Nr. 4 (rifled four pounders)
Total – 3 batteries   592 men   24 guns

Divisional Pioneers (Nassau)   82 men
Medical Detachment (Nassau) 115 men
Medical Detachment (Austria) 46 men

Corps Reserve Cavalry
Commander   Lieutenant-General Entress-Fürsteneck (Württemberg)
General Staff Officer   Oberlieutenant von Maucler
Württemberg 3rd Mounted Regiment (4 squadrons) 700 men
Württemberg 1st Mounted Regiment (1 squadron)   (included in above)
Baden Leib Dragoon Regiment (4 squadrons)   974 men
Baden 3rd Dragoon Regiment (4 squadrons)   (included in above)
Hessian 2nd Mounted Regiment (4 squadrons)   566 men

Artillery
Württemberg 2nd Horse Artillery Battery (muzzle-loading four pounders)
Total – 1 battery   238 men   8 guns
Total, Reserve Cavalry:
17 squadrons, 1 battery   2,478 men 8 guns

Corps Reserve Artillery
Commander   Major Scholl (Hessian)[2]

Württemberg Detachment
1st Twelve pounder Foot Battery (Smoothbores)   238 men   8 guns
4th Twelve pounder Foot Battery (Smoothbores)   238 men   8 guns

Baden Detachment
Six Pounder Horse Artillery Battery (Smoothbores)   159 men   6 guns
3rd Foot Artillery Battery (six rifled six pounders) 159 men   6 guns

Hessian Detachment
Mixed Horse Battery (4 Smoothbore and 2 Rifled
                          Six Pounders)   179 men   6 guns
1st Six Pounder Foot Artillery Battery (Smoothbores) 179 men   6 guns

---

2   Subsequently, Hessian Colonel Seederer.

Nassau Detachment

Six Pounder Foot Battery (Smoothbores)	203 men	8 guns

Munitions Columns

3 Württemberg columns	203 men	2 spare guns
2 Baden columns	218 men	
2 Hessian columns	290 men	
1 Austrian column	101 men	
1 Nassau column	171 men	
Total Reserve Artillery:		
7 batteries	2,412 men	50 guns

Bridging Trains   Colonel von Niethammer (Württemberg)[3]

Württemberg	2½	313 men
Baden	1¼	147 men
Hesse	¾	74 men
Nassau	½	81 men
Total:	5 units	615 men

---

3   Note that these units were intended to combine in this manner for operations.

Appendix IX

Ammunition Expenditure by Prussian units at Kissingen and Friedrichshall, July 10 1866[1]

Unit	Rifle Rounds	Shells	Shrapnel
II/IR 13	nil	–	–
F/IR 13	1,050	–	–
I/IR 15	15,080	–	–
II/IR 15	2,008	–	–
F/IR 15	5,660	–	–
I/IR 19[2]	8,540	–	–
II/IR 19	13,950	–	–
F/IR 19	17,449	–	–
I/IR 53	2,934	–	–
II/IR 53	4,465	–	–
F/IR 53	8,686	–	–
I/IR 55	5,490	–	–
II/IR 55	5,520	–	–
F/IR 55	10,060	–	–
F/Lippe	8,450	–	–
7th Field Artillery Regiment:			
3rd Twelve Pounder Battery	–	99	19
3rd Six Pounder Battery	–	153	22
3rd Four Pounder Battery	–	384	–
4th Four Pounder Battery	–	184	–
3rd Horse Artillery Battery	–	72	–
Total	100,942[3]	892	41[4]

---

1 Hoenig, *Entscheidungskämpfe*, Table 6.
2 Note that IR 19, while present and heavily engaged, was actually a unit of Beyer's division.
3 The precise even numbers reported by a majority of units may well indicate a preference for 'tidiness' on the part of the quartermasters.
4 In addition, von Manteuffel's artillery batteries fired seven rounds at Friedrichshall, and a further 120 rounds at Hausen, ibid.

Order of Battle of the Prussian II Reserve Corps, July 20 1866[1]

Commander	General of Infantry Friedrich Franz, Grand Duke of Mecklenburg-Schwerin
Chief of Staff	Lieutenant-Colonel Veith
Artillery Commander	Colonel von Müller (Mecklenburg)
Engineer Commander	Lieutenant-Colonel Schmidt

Prussian Combined Division

Commander	Lieutenant-General von Horn
Chief of Staff	Major von Bassewitz

Combined Guards Brigade   Colonel von Tresckow[2]
4th Regiment, Foot Guards, Colonel Osten-Sacken
4 battalions   3,910 men
4th Battalions of the 1st, 2nd, & 3rd Foot Guards, 4th Battalion, Guard Grenadier Regiment
4 battalions   3,296 men

Combined Infantry Brigade   Colonel Schuler von Senden
4th Battalions of IR Nrs. 2, 9, 14, 42, & 61
5 battalions   4,120 men
Infantry Regiment Anhalt
2 battalions: 2,050 men

Reserve Landwehr Cavalry Brigade
1st Reserve Landwehr Hussar Regiment
4 squadrons   625 men
1st Reserve Landwehr Uhlan Regiment
4 squadrons   612 men
Total   1,237 men

---

1   Ö.K., Vol. V, Appendices, pp. 32-33. Note that the figures shown represent full strength establishment.

2   Brigade Tresckow was subsequently reinforced by the transfer of the three battalions of IR 19, from Division Beyer.

Artillery
2nd Reserve Field Artillery Regiment
5 four pounder batteries, 6 guns each
3 six pounder batteries, 6 guns each
8 batteries   1,160 men   48 guns

Medical Troops
Two light field hospitals   ?
Division Total: 15,773 men   48 guns

Mecklenburg-Schwerin Combined Division

Commander   Major-General von Bilgner
Chief of Staff   Captain von Koppelow

Mecklenburg Infantry Brigade   Colonel von Jasmund I
Mecklenburg Infantry Regiment, Colonel von Jasmund II
4 Battalions   4,096 men
Mecklenburg Jäger Battalion   1,024 men

Brunswick- Saxe-Altenberg Brigade Colonel von Girsewald
Brunswick Infantry Regiment
2 battalions   2,048 men
Altenberg Regiment
2 battalions   2,048 men
Mecklenburg Dragoon Regiment
4 squadrons   624 men
Brunswick Hussar Regiment
2 squadrons   312 men

1st Mecklenburg Six Pounder Artillery Battery   135 men   6 guns
2nd Mecklenburg Six Pounder Artillery Battery   135 men   6 guns
Brunswick Six Pounder Artillery Battery   68 men   4 guns

Division Total: 9,216 men   16 guns
Corps Total: 26,623 men   64 guns

Appendix XI

Garrison of the Federal Fortress of Mainz, July 11 1866[1]

	A	B	C	D	E	F	G	H
k.k. Austrian artillery & postal depot	7	24	–	–	7	5	29	–
k.k. Engineer Detachment	2	12	–	–	1	91	103	–
I/1st Bavarian Infantry Regt.	26	73	29	1	–	798	900	2
I/Bavarian Leib Infantry Regt.	24	72	30	2	–	832	934	2
Bavarian 2nd Artillery Regt, 2nd Foot Battery	4	18	3	–	–	147	168	3
Bavarian 4th Artillery Regt, 2nd Foot Battery	4	14	3	–	–	138	155	4
I/Kurhessian Leibgarde Regiment	17	53	17	2	16	650	720	8
II/Kurhessian Leibgarde Regiment	19	53	67	2	16	800	920	15
I/1st Kurhessian Infantry Regiment	19	53	17	2	16	610	680	8
II/1st Kurhessian Infantry Regiment	17	53	23	2	16	645	721	3
I/2nd Kurhessian Infantry Regiment	17	53	23	3	16	744	820	10
II/2nd Kurhessian Infantry Regiment	17	56	17	3	28	712	785	3
I/3rd Kurhessian Infantry Regiment	19	53	17	3	16	810	880	8
II/3rd Kurhessian Infantry Regiment	19	53	17	3	16	761	831	3
Kurhessian Jäger Battalion	17	54	17	2	1	461	532	4
Kurhessian Schützen Battalion	17	54	27	2	1	583	664	4
Kurhessian Pioneer Company	3	18	2	–	–	100	120	2
Kurhessian Horse Artillery	4	20	4	–	–	90	114	88
Kurhessian Rifled Artillery	4	22	3	–	–	89	114	36
Kurhessian Twelve pounder Artillery	4	21	2	–	–	99	122	44
Kurhessian Six pounder Artillery	4	13	4	–	–	86	108	39
Kurhessian Labour Company	3	17	1	–	–	47	65	3
Kurhessian Train Detachment	1	5		–	–	97	102	11
Kurhessian Garde du Corps (cavalry)	11	24	12	3	15	199	235	246
Hesse-Darmstadt Artillery	2	7	1	–	2	44	52	2
Saxe-Meiningen Contingent	28	98	64	3	15	726	888	12
Hanoverian Contingent	1	–	–	–	–	–	86	86

---

1   *Österreichs Kämpfe 1866*, Volume V, Appendix 11.

A total of 29 Kurhessian guns were available (no breakdown given).

KEY:
A. Officers
B. NCO's
C. Musicians & Carpenters
D. Medical
E. Other Specialists and Instructors
F. Men
G. Totals of NCO's, Musicians & Carpenters, and men.
H. Horses

Appendix XII

Lippe-Detmold Battalion, July 5 1866[1]

	Officers	NCOs	Musicians	Fusiliers
Staff	2		1	
1st Company	4	11	4	210
2nd Company	3	14	4	214
3rd Company	3	9	4	213
4th Company	4	12	4	209

---

1   *Der Antheil des Bataillons Lippe an dem Feldzuge der Main-Armee im Sommer 1866*, App. 2.

Appendix XIII

Later Breakdown of Hessian Losses, Action of Laufach, July 13 1866[1]

	Killed		Wounded	
	Officers	Men	Officers	Men
Division Staff	1	–	–	–
1st Brigade Staff	–	–	1	–
2nd Brigade Staff	–	–	1	–
1st Infantry Regiment	–	25	4	80
2nd Infantry Regiment	1	3	2	6
3rd Infantry Regiment	5	67	9	148
4th Infantry Regiment	5	66	6	143
2nd Hesse-Homburg Jäger Company		1	1	3
1st Mounted Regiment		1		1
2nd Foot Artillery Battery				2

---

1   These statistics were published in the *Großherzoglich Hessischen Militärverordnungsblatt* of February 28 1867.

A Note on Sources

In the past few years, a number of 'reprints' of contemporary sources have become available from a number of sources. Many of these, often taken from digital copies already available on the internet, vary greatly in legibility, and maps/appendices in particular have suffered in the transition. This should be understood. A notable exception, in general, is the work recently undertaken by the British Library.

Bavarian General Staff, *Antheil der Königlich Bayerischen Armee am Kriege des Jahre 1866.*
The official Bavarian account of the campaign, this work was published in 1868. It covers Bavarian involvement, often in minute detail, but offers little insight into errors or omissions.

Booms, Petrus Gerardus. See bibliography under 'Dutch-language books'.
Colonel Booms, a Netherlands Army officer, later Chief of Staff, and subsequently War Minister, wrote two very valuable works concerning the 1866 campaign. These works are particularly useful, as they are penned by a contemporary outside and unbiased, though reliable, source. He is also an acute observer, though can be unduly harsh.

Cohn, Martin & Mels, August, *Von der Elbe bis zur Tauber : Der Feldzug der Preussischen Main-Armee im Sommer 1866, vom Berichterstatter der Daheim'.*
This is a colourful and well illustrated anecdotal popular history of the campaign, branded by Lettow-Vorbeck simply, and somewhat harshly, as 'unreliable'.

Fontane, Theodor, *Der deutsche Krieg von 1866 (Volume II). Der Feldzug im West und Mitteldeutschland.*
Another most talented contemporary observer, Fontane offers a highly detailed journalistic account of the whole of the war, the second volume of his 1866 work including the 'German' campaign. His agenda is always a plain and simple one, based upon Prussian-inspired and -directed German nationalism and glory. This must always be borne in mind in interpreting his work.

Hoenig, Fritz, *Das Gefecht bei Kissingen am 10 Juli 1866.*
This is a detailed and wide-ranging source for the actions along the River Saale on July 10th.

Prussian General Staff (GGS), *Der Feldzug von 1866 in Deutschland.*
The Prussian General Staff History, originally published in 1867, this is a highly detailed account of the war, including, of course, the events in southern and western Germany. It is an invaluable source, but it is also, obviously, an official history, and additionally, was published before a large number of other important works appeared. Several editions of an English translation exist, entitled, *The Campaign of 1866 in Germany*, the first of which appeared in 1872.

Rüstow, Wilhelm.

A former refugee from the 1848 revolution in Berlin, Rüstow settled in Switzerland, and subsequently wrote comprehensive accounts of then contemporary military campaigns. His coverage of this aspect of the 1866 war is necessarily subordinated to the primary theatre, but it is balanced and, as always, presented with clarity. His unflinching pro-Prussian bias should be noted. Both of Rüstow's brothers died in the 1866 war, Cäsar (Caesar), a Prussian infantry major, being killed in action during the Main Campaign.

Bibliography

German-language books

(Anon.), *Aktenstücke und Verhandlungen in der Klagsache der k. preußischen Staatsanwaltschaft zu Frankfurt a. M. gegen die Redaktion der Frankfurter Zeitung wegen behaupteter Verleumdung und Beleidigung der Führer der Mainarmee und der Militärbefehlshaber von Frankfurt im Jahre 1866* Taken from stenographer's notes,(Ebner, Stuttgart 1869

(Anon.), *Antheil des 1. Rhenischen Infanterie-Regiments Nr. 25 an den Feldzuge der Main-Armee im Jahre 1866,* (Mittler & Son, Berlin 1867)

(Anon.), *Das Treffen bei Kissingen, Winkels, und Nüdlingen am 10. Juli 1866,* (Franz Joseph Reichardt, Kissingen 1866)

(Anon.), *Das VIII und IX Deutsche bundes-armee-corps 1866,* (Confidential Royal Printers, Berlin 1866)

(Anon.), *Der Bundesfeldzug in Bayern im Jahre 1866,* (C.W. Hochhausen, Wenigen-Jena 1866)

(Anon.), *Der Deutsche Krieg von 1866 und dessen Ursprung. Für das Volk erzählt von einem Preußischen Landwehr-Offizier,* (C.F. Conrad, Berlin 1866)

(Anon.), *Der Feldzug der Mecklenburger nach Bayern im Sommer 1866,* (Privately published, 'Stifts Bethlehem', Ludwigsluft 1867)

(Anon.), *Der Feldzug von 1866 in Deutschland,* (Prussian General Staff History, Mittler & Son, Berlin 1867. Subsequent official English translations of this work also exist – see entry in English-language books.

(Anon.), *Der Sieg der Hannoveraner in der Schlacht bei Langensalza am 27 Juni 1866,* (Schulz, Celle 1869 [?])

(Anon.), *Die Bayerische Armee 1866,* (Confidential Royal Printers, Berlin 1866). A low-level Prussian intelligence publication, prior to the outbreak of hostilities. An English translation of this work also exists – see entry in English-language books.

(Anon.), *Die Hannoveraner in Thüringen und die Schlacht bei Langensalza 1866,* (Rockstuhl, Bad Langensalza 2005)

(Anon.), *Geschichte des königlich bayerischen 15 Infanterie-Regiments König Johann von Sachsen im Feldzuge 1866 gegen Preussen,* (Josef Rindfleisch, Neuburg 1867)

(Anon.), *Handbuch für die Offiziere der königlich Preußischen Artillerie,* (Mittler, Berlin 1860)

(Anon.), *Juni-und Julitage 1866 in Frankfurt am Main,* (Karl Luckhardt, Kassel 1866)

(Anon.), *Kurze Beschreibung des Bruderkriegs in Deutschland im Jahr 1866,* (?, Reutlingen. 1867(?))

(Anon.), *Officieller Bericht über die Kriegsereignisse zwischen Hannover und Preußen im Juni 1866* (Carl Gerold's Sohn, Vienna 1866)

(Anon.), *Österreichs Kämpfe im Jahre 1866,* (K.K. General Staff, Volumes I & V, Vienna 1869)

(Anon.), *Wirkungen und Ursachen der preuszischen Erfolge in Bayern,* (G. W. Hochhausen Wenigen, Jena 1866). A riposte to Gemmingen von Massenbach's work, see below.

(Anon.), *Zum Gedenken der Schlacht bei Roßbrunn: 1866 26 Juli – 100 Jahre*, (Hans Beck, Würzburg 1966)

(Anon.), *Zur Beeurtheilung des Verhaltens der badischen Felddivision im Feldzuge des Jahres 1866*, (Eduard Zernin, Darmstadt & Leipzig 1867)

(Anon.), *Zur Erinnerung an den Feldzug 1866: Main-Armee, XIII Division, Oldenburgisch-Hanseatische Brigade, Infanterie-Regiment; 1.-3. Bataillon,* (?, ?, 1870?)

(Anon.),('Landwehr Offizier'), *Die Kriegsbegebenheiten des Jahres 1866, in Deutschland und Italien. Von einem Landwehr-Offizier*, (Sacco, Berlin 1866)

(Anon.),(Royal Bavarian General Staff), *Antheil der Königlich Bayerischen Armee am Kriege des Jahre 1866,* (Hermann Manz, Munich 1868)

Anon ('A Badener'), *Badische Antwort auf das Pamphlet über den angeblichen bad. Verrath an den deutschen Bundestruppen*, (J.H. Geiger, Lahr 1867)

Anon. ('einem deutschen Staatsmanne'), *Tagebuch-Blätter aus dem Jahre 1866*, (Eduard Zernin, Darmstadt & Leipzig 1867)

Alexander, Prince of Hesse, *Feldzugs-Journal des Oberbefehlshabers des 8ten deutschen Bundes-Armee-Corps im Feldzug des Jahres 1866 in Westdeutschland (Im Auszug mitgetheilt und als Manuscript gedruckt)* (G. Otto, Darmstadt, n.d./1866?)

Alexander, Prince of Hesse, *Erläuterungen des Höchstkommandirenden der Südwestdeutschen Bundes-Armee zu dem im Buchhander erschienenen feldzugs-Journal*, (Hermann Manz, Munich 1867)

Aufsess, Baron Werner von und zu, *Manteuffels Operationen in Bayern von den Tauber bis zum Beginn der Waffenruhe 1866: Eine kriegsgeschichtliche Studie*, (Liebel, Berlin 1905)

Aulhorn, Max, *Feldzug 1866: Auszüge aus den Briefen des Premierleutnants und Adjutanten vom damaligen Weimarischen Kontingent Max Aulhorn aus den neutralen Festungen Mainz und Rastatt an seine Frau*, (Scheibe, 1912)

Barsewich, W., *Geschichte des Großherzoglich Badischen Leib-Grenadier-Regiments 1803-1871* (2 vols.), (Muller, Karlsruhe 1893)

Bartels von Bartberg, Eduard, *Der Krieg im Jahr 1866. Kritische Bemerkungen über die Feldzüge in Böhmen, Italien und am Main*, (Otto Wigand, Leipzig 1866)

Baur, Wilhelm, *Reiseerrinerungen aus der Main-Armee*, (Agentur des Rauhes Haus, Hamburg 1866)

Baur-Breitenfeld, Fidel Carl Friedrich von, *Die Operationen des achten deutschen Bundes Corps im Feldzuge des Jahres 1866*, (Eduard Zernin, Darmstadt & Leipzig 1868)

Beaulieu-Marconnay, Carl, *Tagebuch-Blätter aus dem Jahre 1866: Erlebtes und Durchdachtes von einmem deutschen Staatsmanne*, (Eduard Zernin, Darmstadt & Leipzig 1867)

Beck. Bernhard, Dr., *Kriegs-Chirurgische Erfahrungen während des feldzuges 1866 in Süddeutschland*, (F.R. Wagner, Freiburg 1867)

Beck, Fritz, *Geschichte des 1.Großherzoglich hessischen Infanterie-(Leibgarde-) Regiments Nr. 115 1621-1899*, (E.S. Mittler & Son, Berlin 1899)

Beck, Fritz, *Geschichte des Großherzoglich Hessischen Feld-Artillerie-Regiments Nr. 25 (Großherzogliches Artilleriekorps) und seine Stämme 1460-1883*, (E.S. Mittler, Berlin 1884)

Becker, Ernst, *Geschichte des 2. Badischen Grenadier-Regiments Kaiser Wilhelm Nr. 110*, (E.S. Mittler & Son, Berlin 1877)

Beiche, Wilhelm Eduard, *Der deutsche Krieg im Jahre 1866: ein Gedenkblatt für das deutsche Volk*, (Herrosé, Wittenberg 1866)

Besser, L. von, *Die preussische Kavallerie in der Campagne 1866*, (Alexander Duncker, Berlin 1868)

Bezzel, Oskar, *Geschichte des Königlich Bayerischen Heere von 1825 mit 1866*, (Schick, Munich 1931)

Biebrach, *Kritische Beleuchtung der Preussischen und Süddeutschen Kriegsführung im Main-Feldzuge 1866*, (Mainz, Victor v. Zabern 1870)

Blankenburg, Heinrich, *Der deutsche krieg von 1866: historisch, politisch und kriegswissenschaftlich dargestellt*, (F. W. Brockhaus, Leipzig 1868)

Bleibtreu, Carl, *Langensalza – Der Mainfeldzug*, (Carl Krabbe, Stuttgart 1906)

Blomberg, Baron, & Leszcynski, Captain, *Geschichte des 6. Westfälischen Infanterie-Regiments Nr. 55, von seiner Errichtung bis zum 2. September 1877*, (Meyer, Detmold 1877)

Blume, General of Infantry von, *Geschichte des Infanterie-Regiments Herwarth von Bittenfeld (1.Westfälischen) im 19 Jahrhundert*, (E.H. Mittler & Son, Berlin 1910)

Bock von Wülfingen, Julius, *Tagebuch vom 11 Juni bis 3 Juli 1866*, (Gustav Jacob, Hanover 1876)

Bockenheimer, Karl Georg, *Mainz im Jahre 1866*, (P. von Zabern, Mainz 1907)

Borbstädt, Adolf, *Preußens Feldzüge gegen Oesterreich und dessen Verbündete im Iahre, 1866*, (Mittler & Son, Berlin 1866)

Bredow, Gottfried Klaus von, *Geschichte des 2. Rheinischen Husaren-Regiments Nr. 9*, (E.H. Mittler & Son, Berlin 1889)

Broecker, Rudolph, *Erinnerungen an die Thätigkeit der 11. Infanterie-Division und ihrer Artillerie während des Feldzuges 1866: Vortrag gehalten in der militairischen Gesellschaft am 19. Dezember 1866*, (Mittler & Son, Berlin 1867)

Bronsart von Schellendorf, Paul Leopold Eduard, Heinrich Anton, *Taktische Rückblicke von 1866*, (Dümmer, Berlin 1869). A subsequent English translation of this work also exists – see entry in English-language books. In addition, further musings followed in 1870.

Burger, Ludwig, *Erinnerungs-Blätter aus dem Feldzuge der Main-Armee 1866*, (W. Korn, Berlin 1870 – Portfolio of prints)

Caemmerer, Rudolf von, *Die süddeutschen Heeresbewegungen im Main-Feldzug von 1866*, (?, Berlin 1903)

Clotz, Ernst, *Die Süddeutschen Staaten im Kriege von 1866 und die gefechte in Taubergrund*, (Verein Tauberfränk. Heimatfreunde, 1966)

Cohn, Martin & Mels, August, *Von der Elbe bis zur Tauber. Der Feldzug der Preußischen Main-Armee im Sommer 1866*, (Velhagen & Klasing, Bielefeld & Leipzig 1867)

Cordemann, G., *Die Hannoveersche Armee und ihre Schicksal in und nach der Katastrophe von 1866*, (Quellen und Darstellungen zur Geschichte Niedersachsens Vol. 15, Hannover und Leipzig, Hahn 1904)

Cramm, Baron Burghard von, *Aus Langensalza. Ein Erinnerungsblatt*, (G.G. Meinhold & Son, Dresden 1867)

Cramer, Adalbert, *Theilnahme des Königlich Preussischen 5. Westfälischen Infanterie-Regiments Nr. 53 am Feldzuge der Main Armee im Jahre 1866*, (?, Wesel 1869)

Cramer, Alfred, *Geschichte des Infanterie-Regiments Prinz Friedrich der Niederlande (2. Westfälischen Nr. 15) 1813-1911*, (R. Eisenschmidt, Berlin 1911)

Dambrowski, Karl von, *Die Regimentsgeschichte des Infanterie-Regiments Prinz Friedrich der Niederlande (Westf.) Nr. 15*, (Helwing, Hanover 1878)

Dammers, Major-General Georg Friedrich Ferdinand, *Erinnerungen und Erlebnisse des königlich hannoverschen Generamajors G.F.F.D, letzten Generaladjutanten des König Georg V. Hannover,* (Helwing, Hanover 1890)

Delbrück, Hans, *Erinnerungen, Aufsätze und Reden,* (Stilke, Berlin 1905)

Demeter,Karl, *Das Deutsche Offizierkorps in Gesellschaft und Staat 1650-1945,* (Bernard & Graefe, Frankfurt on Main 1962)

Diebitsch, Victor von, Die *Königlich Hannoversche Armee auf ihrem letzten Waffengange im Juni 1866,* (M. Heinstus, Bremen 1897)

Diest, Gustav, *Aus dem Leben eines Glücklichen: Erinnerungen Eines alten Beamten,* (Siegfried Mittler und Son, Berlin 1904)

Dragomirov, Mikhail, *Abriß des österreichisch-preussischen Krieges im Jahre 1866,* (U. Bath, Berlin 1866)

Ecke, Ralf, *Franken 1866.Versuch eines politischen Psychogramms,* (Korn & Berg, Nuremburg 1972)

Emmerling, Ernst, *Actenmäßige interessante Enthüllungen über den badischen Verrath an den deutschen Bundestruppen in dem soeben beendigten preußisch-deutschen Kriege,* (Zamerski, Vienna 1866)

Emmerling, Ernst, *Nochmals der Badische Vorrath,* (Keeblath, Stuttgart 1866)

Fontane, Theodor, *Der Deutsche Krieg von 1866,* (Volume II), *Der Feldzug in West und Mitteldeutschland,* (Royal Press, Berlin 1871)

Förster, Brix, *Der Feldzug von 1866 in Südwest-Deutschland. Militärisch – statistische Notizen,* (J. Lindauer, Munich 1867)

Förster, Rolf, *Die Leistungsfähigkeit der Bayerischen Armee im Feldzuge 1866,* (Dissertation, Munich 1987)

Frauenholz, Dr. Eugen, *Die Heerführung des Feldmarschalls Prinzen Carl von Bayern im Feldzug von 1866 (Darstellungen aus der Bayerschen Kriegs-u. Heeresgeschichte, vol. 25),* (Bavarian Kriegsarchiv, Munich 1925).

Freudenthal, Friedrich, *Von Lüneburg bis Langensalza: Erinnerungen eines hannoverschen Infanteristen,* (Carl Schünemann, Bremen 1894)

Fricke, D., *Aus dem Feldzuge 1866. Briefe aus dem Felde und Predigten und Reden im Felde,* (Fr. Richter, Leipzig 1891)

Friedjung, Heinrich, *Der Kampf um die Vorherrschaft in Deutschland 1859 bis 1866,* (J. G. Cotta, Stuttgart & Berlin 1912)

Galperin, Peter, *Deutsche Wehr im Deutschen Bund 1815 – 1866: mit gesonderten Hinweisen auf die Bewaffnung, die Marine, die Soldatenversorgung, die Wehrfinanzierung,* (Biblio-Verlag, Osnabrück 2000)

Gemmingen von Massenbach, Franz, *Ursachen und wirkungen der Bayerischen Kriegführung im feldzuge 1866,* (Hermann Manz, Munich 1866). This work elicited a riposte – see (Anon.), *Wirkungen und Ursachen der preuszischen Erfolge in Bayern.*

Glasenapp, G. von, *Gedanken über die Verwendung und Ausbildung der Kavallerie, mit besonderer Berücksichtigungdes Feldzuges 1866,* (Berlin 1867)

Goeben, August v. *Das Gefecht bei Dermbach am 4. Juli 1866,* (Eduard Zernin, Darmstadt & Leipzig 1870).

Goeben, August v., *Das Treffen bei Kissingen,* (Eduard Zernin, Darmstadt, 1868)

Göhring, Carl, *Die Kriege Preußens gegen Oesterreich: von 1740 bis 1866, und zwar der Erste und Zweite Schlesiche, der Siebenjährige und Siebentägige Krieg,* (Vol. II – Carl Minde, Leipzig 1867)

Goldbach, School Master, *Bild aus d. Schrecktagen von Aschaffenburg am Main am 13. u. 14. Juli 1866*, (Riecher, Tübingen 1866)

Gollwitzer, Wilhelm, *Das Gefecht bei Seybothenreuth am 29. Juli 1866 mit Allem, was ihm vorausgang und nachfolge*, (Emil Mühl, Bayreuth 1932)

Gotzes, Friedrich August, *Marschnotizen u. Erlebniße aus dem Feldzuge1866 bei der Main-Armee*, (Universitäts und Landesbibliothek 1912)

Guntermann, A., *Mit Badens Wehr für deutsche Ehr: Die Badischen Truppen und ihre Anteilnahme am Einigungskriege*, (?, Freiburg in Baden 1895)

Günther, Adolf, *Das Gefecht bei Aschaffenburg am 14. Juli 1866*, (Wailandt, Aschaffenburg 1902)

Gutbier, Hermann, *Ein Gang über das Schlachtfeld des 27. Juni 1866*, (Drei Türme, Bad Langensalza 1991)

Habermehl, Ferdinand, *Das Gefecht von Frohnhofen, Laufach und Weiler, von einem Augenzeugen,* (Schorkopf, Darmstadt 1867)

Halbreiter, Adolph, *Bismarckfänger. Wie die Bayern letztmals gegen die Preussen zogen. Adolph Halbreiters Erinnerungen aus dem Feldzuge Anno 1866*, (Spätlese, Nuremburg, 1983)

Hamm, Captain & Moewes, Premierlieutenant, *Geschichte des 1. Westfälischen Feld-Artillerie-Regiments Nr. 7,* (E. S. Mittler & Son, Berlin 1891)

Hamm, Walter, & Bergmann, Werner, *Bayern's Anteil am Feldzug gegen Preussen im Sommer des Jahres 1866*, (Eigenverlag, ? 1990)

Hamm, Walter, *Rossdorf im Deutsch-Deutschen Krieg von 1866*, (Roßdorf Museum, Uettingen & Roßdorf 2003)

Harren, Franz, *Gefechts-Album von dem Treffen bei Kissingen*, (Books on Demand, Norderstedt 2009)

Hartmann, Julius, *Meine erlebnisse zu hannoverscher Zeit 1839-1866*, (J. F. Bergmann, Wiesbaden 1912)

Hauff, Ludwig, *Die Geschichte der Kriege von 1866 in Mitteleurope: Ihre Ursache und ihre Folgen*, (E.H. Summi, Munich 1867)

Heinemann, J., *Die Schlacht bei Kissingen und Nüdlingen am 10 Juli 1866*, (A. A. Reichardt, Kissingen 1866)

Helmert, Heinz, *Militärsystem Und Streikräfte Im Deutschen Bund am Vorabend Des Preussisch-Österreichischen Krieges Von 1866,* (Deutscher Militärverlag, East Berlin 1964)

Helmert, Heinz, & Usczeck, Hansjürgen, *Preussischdeutsche Kriege von 1864 bis 1871,* (Deutscher Militärverlag, East Berlin 1984)

Henning von Schönhoff, Otto von, *Sine ira! Die Darstellung des Gefechts von Kissingen, 10 juli 1866, durch dan K. Bayr. Generalstabquartiermeisterstab partiel beleuchtet von Königl. Preussischen Obersten Henning auf Schönhoff…*(Gerold, Königsberg 1869)

Hentz, Ferdinand von, *Geschichte des Infanterie-Regiment Graf Bülow von Dennewitz (6. Westfälisches) Nr. 55*, (Uhland'schen, Stuttgart 1910)

Hepp, Armin und Nickel, Walter: *Bruderkrieg zwischen Preußen und Bayern. Das Gefecht am Nebel bei Rossdorf vor der Rhoen am 4.Juli 1866* (Christel`s Copythek, Seligenthal 1991)

Hiltl, Georg, *Der Böhmische Krieg und der Main-Feldzug*, (Velhagen & Klasing, Bielefeld 1873)

Höhn, *Das Gefecht bei Hammelburg am 10. Juli 1866: kriegsgeschichtliche Geländbesprechnung*, (Infantry School, Hammelburg 1991)

Hoenig, Fritz, Das *Gefecht bei Kissingen am 10 Juli 1866*, (Clement's Buch und Kunsthandlung, Bad Kissingen 1901)

Hoenig, Fritz, *Die Entscheidungskämpfe des Mainfeldzuges and der Fränkischen Saale: Kissingen- Friedrichshall-Hammelburg*, (Mittler & Son, Berlin 1895)

Hoffmann, A. F., Th., *Erinnerungen an Langensalza aus dem Sommer 1866*, (Schmerl & v. Seefeld, Hanover 1867)

Hohenlohe-Ingelfingen, Prince Kraft zu, *Ausfzeichnungen aus meinem Leben*, (E. S. Mittler & Son, Berlin 1906)

Hölzermann, L, *Der Antheil des Bataillons Lippe and dem Feldzuge der Main-Armee im Sommer 1866*, (Meyer'sche Buchhandlung, Detmold 1866)

Hopf, Wilhelm, *Das Jahr 1866: Die deutsche Krisis des Jahres 1866*, (H. Feesche, Hanover 1906)

Horst, Edmund, *Kriegsbilder von den Schlachtfeldern Böhmens und Süddeutschlands, sowie von Italiens Land – und Seekämpfen im Jahre 1866,* (Münchmeyer, Dresden 1870)

Horwitz, J., *Von Berlin von Nikolsburg: Skizzen aus dem Kriegsjahre 1866*, (Springer, Berlin 1866)

Hösslin, Roland von, *Das Gefecht bei Roßdorf am 4 Juli 1866*, (Schmalkalden-Meiningen, Roßdorf 1938)

Hutten-Klingenstein, Moritz von, *Meine Eindrücke aus dem bayerisch-preußischen Feldzuge im Jahre 1866: von einem Augenzeugen*, (Seidel & Son, Vienna 1867)

H v B, *Der deutsche Krieg im Jahre 1866 nach den bis vorhandenen Quellen*, (Neumann-Hartmann, Elbing 1867)

Illing, Oskar, *Das Königlich Bayerische Infanterie-Leib-Regiment 1814 bis 1914*, (Royal Printing Office, Munich 1914)

Jakubaß, Franz A., *Das Gefecht bei Bad Kissingen von 1866*, (Bayerische Rundfunk, Nuremburg 1998)

Jena, Eduard v., *General von Goeben im Feldzuge 1866 gegen Hannover und die Süddeutschen Staaten und meine Erlebnisse in diesem Feldzuge als Generalstabsoffizier der Division Goeben* (R. Eisenschmidt, Berlin 1904)

Jentsch, Emil, *Errinerungen nach dem Tagebuch eines Zwanzigers aus dem Main-Feldzuge 1866*, (Max Babenstein, Rathenow 1899)

Jordan. Walther, *Das Gefecht bei Hammelburg am 10. Juli 1866*, (?, ?, 1938)

Käuffer, Karl, *Geschichte des königlich bayerischen 9. Infanterie-Regiments Wrede: Von seinem Ersprung bis zur Gegenwart*, (Georg Hertz, Würzburg 1888)

Kanngiesser, Otto, *Geschichte der Eroberung der freien Stadt Frankfurt durch Preussen im Jahre 1866*, (Heinrich Keller, Frankfurt 1877)

Kanngiesser, Otto, *Geschichte des Krieges von 1866*, (Swiss Publishing House, Basle 1892)

Kehnert, H., *Die kriegsereignisse des Jahres 1866 im Herzogtum Gotha und die gothaischen sturmer zur zeit das Treffens von Langensalza*, (Friedrich Perthes, Gotha 1899)

Kessel, von, *Die Ausbildung des Preußischen Infanterie-Bataillons im praktischen Dienst*, (Mittler & Son, Berlin 1863)

Klopp, Doctor Onno, *Die hannoveraner von Eisenach am 24 juni 1866*, (Wilhelm Braumüller, Vienna 1869)

Klugmann, Anna, *Reise-Erlebnisse einer preussischen Offiziers Frau im Feldlager der Main-Armee vom 15 bis 23 Juli 1866*, (Privately published, Berlin 1867)

Kluck, Alexander von, *Wanderjahre – Kriege – Gestalten*, (R. Eisenschmidt, Berlin 1927)

Knorr, Emil, *Der Feldzug das Jahres 1866 in West und Süddeutschland*, (Otto Meissner, Hamburg 1867, three volumes)

Kolb, Richard, *Unter Nassaus Fahnen: Geschichte des herzoglich-nassauischen Officiercorps 1803 – 66*, (Bechtold, Wiesbaden 1903)

Kopp, Walter, *Das Gefecht bei Kissingen am 10. Juli 1866*, (Privately published, Würzburg 1968)

Krieg, Captain von, *Kriegs-Tagebuch des 2. Westfälischen Infanterie-Regiments Nr. 15 (Prinz Friedrich der Niederlande) aus dem Feldzuge der Main-Armee 1866*, (Bruns, Minden 1867)

Kunz, Hermann, *Der Feldzug der Mainarmee im Jahre 1866*, (Friedrich Luckhardt, Berlin 1890)

Leeb, W., *Das Kgl. Bayerische 4. Feldartillerie-Regiment "König: Ein rückblik auf seine 50 jährige Entwicklung 1859-1909*, (Uhland, Stuttgart 1909)

Legde, Adolf, *Geschichte des 2. Badischen Dragoner Regiments Nr. 21*, (E.S. Mittler & Son, Berlin 1893)

Leoprechting, Marquard Baron, *Skizzen aus dem Feldzuge 1866*, (Staele, Munich 1866)

Lettow-Vorbeck, Oskar, *Geschichte des krieges von 1866 in Deutschland*, (E. S. Mittler & Son, Berlin, three volumes, 1902)

Linsingen, Erich von*, Die Hannoversche Heeresleitung im Feldzuge 1866 bis zur Schlacht von Langensalza*, (?, 1910)

Losch, Philipp, *Geschichte des Kurfürstentums Hessen 1803 bis 1866*, (Elwert, Marburg 1922)

Luedecke, Max, *Des Krieges Leid und Lust: poetisches Lebensbild aus dem Feldzuge der Main-Armee im Jahre 1866*, (Streiber, Magdeburg 1868)

Marx, Karl Friedrich*, Geschichte des Infanterie-Regiments Kaiser Friedrich, König von Preussen (7. Württembergischen) Nr. 125: 1809 bis 1895*, (E.S. Mittler & Son, Berlin 1895)

Meister, Oskar, *Aus bewegter Zeit. Erinnerungen eines österreichischen Soldaten an den Feldzug im Jahre 1866*, (Olmütz, 1878)

Menzel, Rudolf, *Geschichte des Infanterie-Regiments Kaiser Wilhelm, König von Preußen (2. Württembergischen) Nr. 120 1673-1909*, (Uhlandschen, Stuttgart 1909)

Menzel. Wolfgang, *Der Deutsche Krieg im Jahr 1866: in seinem Ursachen, seinem Verkauf, und seinem nächsten folgen*, (Adolph Krabbe, Stuttgart 1867)

Merkel, Georg, *Erinnerungen an Langensalza: geschrieben im Juli 1867*, (Schmorl & von Seefeld, Hanover 1867)

Moltke, Helmuth Karl Bernhard, Count von, *Moltkes Militärische Korrespondenz: Aus den Dienstschriften des Krieges 1866*, (German General Staff, Mittler & Son, Berlin 1896)

Müller, *Arnold, Das Königlich Bayerische 3 Feld-Artillerie Regiment Königen Mutter 1848 – 1898*, (G. Hafner, Munich 1898)

Müller, Herbert, *Geschichte des 4. Württembergischen Infanterie-Regiments No. 122, Kaiser Franz von Oesterreich, König von Ungarn 1806-1906,* (A. Scheuren, Heilbronn 1906)

Müller, Karl Alexander von, *Bayern im Jahre 1866 und die Berufung des Fürsten Hohenlohe*, (Oldenbourg, Munich 1909)

Müller, Karlheinz, *Preußischer Adler und Hessischen Löwe: hundert Jahre Wiesbadener Regierung 1866 – 1966; Dokumente der Zeit aus den Akten*, (Kultur u. Wissen, Wiesbaden 1866)

Müller, Klaus, *1866: Bismarcks deutscher Bruderkrieg*, (Ares, Graz 2007)

Müller, Wilhelm, *Geschichte der Neuesten Zeit 1816-1866 mit besonderer Berücksichtigung Deutschlands*, (Paul Neff, Stuttgart 1867)

Münich, *Friedrich, Geschichte der Entwickelung der bayerischen Armee seit zwei Jahrhunderten*, (J. Lindauer, Munich 1864)

Münster von Derneburg, Count Georg Herbert, *Hannovers Schicksal, Juni bis September 1866*, (Helwing, Mack, Brunswick 1866)

Neuss, Erich, *Die Schlacht bei Langensalza am 27. Juni 1866: Betrachtungen zur Landesgeschichte und zur Geschichte der Kriegschirurgie unter Zugrundelegung der "Erinnerungen an den Juni 1866 von Schulrat Looff,* (Martin Luther University, Halle-Wittenberg 1966)

Ortenburg, Georg, *Mit Gott für Gott und Vaterland: Das preußische Heer 1807-1914*, (Berlin Universities, Berlin 1979)

Otto, Franz, *Fünfzig Jahre aus Preußens und Deutschlands Geschichte. Preußens Volk in Waffen in Schleswig-Holstein und Dänemark, in Böhmen und Franken, am Main und Neckar*, (Spamer, Berlin & Leipzig 1882)

Paulizky, Otto & Woedtke, Axel von, *Geschichte des 4. Rheinischen Infanterie-Regiments: Ausgaben 1815-1884*, (E. S. Mittler & Sons, Berlin 1884)

Pfeifer, Klaus, *Die Bedeutung der Schlacht bei Langensalza am 27. Juni 1866*, (Drei-Türme-Verlag, Bad Langensalza 1991)

Pfister, Albert von, *Deutsche Zwietracht: Erinnerungen aus meinem Leutnantzeit 1859-1869*, (J.G. Cotta, Stuttgart 1902)

Pfister, Albert von, *Denkwürdigkeiten aus der württembergischen Kriegsgeschichte das 18. und 19. Jahrhunderts, Anschluss am die Geschichte das 8. Infanterieregiments*, (Grüninger, Stuttgart 1868)

Pulkowski & Tidow, *Kurzegefasste Geschichte des Fußartillerie-Regiments General-Feldzeugmeister (Brandenburgischen) Nr. 3*, (E.H. Mittler & Son, Berlin 1914)

Rappert, Dr. Georg, *Chronik der Kriegs-Ereignisse in der Stadt Hammelburg: 1866*, (Hiller, Hammelburg 1866)

Regensberg, Friedrich, *Der Mainfeldzug*, (Frankh, Stuttgart 1908)

Rehmann, Wilhelm, *Das Gefecht bei Frohnhofen*, (?, 1934)

Reichenau, Walther von (ed.),*Schlachtfelder zwischen Alpen und Main*, (Nazi Party Publication, Munich, 1938)

Reitzenstein, Johann Baron von, *Die Königlich Hannoversche Artillerie im Kriege 1866*, (W. Kaune, Bremen 1891)

Riese, Heinz, *Die Badische Wehrmacht 1866-1870/71*, (Dissertation, Gotha 1934)

Rintelen, Wilhelm von, *Geschichte des Niederrheinischen Füsilier Regiments Nr. 39*, (E. S. Mittler & Son, Berlin 1911)

Röder von Diersburg, Carl Christian, *Geschichte des 1. Grossherzoglich hessischen Infanterie (leibgarde) Regiments Nr. 115*, (E.H. |Mittler & Son, Berlin 1899)

Rogge-Ludwig, Wilhelm, *Die letzten Regierungstage des letzten Kurfürsten von Hessen*, (Privately published, Kassel 1886)

Rosenwald, Walter, *Die Herzoglich Nassauische Brigade im Feldzug 1866*, (Schellenberg, Taunusstein 1983)

Rüstow, Wilhelm, *Der Krieg von 1866 in Deutschland und Italien*, (Friedrich Schulthess, Zürich 1866)

Samarow, *Gregor, Memoiren zur Zeitgeschichte: Das Jahr 1866*, (F. W. Brockhaus, Leipzig 1881)

Scherff, Wilhelm von, *Die Division von Beyer im Main-Feldzug 1866*, (E.S. Mittler & Son, Berlin 1899)

Scheibert, Justus, *Die Kriege gegen Dänemark 1864 und Österreich 1866*, (W. Pauli, Berlin 1894)

Scheibert, Justus, *1864 1866, Preussen's Waffengänge zu der Gründung des Deutschen Reich*, (Ernst Finking, Berlin ?)

Schimmelpfeng, Adolf, *Die Kurhessische Armeedivsion im Jahre 1866: Beleuchtung der gleichnamigen Schrift des Generallieutenants z. D., ehemaligen hessischen Hauptmanns, Julius v. Schmidt*, (Hopf, Melsungen 1892)

Schmidt, Julius von, *Die vormals kurhessische Armeedivision im Sommer 1866: Auf Grund d. vorhandenen actenmäßigen Materials sowie d. eigenen Erlebnisse*, (Brunnemann, Kassel 1892)

Schmitt, Ludwig, *Das Treffen bei Kissingen am Kissingen am 10. Juli 1866*, (Otto Levin, Bad Kissingen 1932)

Schneider, K. J., *Der Antheil der Badischen Feld-division an dem Kriege des Jahres 1866 in Deutschland – von einem Angehörigen der badischen Felddivision*, (J. H. Geiger, Lahr 1867)

Schoeps, Julius H., *Bismarck und sein Attentäter. Der Revolveranschlag Unter den Linden am 7. Mai 1866*, (Ullstein, Berlin 1984)

Schulenburg-Hehlen, Count Bernhard von der u.,& Briesen, Franz, *Geschichte des Magdeburgischen Dragoner-Regiments Nr. 6*, (E. H. Mittler, Berlin 1885)

Schüssler, Wilhelm (Editor), *Die Tagebücher des Freiherrn Reinhard von Dalvigk zu Lichtenfels aus den Jahren 1860-71*, (Deutsche Verlags-Anstalt, Stuttgart 1920)

Schwerdt, Heinrich, *Die Hannoveraner in Thüringen und die Schlacht bei Langensalza, Eine Episode aus der neuesten Kriegsgeschichte*, (Wilhelm Klinghammer, Langensalza 1866)

Scriba, J. von, *Die Operationen der Hannoveraner und Preußen und die Schlacht bei Langensalza im Juni 1866: Vorträge mit autorisierter Benutzung der hannoverschen Originalberichte der in der Schlacht thätig gewesenen Einheiten*, (Schweighauserische Verlagsbuchhandlung, Basel 1872)

Sichart, Alexander Eberhard von, & Robert William Georg von, *Der feldzug Preußens gegen Hannover im Jahre 1866*, (Hahn, Hanover & Leipzig 1901)

Sollwitzer, Wilhelm, *Das Gefecht bei Seybothenreuth am 29. Juli 1866*, (Emil Mühl, Bayreuth 1932)

Stade, August von, *Die Schlacht bei Langensalza zwischen Hannoveranern und Preußen am 27. Juni 1866, sammt der in dieser Schlacht gefallenen Hannoveraner*, (Temme, Stade 1866)

Starklof, R., *Geschichte des königlich Württemburgischen vierten Reiterregiments Königin Olga 1805-1866*, (Karl Aue, Stuttgart 1867)

Stein, Hartwig (Editor), *Das Kriegstagebuch des preußischen Gefreiten Albert Koch aus dem West-und Main Feldzug des Jahres 1866*, (Peter Lang, Frankfurt am Main 2009)

Strombeck, Richard Baron von, *Kriegstagebücher aus den Jahren 1864 und 1866*, (Eduard Zernin, Darmstadt 1869)

Strubberg, Friedrich Armand ('Armand'), *In Süd-Carolina und auf dem Schlachtfelde von Langensalza*, (Carl Rümpler, Hanover 1869)

Stumpf, Major v., *Geschichte des Grossherzoglich Oldenburgischen Artillerie-Korps und der Teilnahme seiner ehemaligen Batterien an dem Feldzuge gegen Frankreich 1870/71*, (Gerhard Stalling, Oldenburg ?)

Suckow, Albert von, Suckow, Emma von, & Busch,Wilhelm, *Rückschau des Königl. Württembergischen Generals der Infanterie und Kriegsministers Albert von Suckow,* (J.C.B. M|aur, Tübingen 1909)

Sybel, Heinrich von, *Die Begründung des Deutschen Reiches durch Wilhelm I. Basierend vonehmlich auf den preußischen Staatsakten,* (Hendel, Meersburg 1930)

Tabouillot, Ferdinand von, *Die Dreizehner in Feindes Land; Kriegsbilder aus dem Feldzuge des Jahres 1866,* (E. Obertüschen, Münster 1866)

Tanera, Carl, *Der Krieg von 1866,* (Die Deutschen Einigungskriege, Volume IX, Part Two of Deutschlands Kriege von Feherbellin bis Königgrätz, Beck, Munich 1894)

Tittman, Axel, *Der deutsche Krieg von 1866 im Raum Würzburg,* (Freunde Mainfrankischer Art & History, 1980)

Trinius, August, *Geschichte des Krieges gegen Österreich und den Mainfeldzuges 1866,* (Hempel, Berlin 1886, Volume 2)

Türcke, Baron Ernst von, *Geschichte des 2. Thüringischen Infanterie-Regiments Nr. 32 von Seiner Gründung,* (E.H. Mittler & Son, Berlin 1890)

Voss, Wilhelm, *Illustrierte Geschichte der deutschen Einigungskriege 1864-1866,* (Union Deutsche Verlagsgesellschaft, Stuttgart 1914)

Wabra, Josef, *Rhönfeldzug 1866. Schlacht bei Hammelburg und Bad Kissingen,* (Wabra Verlag, Werneck 1968)

Wacker, Peter, & Rosenwald, Walter, *Die Herzoglich Nassauische Brigade im Feldzug 1866,* (Schellenberg, Taunusstein 1983)

Wallman, Dr., *Feldzug der Preussischen Main-Armee gegen Süddeutschland: insbesondere der Division Goeben im Jahre 1866,* (Vogelsang & Köhler, Minden 1866)

Wengen, Friedrich von der, *Geschichte der Kriegsereignisse zwischen Preussen und Hannover im 1866,* (Friedrich A. Perthes, Gotha 1886)

Wengen, Friedrich von der, *General Vogel v. Falckenstein und der hannoversche Feldzug 1866. Offenes sendschreiben von F. von der Wengen an seiner Kritiker,* (Friedrich A. Perthes, Gotha 1887)

Wienhöfer, Elmar, *Das Militärwesen des Deutschen Bundes und das Ringen zwischen Österreich und Preußen um die Vorherrschaft in Deutschland 1815-1866,* (Biblio Verlag, Osnabrück 1973 – originally thesis, Münster 1971)

Wiese, Premier-Lieutenant P. von, *Das 2. Schlesische Grenadier-Regiment Nr. 11 im Mainfeldzuge 1866: Ein Beitrag zur Geschichte des Regiments,* (E. H. Mittler, Berlin 1870)

Wilhelm, R., *Zum Gedenken der Schlacht bei Rossbrunn: 26 Juli, 100 Jahre,* (Privately published, Rossbrunn 1966)

Willisen, Karl Wilhelm von, *Der Feldzüge der Jahre 1859 und 1866,* (Duncker & Humboldt, Leipzig 1868)

Winterfeld, Karl, *Vollständige Geschichte des Preußischen Krieges von 1866 gegen Oesterreich und dessen Bundesgenossen,* (Gustav Hempel, Berlin 1866)

Wundt, Wilhelm, *Das Land Baden im Kriegsjahre 1866,* (Leipziger Bibliophilen, 1919)

Zaenglein, N., *Zeitstudie der Entstehung und Erhaltung der Denkmale der Schlacht bei Langensalza am 27. Juni 1866,* (Privately published, Langensalza 1991)

Zander, Ernst, *Die bayerische Heerführung und der Chef des Generalstabes Generallieutenant Freiherr v. d. Tann vor den Geschworenen in der zehnstündigen öffentlichen Verhandlung des oberbayerischen Schwurgerichts vom 19. Oktober 1866 gegen den Redakteur des Volksboten Ernst Zander wegen "Amtsehrenbeleidigung",* (Library '...des Expedition der Volksboten', Munich 1866)

Zernin, Gerhard, *August von Goeben in seinem Briefen: mit einem einleitenden Lebenseite,* (E. S. Mittler & Son, Berlin 1903)

Zernin, Gerhard, *Das Leben des Königlich Preußischen General der Infanterie August von Goeben*, (E. S. Mittler & Son, Berlin 1895-1897)

Zerzog, A. von, *Die Bayern im deutschen kriege von 1866*, (Jentsch & Stage, Augsburg 1867)

Ziegler, Peter, *Mit den Preußen kam die Feuersbrust*, (?, ? 1996)

Ziegner, Siegfried von, *Geschichte des Lauenburgischen Jäger-Bataillons Nr. 9 (1866 bis 1897)*, (H.H.C. Freystatzky, Ratzeburg 1898)

Zimmermann, C. von, *Der Antheil der Großherzoglich hessischen Armee-Division am Kriege 1866* – German General Staff, *Kriegsgeschichtliche Einzelschriften*, vols. 22 and 23 -, (E. S. Mittler und Son, Berlin 1897)

Zimmermann, Dr. R., *Illustrierte Kriegsgeschichte des Jahres 1866 für das deutsche Volk*, (Gustav Weise, Stuttgart 1868)

Zöller, Joseph Gabriel, *Nach 30 Jahren!: die Gefechte bei Hundheim, Tauberbischofsheim und Wehrbach am 23 und 24 Juli 1866; mit einem geschichtlichen Rückblick*, (?, ?, 1896)

German-language articles

(Anon.), 'Bayreuth im Sommer des Jahres 1866, das gefecht von Seybothenreuth und die Preußische Occupation', (*Historischer Verein für Oberfranken zu Bayreuth, 1867*)

(Anon.), 'Das Gefecht von Aschaffenburg (1866)', (*Österreichische Militärische Zeitschrift*, Vol. 4, Vienna 1866)

(Anon.), 'Das Gefecht von Fronhofen, Laufach und Weiller am 13 Juli 1866', (*Allgemeine Militärzeitung*, Nr. 50, Darmstadt, 15 December 1866)

(Anon.), 'Der deutsche krieg von 1866, Part 6, Die kriegsereignisse in Mittel und Westdeutschland', (*Unsere Zeit. Deutsche Revue der Gegenwart*, 1867, Vol. 2)

(Anon.), 'Die Armeeführung des Generals Vogel von Falckenstein in den Tagedes 21-26. Juni 1866', (*Jahrbücher für die deutsche Armee und Marine*, June 1886)

(Anon.), 'Die Gefechte der bayrischen Armee mit der preussischen Main-Armee am 2, 3, und 4 Juli 1866', (*Allgemeine Militär-Zeitung*, Year 41, 1866, pp.266-269, 'Officiele Mitteilungen des K. bayerischen Heeres')

(Anon.), 'Die Kriegsoperationen in West Deutschland nach der Schlacht von Langensalza bis zum Abschluß des Waffenstillstandes', (*Allgemeine Militär-Zeitung*, Nrs. 39-41, Darmstadt, 1866)

(Anon.), 'Kriegsnachrichten', (*Landshuter Zeitung*, Landshut, July 19 1866)

(Anon.), 'Preussen – Königliche Ordre, betreffend die gleichmässige Bezeichnung der Kriegerischen Ereignisse des Feldzuges von 1866', (*Staatarchiv, Sammlung der officiellen Actenstücke zur Geschichte der Gegenwart*, Vol. 14, January-June 1868)

(Anon.), Various notices, (*Der Kamerad*, Vienna, 1866, Issues Nrs. 65, 72, 74, 76, 77, 78, 84, 86, 89, 90, 93)

(Anon.), Various notices, *Militär-Wochenblatt*, Berlin

Baumer, Günter, 'Der Krieg des Jahres 1866 und das Hinterland', (*Hinterländer Geschichtsblätter*, Year 45, 1966)

Becker, 'Erläuterungen und Berichtigungen zu der Relation über das Gefecht bei Aschaffenburg (1866)', (*Österreichische Militärische Zeitschrift*, Vol. 1, Vienna 1867)

Bethke, Martin, 'Die Kurhessische Armee', (*Zeitschrift für Heereskunde*, 1979, Numbers 284 & 285)

Böhning, Paul, 'Das Gefecht bei Dermbach: Erinnerungen an die Kriegs- und Schreckenstage von 1866 im Rhöngebiet (4. Juli 1866)', (*Sonntagsblatt der Dorfzeitung*, Nr. 28, 1926, pp.214-220)

Bosl, Karl, 'Die deutschen Mittelstatten in der Entscheidung von 1866', (*Zeitschrift für bayerische Landes-geschichte*, Volume 29, 1966, pp.665-679)

Caemmerer, Rudolf von, 'Die süddeutschen Heeresbewegungen im Main-Feldzuge von 1866', (*Beihest zum Militär-Wochenblatt*, Berlin 1902)

Dambron, Rudolf, 'Mainz – Festung des "Deutschen Bundes" 1816-1866', (*Mainzer Almanach, 1967*, pp.119-126.

Deichmann, Adolf, 'Aus den letzten Tagen des letzten Kurfürsten', (*Hessenland*, Volume 38, 1927)

Delbrück, Hans, 'Langensalza und Vogel von Falckenstein', (*Preussische Jahrbücher,* Volume 59, May 1887, pp.13-47)

Dreher, 'Das Achte Bundesarmeecorps in der Wetterau 1866', (*Friedberger Geschichtsblätter*, 1923

Droll, Hermann, 'Das Reitergefecht beim Hettstadter Hof', (*Rund um den Saupurzel*, Karlstadter Zeitung, 1953, p.4)

Droll, Hermann, 'Der Mainfeldzug 1866', (*Die Mainlande*, Nr. 2, 1951, pp.41-43)

Dungern, Otto Baron von (contributor), 'Max Freiherr von Dungern – Briefe eine nassauischen Leutnants aus dem Feldzug 1866', (*Nassauer Annalen*, Vol. 36, pp.109-132, 1907)

Eckart, Werner, 'Einige Ausführungen über das Minie-Gewehr', (*Zeitschrift für Heeres und Uniformenkunde*, 1939)

Fürchtbauer, Heinrich von (pamphlet), 'Festschrift zur Jahrhundertfeier des K. b. 14. Infanterie-Regiments "Hartmann" von 11. bis 13. Juli 1914 in Nürnburg', (J.L. Stich, Nürnburg 1914)

Ghillany, F. W., (Chronicle of Events), (*Europäische Chronik von 1492 bis ende April 1867*, Volume 3, 1867, approx. pp.183-322)

Glasenapp, G. von, 'Die Werke des Preußischen, Bayerischen, und Oesterreichischen Generalstabes über den Feldzug von 1866', (*Militärische Blätter*, Vol. XXI, Berlin 1869, pp.113-132)

Hagen, C.C. von (editor), 'Bayreuth im Sommer des Jahres 1866, das gefecht von Seybothenreuth, und die Preußische Occupation', (*Archiv für Geschichte & Alterthumstunde von Oberfranken*, Vol. 10, 1867) – see entry under Sollwitzer, in German-language books.

Hess, Leonhard, 'Erlebnisse der Odenwälder Bevölkerung im Kriegsjahr 1866', (*Die Heimat,* Nr. 4, Erbach 1966)

Hirtenfeld, Dr. F. (Editor), 'Ueber die Operationen der Main-Armee von 21 bis 28 Juli 1866', (*Militär-Zeitung*, Year 19, 1866)

Horben, A. von, 'Das Gefecht bei Dermbach am 4. Juli 1866', (*Allgemeine Militär-Zeitung*, Volume 45, Nr. 3, Darmstadt 1870)

Ilgen, O. v., 'Das Gefecht bei Roßdorf 1866', ((*Heimatbuch für das obere Werratal und die angrenzenden Gebiet*, Volume 2, Meiningen 1928, pp.144-149)

Jena, Eduard, 'General v. Goeben im Feldzug 1866 gegen Hannover und die süddeutschen Staaten', (*Rüstung und Abrüstung: eine Umschau über das Heer, -und Kriegswesen aller Länder*, Volume 31, Berlin 1904)

Lehmann, Max, 'Der Krieg in West-Deutschland und die vorhangenden Unterhandlung des Jahres 1866', (*Historischer Zeitschrift*, Volume 22, Munich 1869)

M., F. von, 'Von Schriften über den Krieg von 1866', (*Historischer Zeitschrift*, Volume 18, Munich 1867, pp.430-433)

Neubecker, Dr. Ottfried, 'Welche Fahnen bei Langensalza?',(*Hannoversche Geschichtsblätter*, New Series, Volume 4, Hanover 1936/37)

Oberländer, Karl, 'Was die Großmutter als Vetreranen von 1866 zu erzählen weiß', (*Heimatbuch für das obere Werratal und die angrenzenden Gebiet*, Volume 2, Meiningen 1928, pp.132-143)

Petzler, Dr. Wilhelm, 'Die Hannoverschen Fahnen im Vaterländischen Museum der Stadt Hannover', (*Hannoversche Geschichtsblätter*, Volume 26, Hanover 1923)

'R.M.', 'Studien über der Main-Feldzug im Jahre 1866', (*Allgemeine schweizerische Militärzeitung*, Year 36, Nrs. 1, 2, 3, 4, 7, 8, 9,10 & 11, Basle 1870)

Rüttenauer, Benno, 'Der Tag von Tauberbischofsheim: anno 1866', (*Der Frankische Landbote für die Landkreise Tauberbischofsheim*, Bad Mergentheim 1966)

Siebert, Karl, 'Das Gefecht bei Hünfeld am 4. Juli 1866', (*Hessenland*, Year XXII, Nr. 16, 1908, pp.222-225)

Seußler, Wilhelm, 'Der Krieg von 1866 und die Zivilbevölkerung im Bezirk', (*Badische Heimat*, Vol. 73, Tauberbischofsheim 1993)

Trittler, Bonifatius, 'Meine erinnerungen an die Schlacht bei Tauberbischofsheim 1866', (*Hohenloher Chronik*, Nr. 13 1966)

Umminger, Gernot, 'Das Gefecht bei Hundheim: im deutschen Schicksaljahr kämpfen am 23. Juli 1866 auf der Höhe zwischen Miltenberg und Wertheim die 113er aus Freiburg gegen die Preußen', (*Badische Heimat*, Vol. 48, 1968, pp.402-406)

Weiß, Berichtigung zur den Aufsatze, 'Der Tag von Aschaffenburg', (*Österreichische Militärische Zeitschrift*, Vol. 3, Vienna 1869)

Wenigen, Fr. von der, 'Der letzte Feldzug der Hannoverschen Armee 1866', (*Jahrbücher für die deutsche Armee und Marine*, Nrs. 357 & 358, Berlin 1901)

English-language books

Brackenbury, Henry, *The Last Campaign of Hanover. A lecture delivered at the R.U.S.I.*, (W. Mitchell & Co., London 1870)

Bronsart von Schellendorf, Paul Leopold Eduard, Heinrich Anton, *The Prussian Campaign of 1866. A Tactical Retrospect,-* translated by Colonel Henry Aimé Ouvry – (Mitchell & Co., London 1870). For details of the German language original, see listing in German-language books section. Further musings in both languages appeared soon after.

Dicey, Edward, *The Battlefields of 1866*, (Tinsley Brothers, London 1866)

Hallett, Gerard Ludlow, *A memento of Kissingen, 1866*, (A sermon given on July 15th, 1866, London 1866)

Hozier, Henry, *The Seven Weeks War and its Antecedents*, (Macmillan & Co., London 1867)

Malet, Sir Alexander, *The Overthrow of the Germanic Confederation by Prussia in 1866*, (Longmans, Green & Co., London 1870)

Malleson, George Bruce, *The Refounding of the German Empire 1848-1871*, (Charles Scribner, New York 1893)

Pocock, John, *Langensalza 1866, Hanover's Last Stand*, (Continental Wars Society, Harrow, London 2002)

Showalter, Dennis E, *Railroads and Rifles*, (The Shoe String Press, Hamden 1986)

Strauss, Gustave Louis Maurice, *Men who have made the new German empire: A series of brief biographic sketches*, (Tinsley Brothers Ltd., London 1875)

Ward, A.W., & Wilkinson, S., *Germany 1815-1890*, (Cambridge University Press, Cambridge 1916-1918, Vol. II)

Wright & Hozier (Translators), *The Campaign of 1866 in Germany*, (Her Majesty's Stationery Office, London 1907. English translation of the Prussian General Staff History of 1866 – see entry in German-language books. Several other editions also exist.

Wyatt, Captain W.J., *A Political and Military History of the Hanoverian and Italian War*, (Edward Stanford, London 1868)

English-language articles

Ainsworth, William Harrison (editor), 'The Campaign in South Germany', (*The New Monthly Magazine*, London 1867)

(Anon.), 'A Review of the Continental War', (*Blackwoods Edinburgh Magazine*, Volume 100, August 1866)

(Anon.), 'How Vogel von Falkenstein became a Soldier', (*Once a Week: an Illustrated Miscellany of Literature, Art, Science, and Popular Information*, Volume 4, July 1867)

(Anon.), 'The Battle of Kissingen', (*Macmillan's Magazine*, Volume 16, July 1867)

Brackenbury, Henry, 'The Last Campaign of Hanover', (*Journal of the Royal United Services Institution*, Volume XIV, London 1870)

Chesney, Captain C.C., 'The Campaign in Western Germany', (*Blackwood's Edinburgh Magazine*, January 1867, pp.68-82)

Crowe, J. A., 'The Prussian Campaign of 1866', (*The Edinburgh Review*, Vol. 125, 1867)

Hale, Lonsdale, 'The Fog of War', (*Vol. 58, Aldershot Military Society Lecture*, Edward Stanford, 1896)

Schmitt, Hans A., 'From Sovereign States to Prussian Provinces: Hanover and Hesse-Nassau 1866-1871', (*The Journal of Modern History*, Volume 57, Nr. 1, March 1985)

Schmitt, Hans A., 'Prussia's Last Fling: The annexation of Hanover, Hesse, Frankfurt and Nassau June 15–October 8, 1866', (*Central European History*, Volume 18, Issue 4, 1975)

Sterne, Margaret, 'The End of the Free City of Frankfort', (*The Journal of Modern History*, Volume 30, Nr. 3, Chicago, September 1950)

Sherwood, John D., 'The Battle of Kissingen', (Letter to *The New York Times*, January 20 1867)

Sherwood, John, D., 'What I saw at the Battle of Kissingen', (*Hours at Home*, Volume 4, February 1867)

Teichman, Oskar, 'The Hanoverian Cavalry in 1866', (*The Cavalry Journal*, Royal United Services Institution, Volume 29, London 1939)

French-language books

Anquetil, Thomas, *La Guerre 1866*, (Renault, Paris 1866)

Belet, P., & Ketteler, Mgs de, *L'Allemagne après La Guerre de 1866*, (Gaume Brothers & J. Duprey, Paris 1867)

Brugère, Joseph, *Tactique de l'artillerie pendant la guerre de 1866*, (Berger-Levrault & Co., Paris 1877)

Crousse, Franz, *Les Luttes de l'Autriche en 1866; Rédigéd'apres Documents Officiels,* (C. Mucquardt, Brussels, Leipzig, & Ghent 1868)

Fay, Charles Alexandre, *Étude sur la Guerre D'Allemagne de 1866*, (J. Dumaine, Paris 1867)

Fay, Charles Alexandre, *Exposé sommaire de la campagne d'Allemagne en 1866*, (J. Dumaine, Paris 1869)

Ladimir, Jules, & Tranchant, Alfred, *La guerre de 1866: ses cause directes et indirectes,* (F. Carnol, Paris 1866)

Lecomte, Ferdinand, *Guerre de la Prusse contre L'Autriche et la Confédération Germanique en 1866*, (Charles Tanera, Paris 1868)

Malo, Charles, *Précis de la Guerre de 1866 en Allemagne & en Italie*, (C. Mucquardt, Brussels 1886)

Renémont, Charles de, *Campagne de 1866: etude militaire, rédigée conformément au programme des examens d'admission à l'ecole supérieure de guerre*, (War College, 1900)

Vandevelde, Louis, *La guerre de 1866*, (C. Mucquardt, Brussels 1869)

Vilbort, J., *L'Oeuvre de M. de Bismarck 1863-1866: Sadowa et le Campagnes des Sept Jours*, (Charpentier & Co., Paris 1869)

French-language articles

(Anon.), 'La Guerre de L'Allemagne en 1866 – le Role et les Développements de la Prusse dans La Campagne de 1866', (*Revue des Deux Mondes*, Paris, 15 October 1868)

(Anon.), 'La guerre de Sept Jours: Campagne de 1866 en Allemagne', (*Revue Contemporaine*, Year 7, Paris 1867)

Anon., 'La Charité Chrétienne dans La Guerre D'Allemagne de 1866', (*Revue Générale*, Volume 5, Year 3, Brussels 1867)

'Gandolfi', 'Le Hanovre et la Prusse', (*Revue Générale*, Year 3, Nr. 5, Brussels 1867)

Heydt, E., 'Le fusil à aiguille, notes et observations critiques sur le l'arme àfeuse chargeant par la culasse', (*Le Spectateur Militaires*, Paris, July & August 1866)

Lacombe, Ferdinand de, 'Opérations Militaires du nord de l'Allemagne', (*Le Spectateur Militaires*, Paris, July, August, & September 1866)

Dutch-language books

Booms, Petrus Gerardus, *Kissingen. Eene Episode uit den Oorlog van 1866 in Duitschland*, (Roelants, Schiedam 1870)

Booms, Petrus Gerardus, *Oostenrijk in Zuid-Duitschland in den oorlog van 1866 tegen Pruisen*, (H. Roelants, Schiedam 1867)

Brouwer, E. H., *De veldtogt van het jaar 1866 in Duitsland*, (Kemink, Utrecht 1869)

Ising, Arnold Leopold Hendrik, & Rietstrap, Johannes Baptist, *De oorlog in Duitschland en Italie*, (H. Nijgh, Rotterdam 1866)

Meydt, Friedrich von der, *Veldtogt en overwinning van Pruissen in den zomer van 1866*, (Kemmer, Utrecht 1866)

Dutch-language articles

Van der Hegge, H. O., 'Aanteekeningen over den Oorlog den Duitschen Oorlog van 1866', (*Nederlandsch Tijdsschrift vor Geneeskunde. Trevens organ der Nederlandsche Maatschappj tot Bevordering der geneeskunst*, Year 4, Amsterdam 1868)

Swedish-language books

Henning, Hamilton, *Kriget I Tyskland År 1866*, (P.A. Norstedt & Sons, Stockholm 1869)

Index

INDEX OF PEOPLE

INDEX OF PLACES

INDEX OF MILITARY UNITS

Bavarian II/14th Infantry Regiment, 73
Bavarian I/15th Infantry Regiment, 96, 105, 110
Bavarian II/15th Infantry Regiment, 96, 102, 169
Bavarian III/15th Infantry Regiment, 96-97, 104, 107
Bavarian 1st Jäger Battalion (listed as separate companies), 73, 91-92, 169
Bavarian 2nd Jäger Battalion, 112, 171
Bavarian 4th Jäger Battalion, 168
Bavarian 5th Jäger Battalion, 96-97, 109
Bavarian 6th Jäger Battalion, 77, 96-97, 102
Bavarian 7th Jäger Battalion, 102-103, 107
Bavarian 8th Jäger Battalion, 116, 179
Miscellaneous:
Bavarian Battery Hang, 80
Bavarian Battery Hutten, 111
Bavarian Battery Königer, 80
Bavarian Battery Lepel, 112
Bavarian Battery Lottersberg, 93
Bavarian Battery Mussinan, 111-112
Bavarian Battery Redenbacher, 96-97, 99-100, 105
Bavarian Battery Schuster, 96, 111
Bavarian Battery Zeller, 105-106
Bavarian Horse Artillery Battery La Roche, 89
Bavarian Horse Artillery Battery Lepel, 108, 111
Bavarian Horse Artillery Battery Massenbach, 82, 93
Bavarian Horse Artillery Battery Metting, 72, 75, 89
Bavarian Reserve Artillery, 117, 120-121, 171, 173, 178, 186-187

Hanoverian Military Units

Brigades:
Hanoverian Cavalry Brigade, 59, 64
Hanoverian 1st Brigade, 57-58, 60, 62
Hanoverian 2nd Brigade, 55, 57-58, 60, 62
Hanoverian 3rd Brigade, 55-56, 57-58, 62
Hanoverian 4th Brigade, 50, 57, 59, 61
Regiments:
Hanoverian Cambridge Dragoons, 55, 64
Hanoverian 'Garde du Corps', 64
Hanoverian Leib Regiment, 60
Hanoverian 4th Infantry Regiment, 51
Battalions:
Hanoverian 1st Jäger Battalion, 55, 60
Hanoverian I/2nd Regiment, 60
Hanoverian II/2nd Regiment, 60

Hanoverian I/3rd Regiment, 60
Hanoverian II/3rd Regiment, 60
Hanoverian II/5th Regiment, 49, 62
Hanoverian 2/Cambridge Dragoons, 64
Hanoverian 2/Guard Hussars, 54
Hanoverian 4/Guard Cuirassiers, 55
Hanoverian 4/Queens Hussars, 55
Hanoverian 3rd Jäger Battalion, 59, 62
Miscellaneous:
Hanoverian Horse Artillery, 59
Hanoverian Reserve Artillery, 57, 59
Hanoverian 9th Foot Artillery Battery, 51

Württemberg Military Units

Divisions:
1st Division, VIII Corps (Württemberg), 122, 146, 154-155, 174, 186
Brigades:
Württemberg 1st Brigade, 157
Württemberg 2nd Brigade, 155-156
Württemberg 3rd Brigade, 157
Regiments:
Württemberg 2nd Mounted Regiment, 154
Württemberg 7th Infantry Regiment, 68, 156, 161-162, 164
Battalions:
Württemberg II/1st Infantry Regiment, 160
Württemberg I/2nd Infantry Regiment, 176
Württemberg I/5th Infantry Regiment, 158
Württemberg II/5th Infantry Regiment, 157-158
Württemberg I/7th Infantry Regiment, 161
Württemberg II/7th Infantry Regiment, 161
Württemberg I/8th Infantry Regiment, 158
Württemberg 1st Jäger Battalion, 71
Württemberg 2nd Jäger Battalion, 156, 161
Württemberg 3rd Jäger Battalion, 158
Miscellaneous:
Württemberg Battery Roschmann, 188
Württemberg 1st Horse Artillery Battery, 188

Grand Duchy of Baden Military Units

Divisions:
2nd Division, VIII Corps (Baden), 122, 146, 150-151, 154, 162-163, 173-174, 186, 192
Brigades:
1st Baden Brigade, 151, 162
2nd Baden Brigade, 151, 162
Regiments:
Baden Grenadier Regiment, 151

MISCELLANEOUS